Education Around the World

Available and Forthcoming Titles in the Education Around the World Series

Series Editor: Colin Brock

Education in South-East Asia edited by Lorraine Pe Symaco

Forthcoming volumes:

Education in Australia, New Zealand and the Pacific edited by
Michael Crossley, Greg Hancock and Terra Sprague
*Education in the Commonwealth Caribbean and
Netherlands Antilles* edited by Emel Thomas
Education in East Asia edited by Pei-tseng Jenny Hsieh
Education in Eastern Europe and Eurasia edited by Nadiya Ivanenko
Education in Southern Africa edited by Clive Harber
Education in West Africa edited by Emefa Amoako
Education in West-Central Asia edited by Mah-E-Rukh Ahmed

Education Around the World

A Comparative Introduction

Colin Brock and Nafsika Alexiadou

B L O O M S B U R Y
LONDON • NEW DELHI • NEW YORK • SYDNEY

Bloomsbury Academic

An imprint of Bloomsbury Publishing Plc

50 Bedford Square	175 Fifth Avenue
London	New York
WC1B 3DP	NY 10010
UK	USA

www.bloomsbury.com

First published 2013

British Library Cataloguing-in-Publication Data
A catalogue record for this book is available from the British Library.

ISBN: PB: 978-1-4411-6940-2
HB: 978-1-4411-0501-1
PDF: 978-1-4411-7809-1
ePub: 978-1-4411-4046-3

Library of Congress Cataloging-in-Publication Data
Brock, Colin.
Education around the world: a comparative introduction/Colin Brock and Nafsika Alexiadou.
pages cm
Includes bibliographical references.
ISBN 978-1-4411-6940-2 (pbk.) – ISBN 978-1-4411-0501-1 (hardcover) – ISBN (invalid)
978-1-4411-7809-1 (ebook (pdf)) – ISBN (invalid) 978-1-4411-4046-3 (ebook (ebook))
1. Comparative education. 2. Education–Cross-cultural studies. I. Title.
LB43.B76 2013
370.9–dc23
2012040666

Typeset by Deanta Global Publishing Services, Chennai, India
Printed and bound in Great Britain

Contents

Acknowledgements

We would like to thank Rachel Dowling for her advice on the USA, Shirley Brock for undertaking the task of compiling the index, and Anna Fleming and Rosie Pattinson of Bloomsbury for their patience and support.

Preface

Education Around the World aims to introduce the field of Comparative and International Education to those beginning to study, or take an interest, in it as educational practitioners of one kind or another. That includes undergraduate and graduate students, teachers at various levels, administrators, politicians and professionals in the field with non-governmental organizations (NGOs). For more advanced methodological issues, recourse should be made to Phillips and Schweisfurth (2008) and Bray et al. (2007) as well as to the specialist journals mentioned in Chapter 2.

This book also acts as an introductory volume to the series *Education Around the World*. All other volumes in the series are regionally based with one or more chapters on each country, about 200 overall. These will present a descriptive analysis of education in each and also highlight key issues of contemporary interest, development and concern.

Here we offer a description of the emergence of the field though a small group of 'founding fathers', and its development as a sub-discipline of educational studies, one of the education foundations. The nature of education 'the discipline' is discussed as an interdisciplinary field of study drawing on a range of contributing disciplines that are necessary for the analysis of educational activity and provision in comparative perspective. Emphasis is laid on the fact that education is not just formal in nature, but non-formal and informal as well.

Broad themes are addressed, such as the significance of scale: temporal and spatial, and globalization, as well as regions and groups of nations such as Europe, sub-Saharan Africa and the emergent BRIC states: Brazil, Russia, India and China. The United States of America and the small states of the world are used to illustrate the central issue of scale. These are not studies of these countries as such, but as means to illustrate issues of significance in the field. Country studies reside in the other volumes in the series, which may also contain regional overviews.

Recourse has been made to a wide range of published sources, both historical and contemporary. Relevance to the discussion, rather than date, has been a guiding principle. Hopefully the outcome will engender an interest to follow the field as it develops further over the coming years through its teaching, research and publications, including the other volumes in the series as they emerge.

1

Why it is Important: The Story so far

What is education for?

preceded

Comparative education is important because education is important, both as a phenomenon and as a discipline. Necessarily, education the phenomenon preceded education the discipline, so we have to consider that first. Education as a phenomenon is easy to define since it comprises just two basic activities: learning and teaching. The discipline of educational studies is more wide-ranging, including such issues as how education, especially formal education, is organized, controlled, administered, funded and evaluated. In short, one may suggest that education is culturally based and politically administered. But, what is it for?

The levels of sophistication and capacity apparent in the ability of *homo sapiens* to learn and to teach are so much greater than that of other primates that we may regard education as one of the key features of humanity. Yet, education is also self-evidently involved in man's inhumanity to man, as also recognized in the growing literature on education and conflict (Davies 2004; Brock 2011a and b). Whether all humanity survives even the twenty-first century is a matter of serious concern (Bizony 2011; Martin 2011) as the capacity of human beings to destroy their physical and bio-diversified environments is self-evident.

Sapiens, of course, means 'wise'. To be wise is a higher order of accomplishment than to be intelligent, and intelligence is of a higher order than cleverness. David Orr (1994) made an important distinction between 'human intelligence' and 'mere intellectual cleverness' (p. 17). He rightly ascribed the dominance of the latter over the former to formal education. In all countries, non-formal education contributes to systematic learning and teaching through agencies that are not part of the system as such, but contribute to the stock of education. For example, a massive amount of formal learning and teaching takes place in the workplace, be it a small company or a massive multinational corporation. There are also many Non-Governmental Organizations (NGOs) contributing to various aspects of education in all countries. In many countries of the world that are economically poor, national systems of formal educational provision are incomplete in one way or another. In many cases, they may not yet have been able to make even primary schooling available to all. This makes access to secondary schooling even more selective than it would otherwise be, which in turn, limits access to further and higher education.

The drive towards complete national education systems across the world is conventionally perceived to be an unqualified good. It has become lodged into the global psyche as an item of conventional wisdom. As such, it is rarely questioned, and so the question 'what is education for?' is rarely asked. Certainly, access to basic education is included in the *Universal Declaration of Human Rights* (1948) for all individuals, and rightly so. In practice, this has been translated in the early twenty-first century into 'Education for All' (EFA) through the Millennium Development Goals (MDGs), especially MDGs 2 and 3 (Table 1.1).

The key word in relation to the MDGs is 'development'. This gives a clue as to what formal education is conventionally reckoned to be for – namely, the enhancement of national development, especially economic development. This is despite the fact that there is no clear, direct causal connection between investment in formal education and national economic growth. There is, of course, a connection but it is extremely complex and, as yet, little understood. Is it the case that well-developed nations with diversified economies owe their situation primarily to investment in formal education? In the United Kingdom, and especially in England, its position at the turn of the twentieth century as the world's economic superpower was reached with a public education system virtually confined to primary levels, but it had a global exploitive trading and military network that was second to none. An extremely strong private sector of schooling had developed over centuries, especially in the nineteenth century, for the benefit of the wealthy and socially privileged elite of Britain. What was it about that private schooling that indicated its purpose and drove its contribution to the nation? It was their preparation for leadership. This particular national case may be unusual, but it reminds us that in all countries of the world, there is a private education sector, and if that is not taken into

Table 1.1 Millennium development goals, UNESCO (Brock 2010, p. 10)

Goal	Summary of Targets (T)
Eradicate Extreme Poverty and Hunger	T1: considerably reduce percentage of people on US$ 1 per day T2: full productive work for all T3: considerably reduce percentage of people who suffer hunger
Achieve UPE	T1: completion of full primary course for all by 2015
Gender Equality	T1: achieve at primary and secondary levels by 2005 and all levels by 2015
Reduce Child Mortality	T1: considerably reduce the child mortality rate by 2015
Improve Maternal Health	T1: reduce maternal mortality rate by 75 per cent T2: achieve universal access to reproductive health
Combat HIV/AIDS, Malaria and other Diseases	T1: reduce by 50 per cent and begin to reverse HIV/AIDS T2: universal access to treatment for HIV/Aids by 2010 for all who need it T3: by 2015, to halt and begin to reverse the influence of malaria and other major diseases
Ensure Environmental Sustainability	T1: get sustainable development into national policies and conserve environmental resources T2: reduce biodiversity loss considerably by 2010 T3: reduce by 50 per cent the proportion of people with no sustainable access to safe drinking water and sanitation T4: To achieve, by 2020, a significant improvement in the lives of at least 100 million slum dwellers
Develop a Global Partnership for Development	T1: address the special needs of the least developed countries, landlocked countries and developing small island states T2: develop an open, rule-based, predictable non-discriminatory trading and financial system T3: deal comprehensively with developing countries' debt T4: work with pharmaceutical companies to provide access to affordable essential drugs in developing countries

account when evaluating or comparing education within, between and across nations, the outcome of the exercise must be flawed, to say the least. Whatever the mix of public and private elements of education, governments of most countries remain fixated with a presumed causal relationship between progress in schools – in terms of assessment of achievement as measured by examination results – and national well-being – as measured by GDP. Clearly, they believe that is what education, especially schooling, is for. But is it? Or should it be?

Table 1.2 Global monitoring reports

2002	Education for All: is the World on Track?
2003/4	Gender and Education for All: the Leap to Equality
2005	Education for All: the Quality Imperative
2006	Literacy for Life
2007	Strong Foundations: Early Childhood Care and Education
2008	Education for All by 2015: Will We Make It?
2009	Overcoming Inequality: why Governance Matters
2010	Reaching the Marginalized
2011	The Hidden Crisis: Armed Conflict and Education
2012	Food Prices, Nutrition and the Millennium Development Goals

Source: UNESCO

We need to consider the EFA Global Monitoring Reports (GMRs), which are annual assessments of progress towards the MDGs as far as education is concerned. EFA is interpreted as 'basic schooling for all' and is considered country by country (Table 1.2).

Having all the nations of the world included in these annual reports reinforces the tendency to consider education, and what it is for, only at the national level. Casual involuntary comparisons are inevitably made by readers, with little understanding of and, therefore, regard for the context of each country. Like most systematized and bureaucratized activities, formal educational provision becomes subject to institutionalized inertia. Only political upheavals of extreme revolutionary proportions, such as those creating the USSR in 1917, the Third Reich in Germany in 1933 or the Peoples' Republic of China in 1949, tend to shake this inertia. Even then, national systems of education may regain a strong element of latent inertia in post-revolutionary times. The relative stability of these nation states was preceded by numerous smaller territorial units as control over groups of people gave way to control over areas of land on an increasingly secure basis (Dodgshon 1987). In Europe, some of these units were just fortified towns, others 'statelets', of which hundreds comprised the Holy Roman Empire, precursor of modern Germany. Conflict was endemic as the dominant religious power of the time, the Catholic Church, vied with the Lutheran Reformation for control over key towns and cities and their hinterlands (Brock 2010). By this time, the realization that 'knowledge is power' was well established and three main agencies competed for its control and for different purposes: religious, political and economic. Their objectives were somewhat different – control over thought, people and money, respectively. Exercising and maintaining that control became a prime function of formal education; that is to say, what such education was deemed to be for, and largely still is.

Why is education around the world so comparable?

We need to take a step back to trace some of the origins of this prime function of formal education as a social and political control mechanism and to see why education systems are so comparable though, in truth, only superficially. It is partly due to a conventional wisdom that 'education' means formal education, which for most people means 'schooling'. The other two forms of education, non-formal and informal, are relatively neglected in the literature as well as in conventional wisdom. This is despite the fact that, for most people, more is learnt outside the formal system than within it. This is an issue as much neglected by comparative and international education as by other foundation disciplines of educational studies. The situation has arisen because of the dominance of one model of formal education derived from Europe. Given the enormous range and variety of human conditions from, say, mid-town Manhattan to the highlands of Papua New Guinea, this is remarkable. Yet, few seem to think so.

Human communities have been learning and teaching since even before *homo sapiens* emerged as the dominant and only surviving human species some 200,000 years ago. Such education was concerned entirely with the survival of relatively small communities. This necessitated a stable relationship with the natural environment within, in most cases, a regular geographical space, even if it involved pastoralism. There were, inevitably, conflicts over territory. Education was informal and non-formal. Everything was on a relatively small scale. Harmony with the natural environment was paramount (Forde 1939), often involving a spiritual dimension as within indigenous communities even today (King and Schielman 2004).

Around the last quarter of the first millennium BC, a new dimension of education began to appear – the religious and formal. It was manifest in two Buddhist seminaries in what is now India, at Nalanda and Vilabhi, respectively. They are now normally recognized as the world's first universities and were only for selected males. The majority of human beings remained with a form of localized community-based learning, and the question 'what is education for' was about to demand more complex responses. The context of this development was the first of three urban revolutions that have signified the development of human society, which is now nearly two-thirds urban. The first urban revolution was associated with the emergence of towns asplaces of exchange. They developed because of the diversification of economies and occupations. New functions developed in association with exchange, such as manufacturing, trading and administration. These activities were supported by informal and non-formal modes of education, as in the predominantly rural populations that still formed the majority, but were in towns for wealth-creation and development rather than survival.

Now, in the first century of the second millennium, we talk as if the connection between knowledge and power has just been discovered. We talk of the knowledge economy and the knowledge business, a new conventional wisdom but with the education/economy connection still at the fore. In reality, this was already well understood by those with influence in the classical Greco-Roman era, embracing as it did, in its declining years, the emergent Roman Catholic Church. Control over knowledge was then, as now, contested by the elites. While classical Greek scholarship achieved remarkable insights into mathematics and science, as still acknowledged by today's leading scientists, such as Stephen Hawking (2011), it was confined to an urban-based elite. Slaves and the rural majority would acquire only the technical skills of the day through informal means. Although elite females would receive formal education, its content was restricted to the roles and skills required of their subordinate position in the social hierarchy. This sexist approach was reinforced by the early Christian Church, with its preoccupation with selecting young males for priesthood. Indeed, when asking 'what is education for', it is clear, in the formal setting, that the function of selection was even then closely allied to that of social and political control (Hopper 1968).

The second urban revolution is popularly known as the Renaissance. It followed several centuries of decline in Europe; during those centuries, the seeds of learning had been nurtured by individuals and institutions in the Arab world and boosted by the emergence and expansion of Islam. Many important intellectual, especially scientific, advances were made from Baghdad in the east to Fez in the west. At the same time, on the north-western fringes of Europe, Christian communities were preserving and advancing their forms of learning, especially in Ireland (Cahill 1998).

Around the turn of the first millennium AD, a long period of relative political stability returned to Western Europe. This enabled the establishment of colonizing towns with their trade and wealth creation. The wool trade, especially, supported manufacture in the city states of Flanders and Northern Italy. Wealthy patrons supported scholarship and the arts, enabling the creation of the first modern universities. The story is well known (Anderson 2004; Ruegg 1992) and battle lines were drawn as much in economic and political terms as theological ones, during the period of the aforementioned Lutheran Reformation. Education in its institutionalized form was still related to social, economic and political control and to the enhancement of relevant knowledge and skills for competing male elites. The Renaissance had been true to its classical forbears in its educational content, if not its purpose. The 'European Model' (Mallinson 1980) began to be exported through the so-called Age of Discovery. Boston, Massachusetts was founded as a 'Renaissance City' with Harvard as a Renaissance university, while 'as early as 1642 and 1647 the Massachusetts Bay Company passed laws requiring all towns to establish and support elementary schools out of local taxes' (King 1965). Although only a colony at the time, this emergent system preceded the earliest national school systems in Europe as well as the third urban revolution.

This was the industrial revolution in Britain, closely followed by other European countries and the USA, which led to urbanization on a massive scale, fierce commercial and military competition and the firming up of nation states. Such states could now defend or even extend their control over geographic space. Developing national systems of education still had two main purposes – political and economic. This was merely the extension of the competition for control over knowledge and skills at all levels – from towns and cities to entire countries. The third dimension, organized religion, also extended its influence to varying degrees, according to the relationship between the church and the state in each young nation. By the turn of the nineteenth century, the newly independent USA had barred religious education from public schools. By contrast, England relied entirely on the established church to provide popular education, whenever and wherever it wished to do so. The government was disinclined to establish a national system and it was left to the Christian churches to play an active role in the establishment of primary schools in the bourgeoning industrial towns and cities.

In the emergent nation states, fiercely competitive in military and colonial as well as economic terms, the acquisition of basic literacy and numeracy became increasingly important. As child labour became outlawed, schools were needed not only for learning purposes but also as custodians during the day. This had not been a problem in pre-industrial rural communities, but gave formal schooling an additional function. Formal education systems were not only becoming more numerous, but also, superficially at least, comparable. This phenomenon had been extended to all other continents by the establishment of colonies by European powers. Very few countries outside Europe escaped the imprint of a colonially derived European model of education, and major examples that did, such as China and Japan, turned to Europe and North America as exemplars for major reforms of their educational provisions in the late nineteenth century. Curiously, England lagged behind, and did not achieve a universal system of state schooling at the secondary level until after the Second World War, as a result of eventually fully implementing the Education Act of 1944. This was little more than a decade after comparative education had joined the other foundations of education disciplines at university level, with programmes at Teachers' College, Columbia University, New York and the University of London. However, the seeds of the field had been sown in the nineteenth century.

The emergence of comparative education

Brickman (1966) published a book on *The Pre-history of Comparative Education to the end of the Eighteenth Century,* in which he traced the interest back as far as Herodotus. Nonetheless, the first known systematic study in comparative education is normally acknowledged to be that of Marc-Antoine Jullien de Paris in 1817. However, this did not come to light until 1942 (Trethewey 1976). Consequently, it is not appropriate to regard him as the founding father of the field as such. The real founding father of comparative education must surely be Michael Sadler, whose contribution was profoundly seminal, and will be discussed further below. First, however, we must not neglect to mention the prior occurrence of what has come to be known in the literature as so-called 'travellers' tales' about education in different countries during the eighteenth and nineteenth centuries. They range from trivial and superficial comments about aspects of education gathered by chance from excursions and expeditions, to more purposeful visits to gather specific information about systems of education sponsored by rival nation states. Even the latter were not seriously comparative but sought to identify features that might be copied and inserted into the system of the observer. This practice has become known as 'borrowing', which was, and is, neither an accurate description nor an advisable practice as such, as David Phillips observed in his discourse *'Neither a Borrower or a Lender Be?'* (1989). It is a matter of regret that this stricture, based on a profound understanding of the perils of educational comparison, remains unheeded by politicians whose mindset of competition is unchanged a century and a half later. Like their forbears, they remain uncritical, instrumental and lacking in any analysis of the cultural context.

The contribution of Michael Sadler

Sir Michael Sadler, as he later became, has no serious rivals for the designation as 'founding father of comparative education'. He spent significant periods of his career at Oxford, but was never fully accepted there, which tells us as much about the institution as it does about the man. Indeed, his conflicts there were mostly concerned with the petty private world of college life (Phillips 2006). Sadler was not one for debates about lost causes but was, rather, a man of action, especially with regard to the neglect of secondary, further and adult education in England in the late nineteenth and early twentieth centuries. In 1885, Sadler was appointed to two positions at Oxford: as Steward of Christ Church, one of the most privileged of Oxford colleges, and as Secretary of the Oxford Delegacy, an organization dedicated to bringing educational opportunities to adults in many locations throughout the country. Sadler was indefatigable in his travels and lectures, and always keen to learn himself about the innumerable variations of circumstance and initiative that were to be fundamental to his understanding the significance of context and scale to the analysis of educational problems and initiatives. It is, perhaps, no surprise that in 1891, his co-author of *University Extension, Past Present and Future* was none other than the renowned Halford Mackinder, Professor of Geography at Oxford.

But, it was the minimal and complex state of an evolving provision for state secondary schooling in England that most concerned Sadler. He was appointed to 'The Bryce Commission' and reported in 1895. It led to a rationalization of the roles of the emergent County Councils, state initiatives such as the 'science schools' movement, private institutions such as charities and eventually to the Education Act of 1902. In his leading role in the Commission, Sadler had taken some account of the observations of some of the authors of the so-called 'travellers' tales' about education in other countries, one of whom was Matthew Arnold, son of the famous headmaster Thomas Arnold of Rugby School, Michael Sadler's *alma mater*. Although not strictly empirical evidence, such information led, in part, to the establishment in 1895 of an 'Office of Special Enquiries and Reports' in a proto-ministry known as the Education Department, and Sadler was appointed Director. It was in this role over the following eight years that Michael Sadler in effect laid the foundations of comparative education. In addition to examining the state of public education in the emergent local authorities in England, he also researched the accumulation of reports on foreign systems of education that he discovered lying dormant in the basement of the Education Department. Gosden (1989) commented, "They now constitute some of the most valuable material in the DES Library" (p. 10).

During his eight years as Director, Michael Sadler made foreign visits of his own to many of the major education systems of Europe and North America, thus adding a contemporary layer of information at the international level to the local studies being made, many by himself, within England, and to the historical material mentioned above. He never wrote a seminal work on comparative education as such, and this may well have been a very good thing. Instead, he lived it, gaining perspectives from proximity to policy makers and school students alike. He instinctively appreciated the wide range of factors affecting education and how they came to mediate the outcome of national policies at the local level. This involved an appreciation of the additional, indeed greater, effects of informal and non-formal education. In short, Michael Sadler understood that education in all its forms is culturally embedded, as may be illustrated by the following extract from his famous 'Guildford Lecture' of 1900:

> When we compare different systems of education we are often in grave danger of slipping unconsciously into expressions which implicitly carry with them the idea that an educational system is nothing more or less than a system of schools, perfectly tidy and neat, known to everybody in the street, an object of local satisfaction and immense boasting; you may multiply it by a thousand and call it a national system of education; and yet all the time you may be actually having less of a really national system of education than is enjoyed by a free country which possesses a strong tradition of national unity, and knows that education is not a matter of schools or book-learning alone. Therefore, if we propose to study foreign systems of education we must not keep our eyes on the brick-and-mortar institutions, nor on the teachers and pupils only, but we must also go outside into the streets and into the homes of the people, and try and find out what is the intangible, impalpable, spiritual force which, in the case of any successful system of education, is in reality upholding the school system and accounting for its practical efficiency' (Higginson 1979, p. 49).

Michael Sadler left government service in 1903 as a result of an internal dispute and proceeded to a Chair in the History and Administration of Education at the University of Manchester. It was during his years there that he compiled reports on education in a number of the newly created Local Education Authorities as a result of the Education Act of 1902, thus illustrating the significance of disparities in educational provision and experiences at varying scales, from local to national. Throughout his time at Manchester and, subsequently, as Vice-Chancellor of the University of Leeds (1911–23) and, later, Master of University College, Oxford (1923–34), Sadler continued his indefatigable efforts on behalf of popular educational provision and the understanding of it, right up to his death in 1943. While at the University of Manchester, Michael

Sadler had tutored a young Isaac Kandel, who turned out to be probably the leading figure in establishing comparative education as one of the educational foundation disciplines.

Pioneers of comparative education in Anglo-American Universities

A trio of scholars can arguably be identified as establishing comparative education as a specialist academic field: Isaac Kandel (1881–1965), Nicholas Hans (1888–1969) and Joseph Lauwerys (1908–80). There were other pioneer scholars in Europe and the Far East, but these three established an Anglo-American tradition, necessarily operating in English and establishing the World Yearbooks in Education from the 1930s. All three came to England from continental Europe – Kandel from Romania, Hans from Russia as an *émigré* from the Bolshevik revolution and Lauwerys from Belgium. All had cross-cultural personal experiences and were at least bilingual, if not multilingual. This kind of background enabled them to gain insights that might elude the monocultural and/or monolingual experience of the majority of people, including many students and even tutors of comparative education today. The polymath challenge is one of the greatest facing all students of education, as a holistic view of this diverse phenomenon is a necessity, though often disregarded.

Isaac Kandel moved from Manchester to teach in Ireland in schools before heading on to the USA and Columbia University, New York (Pollack 1993). His educational interests and activities were eclectic, but Isaac Kandel's most lasting achievements were in comparative education as he was intensely international (Kandel 1933). Just before retiring as Emeritus Professor in 1947, he took a keen interest in the newly formed UNESCO's programme of 'fundamental education' founded the previous year. According to Watros (2010):

> Isaac Kandel warned against simple concerns about illiteracy. Kandel recommended that the Committee avoid technical issues of how to teach local people to read and consider the larger problems of what reading and writing could add to people's lives. In raising this issue Kandel suggested that the Committee members should recognise that education could help students understand and improve the environment in which

they lived. He added the problem that a problem in many in developing countries was that people used the ability to read and write to escape the everyday tasks of the community by taking on some form of government employment. To suggest a way of avoiding such abuses of education, Kandel quoted educational leaders from the United States, France and England who advocated that schools should help students learn to work within their communities in ways that brought about a more humane society (p. 223).

Michael Sadler would have approved, but it did not stop UNESCO from embarking on a series of massive basic literacy programmes, which failed because they paid little regard to context, and modes of literacy acquisition that were functional. Rather, they aimed at wider provincial or even national levels. More importantly, for this discussion, this assessment of Kandel's recognition of the importance of community and, therefore, informal education, is an indication of where we could be now in this field, had things developed differently.

Nicholas Hans came to London in 1919 and joined King's College, London (KCL). He had previously been at the University of Odessa from 1907 to1912. He left Russia as a result of the Bolshevik revolution but always retained a keen scholarly interest in Russian history and education. In 1920, he began to work on the *World Yearbook in Education*, which brought him into contact with Isaac Kandel. From 1939 to 1945, Hans was a civil servant before returning to comparative education. Like Kandel (1933), Nicholas Hans composed a textbook on comparative education (1949), which became a key reader for new courses in the field that developed in the 1960s, a period of funding and expansion in the social sciences.

Joseph Lauwerys came to England in 1914 at the age of twelve. After graduating in natural sciences and then teaching, he joined the University of London, Institute of Education (IOE) in 1932 as a science educator. With wide international interests and connections, Lauwerys too developed an involvement in comparative education and the *World Yearbooks in Education*, which he then took over at the London end with Nicholas Hans, and across to Teachers College, New York and Isaac Kandel. As Kandel retired in 1947 and Hans in 1953, Lauwerys continued until his own retirement as Professor of Comparative Education at IOE in 1970. That was, and still is, the only established chair in this field in the United Kingdom, though it has been renamed, a sobering thought in itself.

The original *World Yearbooks in Education* were a very important part of the establishment of comparative education as a university discipline. Each year, a particular theme was selected and contributions collected from around the world. Also under the supervision of these three pioneers, doctoral students began to produce theses and comparative education acquired a firm status alongside the existing educational foundations disciplines.

International education

The field that has developed from these beginnings went under the name 'Comparative Education' for many decades, but is now conventionally known as 'Comparative and International Education'. There are a number of reasons for this. First of all, as Michael Sadler illustrated through his work, undertaking comparative studies in education does not have to be cross-national in scale. Secondly, if one reviews the titles of the majority of articles in the established journals in the field, discussed in the following chapter, only a minority are actually comparing even cross-nationally. Phillips and Schweisfurth (2008) have a chapter under the heading of 'Domains of Practice and Fields of Enquiry in International Education' in which they recognize six dimensions of 'international education' (pp. 42–59). Of these, 'Education and Development Studies', more commonly known as International Educational Development, is the most prominent in the field today. Their discussion of these forms of international educational studies has much to do with methodological considerations, but also reflects important dimensions of the practical growth of the field and key individuals or innovations within it.

Alec Peterson (1908–88) was of the same vintage as Joseph Lauwerys. After a career in public schools and in the military, culminating in the headship of Dover College, where he created an international sixth form, a unique innovation in England at the time, Peterson moved to the university world in 1958 as Director of the University of Oxford, Department of Education. In 1964, he was one of founders of the now-prestigious academic journal *Comparative Education*. He combined his university work with the founding of the International Baccalaureate (IB) and, in 1968, became the Director-General of the IBO until 1977, having retired from Oxford in 1973. Along with the IB, he was associated with the United World Colleges movement, pioneering international schools. A year before his death, he published the seminal *Schools Across Frontiers: The Story of the International Baccalaureate and the United World Colleges* (1987).

In 1931, a year before the arrival of Joseph Lauwerys at the Institute of Education, University of London, there had been discussion of the need for: 'The creation in London of a strongly-equipped centre for the continuous discussion and investigation of educational problems that are important to the constituents of the British Commonwealth' (Government Papers quoted in Aldrich 2002, p. 103). In 1934, the appointment was made of W. B. Mumford as 'Lecturer in the education of primitive peoples', the title giving some idea of the paternalism of the day. He was also Director of a new Colonial Department, which soon became part of a larger Overseas Division of the Institute, with generous funding from the Carnegie Trust. This also funded Carnegie Fellows from various countries of the 'Old Commonwealth'. In due course, the Overseas Division became the Department of Education in Tropical Areas, a development supported by Joseph Lauwerys, who had been appointed Professor of Comparative Education in 1947. At that juncture, therefore, there was considerable synergy between comparative education and what was to become known as education in developing countries, with Lauwerys at the helm. His extraordinary contribution is summed up by Aldrich (2002) in the following terms: 'By 1970, the year of his retirement, at the age of 67, few members of the Institute could remember a time when Joseph Lauwerys had not been a member of staff . . . and as the leading campaigner for an established chair in comparative education' (p. 182).

With the aftermath of the 1939–45 Second World War came a new spirit of international co-operation, with the new United Nations Organization at the forefront. The United Nations Education, Scientific and Cultural Organisation (UNESCO) was established in Paris, and Joseph Lauwerys was an immediate and enthusiastic supporter.

It is clear from the record of the five important pioneers of comparative and international education outlined above: Michael Sadler, Isaac Kandel, Nicholas Hans, Joseph Lauwerys and Alec Peterson, that they were all generalists and/or polymaths. They all had significant cross-national personal experience before becoming involved in the academic world. The comment made of Peterson in one personal profile that he was 'a visionary with his feet on the ground' applied in some degree to all five, especially to the founding father, Michael Sadler. A firm foundation had been laid for the study of comparative and international education, and in the following chapter, we will see how both developed in the new, more expansive context of post-war reconstruction and development. This was to take place also in the context of an expansion of the social sciences in general, with significant implications for the methodologies for study and research employed.

2

The Nature of the Interdisciplinary Field and its Development

Introduction

The pioneers of comparative and international education appreciated the essential interdisciplinary nature of educational studies – comparative and international education included. All informed the thinking, teaching and writing of a new generation of leaders who also came from a variety of disciplinary backgrounds, but operated within increasingly institutionalized settings. This was a period of relatively generous funding of higher education. It was also one of a greater generation of theory throughout the social sciences. A number of seminal comparative education texts were published at this time in addition to the creation of learnt societies of comparative education and new academic journals.

The nature of education: An interdisciplinary field

The two educations – 'the phenomenon' and 'the discipline' – were introduced earlier. The nature of the latter should necessarily reflect that of the former but unfortunately does not always do so. Although 'education the phenomenon' – that is, the activities of learning and teaching – may seem to be a simple set of relationships, it is in reality extremely complex. It is also of crucial importance to the development of individuals and of the families, communities, regions and nations in which they live and interact. Now, in the early twenty-first century, the well advanced phenomenon known loosely as 'globalization' has produced a new dimension. Human beings need to come to terms with its negative as well as positive attributes (Barber 1995) in order that the potential of education to help the survival of the species and the environment may be maximized: As Aldrich (2010) reminds us:

> Existing aims, such as education for salvation, education for the state and education for progress must be modified, replaced even, by the goal of education for survival' (p. 1).

In order for that potential contribution to be realized, all three forms of education need to be fully recognized and utilized: formal, non-formal and informal. Unfortunately, 'education the discipline' does not in general reflect this. It is overwhelmingly concerned with the formal mode, and within that, 'schooling'.

The totality of 'an education', whether individual or collective, is dependent on the relative influences of a range of *external factors* that impinge on teaching and learning, the main ones being: sociocultural and demographic, historical, geographical, philosophical, economic, political and managerial. All can, and do, operate on a range of scales, from individual to international. Fig. 2.1 illustrates the main factors influencing 'education the phenomenon' and their relationship to the contributing sub-disciplines of 'education the discipline'.

'Comparative and International Education' is simply educational studies perceived through a different lens in order to gain insights that would not otherwise become apparent. First, it is necessary to grasp the 'essence' of education. This is defined as: 'the formation, operation and dissemination of curricula' in Fig. 2.1.

From the holistic view of education being promoted here, 'curricula' means everything that an individual actually learns throughout their lifespan, not just what they have learnt in school. Indeed, despite the sophisticated industry of examinations and assessments, we do not actually know what each individual has actually learnt from formal curricula. We do know that people learn more from non-formal (e.g., in the workplace) and informal education. In the world of informal learning, the 'teaching' component may come from a wide variety of sources, including the media, an ever increasing and sophisticated source boosted by Information Communications Technology (ICT). Much learning is, therefore, involuntary. Such a holistic view is necessary because it attempts to deal with educational reality. Furlong and Lawn (2011) provide a welcome

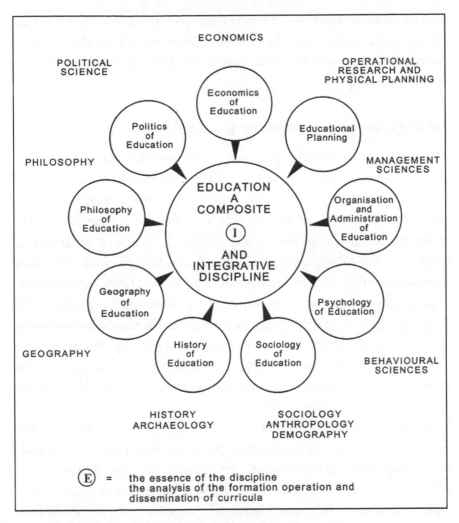

Figure 2.1 Education: A compositive and integrative discipline

reminder of the foundation sub-disciplines, for much educational research has become narrowly instrumental.

Factors and sub-disciplines

For those involved in comparative and international education, a sound general knowledge of the range of factors influencing education, and the sub-disciplines that examine them, is essential. One way of presenting these is to adopt the perspective of a drama being performed in a theatre. So, let us imagine: (a) a stage, (b) a duration of performance, (c) the play: a cast of characters and actors, (d) the media through which they perform and (e) some kind of authorship.

The stage: Geography and the geographical factor

All educational activity takes place somewhere, and that 'somewhere' is not coincidental. Geography is 'the spatial and locational analysis and cartographic representation of the earth's surface phenomena' (Brock 1992). Its realm comprises: (a) the natural and the built environment, (b) the atmosphere above and (c) the lithosphere below. There is, of course, a geography of outer space beyond the atmosphere, the home of the cybernetic revolution in education (Castells 1996; Dodge and Kitchin 2001). An outdated view of geography is that it is strictly divided into physical and human strands. In reality, there is little of the physical world that is totally untouched or unaffected by the actions of human beings, as shown by Thomas (1956), Goudie (2006) and Smawfield (2012). The geographical factor is at the forefront of the challenge facing education's contribution to survival in the twenty-first century (Martin 2011).

Just like the modern stage sets in a theatre, geography is dynamic, and recognizes three dimensions of spatial activity: (a) along lines – for example, information flows; (b) within areas – for example, educational zones within cities and (c) at specific points – for example, in the classroom (Brock 1985). Despite the obvious dynamism inherent in changes in both natural and built environments, there is also a tendency for some activities to cluster in areas where they are already established. This is called geographical inertia and leads to what are called 'surfaces', usually within towns and cities, where educational land use predominates. On the other hand, whereas learners in the past would travel to where their teachers were located, modern forms of ICT allow for information to be brought to the learner almost anywhere. Education is a space-saving mechanism.

Central to geographical observation, data gathering and analysis is the issue of scale. There has been a tendency in comparative and international education to operate mainly at the national scale. While this may be the appropriate scale for some enquiries, such as policy studies, it is rarely the right scale at which to observe educational reality. The issue of scale is discussed in Chapter 4 of this book. Although the geographical factor is clearly a profound influence on educational activity, *The Geography of Education* as a sub-discipline has been slow to develop (Brock 1992; Taylor 2009) and has not yet taken its rightful place alongside the other educational foundations. This compromises the field of comparative education and diminishes it.

Time and duration: History and the historical factor

Educational activity is not only dynamic over space, but also over time. Any educational 'drama' will be set at a certain period of time and will run for a particular duration. The spatial and the temporal go hand in hand, and the legacies of past educational policies, decisions and actions lurk beneath the surface of today's educational landscapes like hidden strata. They may sometimes break through the current surface to explain an educational situation, or they may merely contribute to the evolution of its culture. Understanding gained from the history of education of any place may be crucial to the success, or otherwise, of an innovation or reform. Within this factor, the issue of periodization is important. Broad periods with parameters of little meaning, such as 'nineteenth-century', are inadequate. Selected periods of time must be based on the durations of comparable happenings in education, as illustrated by Phillips (1994 and 2002) with regard to England and Germany.

The History of Education is a well-established member of the family of educational foundations with a sizeable canon of literature. Its importance is well illustrated by Aldrich (2006) and its numerous publications range from studies covering a large expanse of time and space, such as Boyd and King (1995) on Europe, through many on specific countries and some examining the influence of one country on the education of another (Armytage 1968).

Dramatis personae

We may now turn to the action. The *dramatis personae* are the actors who play out the main forces that bear upon educational activity of various kinds. As in any real drama on stage, they will have greater or lesser parts to play, according to the story in question.

Political science: Control, management and administration

Formal and non-formal education may be culturally based but they are politically delivered. As far as national (or in some countries, provincial) systems of formal provision are concerned, control is a prime consideration of those in power. Political science is the study of power and administration, and the political factor is often the most influential one in determining decisions and outcomes. One of the prime functions of formal systems of education is to engender conformity, especially during the period of compulsory schooling. Education systems are an important part of the apparatus of the nation state. There are very few countries in the world where a period of schooling is not compulsory, though there are many countries in the world where this has not yet been achieved. This may mean that control of schooling in such cases is not in the hands of remote government departments, but *de facto*, with more local political forces such as tribal elders, religious missions or even NGOs.

Even in some fully operational systems, power may be formally devolved to regional or local political units, such as the states and school districts of the United States of America and the länder of Germany. Such decentralization of authority over formal education may take many forms: political, curricular or financial. For example, in England, at the time of writing (April 2012), state schools are subject only to the highly centralized political authority of the Minister of Education, who also controls the curriculum of the majority. Local Authorities in England have been progressively stripped of their powers by successive governments since the Education Reform Act of 1988.

The Politics of Education is an established member of the educational foundations. Some of its literature is concerned with power, but much is increasingly to do with policy studies. Cross-national policy borrowing is an issue of obvious interest – for example, Trans-Atlantic (Finegold et al. 1992 and 1993) and Eastern European (Phillips and Kaser 1992). This is related to the transition of formal systems of education in a wide range of circumstances (Griffin 2002). What is less evident in this sub-discipline is the *realpolitik* on the ground at local level, where national policies are often mediated (Griffin 2001). Within the discipline of politics, education is a relatively neglected field, although there are signs that political scientists have begun taking an active interest in the institutional frameworks that govern education, its delivery, and its regulation (Jakobi et al. 2010).

Economics, financial and commercial issues

The social science 'Economics' has to do with actions and systems of production and exchange. Such activities grew significantly in relation to the three urban revolutions: neolithic, renaissance and industrial. Each had profound implications for the development of education in all its forms.

The contemporary discipline of Economics is concerned with the study of resource allocation with the view of improving welfare. The *Economics of Education* branch of the discipline studies the decisions by individual actors or/and states to allocate resources to invest in education (Blaug 1987). In particular, economists research the extent to which one should invest today's resources in future cohorts and are concerned with the efficiency of all aspects of the system (including technologies and processes) as well as with the consequences of these decisions. Given the resource-intensive nature of constructing and maintaining high quality education systems, and the significance individuals in developed economies have attributed to education, the economics of education has been, to a large extent, 'high-jacked' by governments, international organizations and businesses, who link it to political and business objectives.

Education is both a consumer and a producer of financial resources. The economics of education has not only to do with the financing of this service industry, but under the influence of neo-liberal economists in recent decades, its marketization as well. Education has become a commodity (Alexiadou and Brock 1999). Now, we have 'the knowledge business', where a range of educational activities have become wealth creating, in association with globalization (Burbules and Torres 2000). Education, in terms of trading information, is now subject to the General Agreement on Tariffs and Trade (GATT), but is difficult to regulate.

Governments see investment in education, especially formal schooling, as being made in order to foster the economic development of their countries. There must be a connection but it is very complex and unclear. For the more advanced countries, the work of the Organization for Economic Cooperation and Development (OECD), especially its Programme for International Student Assessment (PISA), has become a quasi-comparative education exercise of some influence. This is with regard to prognostications made in relation to national economic development. They are clearly partial as far as predictions are concerned as they take no account of educational inputs other than in a limited number of subject areas for the early teens. It is as if no other component of learning, such as university education and non-formal education at home or in the workplace, makes any contribution at all!

The complex connections between economic and social development and educational input are of even more fundamental concern for less developed countries. Many such countries are former colonies of imperial powers. On independence, their initial policies for development were based on the assumption that the education systems of industrialized nations had a direct and causal relationship to their development, which is simplistic. The result was an over-investment in formal schooling, already burdened with colonially derived curricula. This was at the expense of the development of necessary infrastructures and the acquisition of instrumental literacies by adults on whom increased productivity actually depended.

The nature of aid programmes and their educational dimensions (King 1991; Karpinska 2012) have, in general, not been sufficiently helpful, to say nothing of the disastrous effects of the World Bank's structural adjustment policies in the 1980s, slavishly replicated by other multilateral and bilateral development programmes. Work on the economic factor by some comparative and international educators, notably Colclough et al. (2003), Lewin and Caillods (2001) and Lewin (2008), have been informative, but the divergent views of influential experts, such as Sachs (2005) and Easterby (2006), serve to illustrate the ongoing lack of consensus on relationships between economic policy and sustainable development. The global economic crisis evident in the first decade of the twenty-first century is, likewise, extremely complex and unhelpful (Cable 2009).

A private sector of educational provision exists alongside the public in all countries. Its nature, extent and influence are unique to each country, but it is always significant in economic terms. Stark contrasts between countries in this regard can be illustrated by the considerable influence of private higher education in the United States of America and its virtual absence in the United Kingdom. Conversely, in England, the massive influence of private primary, and especially secondary, schooling contrasts markedly with comparable European nations. New-fangled public–private initiatives are edging into state schooling in England with, as yet, little accountability and uncertain outcomes. As Grayling (2001) has wryly observed:

> Education, and especially 'liberal education' is what makes civil society possible. That means it has an importance even greater than its importance to economic success, which, alas, is all that politicians think it is for' (p. 157).

In closing this section, we want to reaffirm the distinction between (a) the discipline of *Economics of Education* that produces research and theory on the investment of resources in human capital and (b) the uses (and often abuses) of this research by political organizations (including governments) that pursue their own agenda, not necessarily heeding the complexities and conditions under which research results are presented.

Sociology and anthropology: Social and demographic issues

Sociology and Social Anthropology have to do with the study of human groups, though their methodologies are divergent. At a simplistic level, social anthropology, the elder, has been associated with less developed societies and sociology with the more industrialized and modern ones. Social and cultural are not the same, but social anthropology, being more holistic in its approach, can accommodate the cultural – that is to say, overall 'way of life' of a group (Camilleri 1986).

The Sociology of Education is a major and well-established member of the educational foundations, with a strong canon of literature. Karl Mannheim (1893–1947) is sometimes seen as the father of the Sociology of Education. Born a Hungarian Jew, he came as a refugee from Germany to England in 1933 and eventually became Professor of the Sociology of Education at the Institute of Education. With his particular multinational background and zeal for the part education could play in the creation of more just societies, Manheim contributed to the evolution of comparative and international education championed by Hans and Lauwerys. Despite the more liberating ambiance of London academic life, he was immediately 'conscious of the extent to which British society was shot through with divisions and inequalities based upon class and wealth' (Aldrich 2002, p. 124).

Industrialized societies, such as in Europe and North America, were becoming increasingly diversified at this time. This was expressed spatially in more differentiated urban morphologies associated with *de facto* social and occupational segregation. Only in a few places did this become *de jure* segregation, as in the southern states of the United States of America and the emergent South Africa. The provision and expansion of schooling became part of these social structures and key issues for the growing sociology of education, such as class, occupation, gender, race and ethnicity.

These are also aspects of *demography*, a related and important social science in its own right with two main dimensions: population change and population structure. The former has to do with increase or decrease in population numbers due to the balance between birth rates, death rates and migration rates. Population structure has to do with how the population of any place is made up in terms of the same issues as interest the sociologist. Detailed demographic knowledge is, obviously, important for educational planning for all age groups.

The literature of the sociology of education includes classic texts derived from different scales of observation from selected social groups: for example, a community (Young and Willmott 1957), a specific group (Furlong 1992), a single institution (Lacey 1971), a social class (Whitty et al. 2003) or a general text (Ballantyne and Hammack 2011). It also has an international dimension, as represented in the prestigious journal *International Studies in the Sociology of Education*.

The 'Anthropology of Education' examines key issues in human groups that affect their operation, survival, development and distinctive culture. The cultural context of learning was illustrated over four decades ago by Cole et al. (1971) in respect of Bong Country, Liberia. Another example is Todd's classic text (1987), which concentrates on family structures and forms of literacy. Families, rather than governments or other official bodies, are the locations of most decision-making about actual educational participation and performance. Issues such as the age/sex hierarchy in subsistence communities and the relative levels of literacy as between parents, both discussed by Todd, are fundamental. Kinship can also be important, since the majority of systems are patriarchal, which in general adversely affects the educational chances of women and girls. Indeed, the issue of *Gender and Education* is the most important single factor for development, not only for economic reasons but clearly also with regard to natural justice. Gender parity with regard to education is the target of one of the MDGs. The target date of 2007 was set for its achievement at primary level, but it was far from being realized and is now set for 2015. That too is unlikely to be met. Even in more industrialized societies, the issue has not been totally resolved but rather shunted up to higher age groups and the workplace. The issue of gender and education will recur in Chapter 7 in relation to Sub-Saharan Africa. The key role of Lalage Bown (2000a) needs to be recorded here, as does that of Nelly Stromquist (1997). Bown's well-known phrases 'women are development' and 'without women no development' may be laconic but they are fundamentally true.

Modus operandi: Language and communication

Those involved in Comparative and International Education must also understand the medium through which any educational activity is conducted and through which it may be most appropriately and effectively researched, understood and communicated. This means language and mathematics – the latter being a form of language where numbers and symbols are used, rather than words. This has resonance with anthropology, as Edmund Leach encapsulated in the title of his 1976 book, *Culture and Communication: The Logic by Which Symbols are Connected.*

Language is a distinctive feature of the human species that sets it well apart from other higher primates. It is mainly through language and literacy that learning and teaching operate in all three forms of education. This is especially significant in the early years of childhood and within the family, that is to say informal learning, whether it be in a privileged or a disadvantaged setting.

Literacy and numeracy take many forms, including the visual. Paulo Freire, working in north-east Brazil, not only engendered literacy acquisition within the community of adults, but also created a mode of learning and teaching through the forms and symbols of communication already operated by them (Freire 1970). David Archer and Patrick Costello (1990) followed the issue of literacy and power in Latin America by concentrating on little-studied Central America, as did Stromquist (1997), with a study on Brazil. Meanwhile, Archer built on the methodology of Freire in creating and delivering the highly successful literacy programme REFLECT through the agency of the NGO Action Aid. This has been applied successfully in over 60 countries through roughly 450 agencies, ranging from multinational development organizations to small, highly localized NGOs.

Language learning, in whatever context, from primary school to adult literacy initiatives, attracts both theories of acquisition and political action. The issue of national language policy relates to both. Governments decide on the official medium of instruction (MOI), but in situations where the language of the home and family is different (as in most of the less developed countries and many metropolitan cities), use of that 'social language' may be permitted because it engenders more meaningful language acquisition overall. Language policy can be a strongly contested issue at the national level and may take contrasting forms. For example, newly independent Malaysia decided to try to create a particular national identity by making Bahasia Malaysia the MOI for formal education at all levels, including higher education. This was in order to engender a kind of unity under the ruling Malays and control the educational advance of the Indian and Chinese Malaysians. It has proved problematic, as English has become a global language of international discourse, including rapidly advancing scientific and technological innovation. By contrast, on independence, Nigeria, with three major internal languages – Hausa, Ibo and Yoruba – as well as hundreds of local languages, opted to adopt English as the national language and MOI. In present-day USA, there are calls for the recognition of Spanish as an official language alongside English, and as a MOI in schools where there are Spanish-speaking majorities. In this type of situation, bilingualism has become another contested area of policy. Among contemporary comparative educationists, Keith Watson (1992 and 2011) has taken a detailed interest in matters of language policy.

With respect to undertaking educational studies in a culture and language other than one's own, George Bereday, successor to Issac Kandel in New York, was of the view that only many years of immersion in the other culture would enable the researcher to understand educational processes and policies there. Certainly, the whole issue of language is an extremely difficult one for the student or researcher in comparative and international education, and full of potential pitfalls. This is true of the other area of communication, mathematics. Statistical data is massively available in documentary form.

It can also be generated through empirical research, mainly in quantitative mode. For its analysis, some understanding of statistics is essential. The assembly, presentation and manipulation of statistical data by governments are nearly always partial and, in the case of many less developed countries, inevitably incomplete. International and regional datasets rely on what governments contribute to the compiling agencies. So, both students and scholars in comparative and international education have to tread cautiously through this information minefield of dubious veracity.

Authorship: Culture and philosophy

There are multiple authorships of the drama of educational experiences, and not just one playwright, as it were. Both learners and teachers make their distinctive inputs, while the actors outlined above add theirs as well, according to context.

Education, in all its forms, is culturally based. Society is not the same as culture but merely part of it, and susceptible to sociological and anthropological analysis. Culture is the totality of the character of a human group, and gives expression through what might colloquially be termed 'a way of life' or 'a way of doing things'. For most of human existence, groups have been relatively self-contained. As the modern nation state developed, this became even more so, through the establishment of relatively secure borders. Even in Europe, where there have been numerous adjustments of borders over recent centuries, there was little physical migration until the mid-nineteenth century.

Official nationality can change without a person even moving, but this does not mean that culture changes too. Cultural roots run deep. Over the last century and a half, millions of Europeans have emigrated and settled, mostly in locations relatively conducive to their previous climatic experience – the temperate latitudes. In their new locations, they have created variants of a broad European culture based on Greco-Roman and Christian legacies. Such traditions indicate the two main cultural traits: language and religion. Both have, over the centuries, spawned variants such as Romance and Germanic languages and Catholic and Protestant denominations. Nonetheless, they have carried with them what Mallinson called the 'Western European Idea of Education'. Through colonialism (Altbach and Kelly 1978), this idea of the culture of education has spread virtually worldwide. Even major cultures not subject to what they call 'classical colonialism', such as the Chinese and Japanese, took this idea on board partly through the influence of Christian missions and partly through national political decisions to reform formal education in the interests of modernization. In these two cases, as well as what might broadly be called 'the Islamic world', taking on board a European idea of education in systemic terms is not the same as absorbing a whole culture. Consequently, Chinese, Japanese or, for example, Egyptian and Indonesian educational cultures, emerged or re-emerged within the derived European frameworks of educational administration and formal curricula. They carry the linguistic, philosophical and religious dimensions of the indigenous culture – their own 'ways of doing things'.

In those extra-European locations that became fully subjected to classical colonialism, dual cultures have tended to emerge, reflected in their overall educational experiences. For example, in sub-Saharan Africa, indigenous education survived alongside the derived formal schooling of colonialism (Brown and Hiskett 1975). In this region, this is especially so, since most of the countries have derived systems that are far from complete. In these and other poverty-stricken populations in parts of South Asia and Latin America, non-formal and informal modes of learning and teaching hold sway. They operate through their own local economies, cultures and languages, often geared to survival. They too have their own 'ways of doing things', their own philosophies of life, even though many are becoming connected with the globalization of information through ICT, though this is inevitably disparate and partial.

In the worlds of truly indigenous and, to some extent, travelling communities, their approaches to education are holistic (UNESCO 2004), at the heart of which is some form of spirituality that places environmental considerations at the centre. That is to say, their philosophies of education incorporate a kind of religious dimension. This dimension in the 'European idea' has certainly informed the history of education but does not necessarily dominate the philosophical factor. According to *The Oxford English Dictionary*:

> Philosophy is the use of reason and argument in seeking truth and knowledge of reality, especially in the causes and nature of things and the principles governing existence'

The Philosophy of Education is a well-established member of the family of education foundation disciplines. It is the nearest we can get to an author for the drama of education. This is symbolized in the naming of the highest degree obtained by a course of study and research, the PhD/Doctor of Philosophy, whatever the field of study the work is in. As those who have worked for this degree, at least in the humanities and social sciences, will know, the problem or issue in question may be very focused but the research necessary to address it nearly always involves a number of disciplines.

Continuing the story of comparative education

The founding fathers were mindful of the fact that education, in all its forms, was subject to many external influences – 'the things outside the schools matter even more than the things inside the schools and govern and interpret the things inside', as Sadler put it in 1900 (Phillips 2006, pp. 45–6). Kandel, Hans, Lauwerys and Peterson, all understood this too and promoted the subdiscipline as an interdisciplinary field. By the 1960s, they had been joined or succeeded by other scholars who would play their part in expanding graduate programmes and writing textbooks of comparative education. In the United Kingdom, in addition to Nicholas Hans (1949), Vernon Mallinson (1957), Edmund King (1958 and 1968) and Brian Holmes (1965), all laid down markers. Likewise, in the United States of America, Arnold Anderson (1961), George Bereday (1964), Kazamias and Massialas (1965), Harold Noah and Max Eckstein (1969), Kalil Gezi (1971) and others made important contributions.

Over some twenty years, these academics assembled a putative canon of comparative education literature that marked its coming of age as a specialism and, thereby, created a potential problem. From the 1960s into the 2000s, specialization became the mantra of academia in the social sciences and humanities. There was in the early days sufficient funding and therefore demand to create what Becher, in 1989, called 'academic tribes and territories', in his anthropological investigation of higher education. He recognized the limitation of perspectives that had emerged with specialisms which: 'it might seem can only be defined in terms of the labels with which groups of people choose to identify themselves at any given time' (p. 44). He goes on to discuss 'aspects of community life' and 'patterns of communication' within, and between, academic tribes.

For the emergent sub-discipline of comparative and international education, this took the form of defining an identity, forming societies of members in different countries and regions and founding learned journals. Positive and negative aspects of this period of the sub-discipline's growth were discussed by Fletcher (1974), Halls (1977) and McDade (1982). The issue of identity became particularly fraught, as protagonists engaged in arcane, usually sterile and sometimes acrimonious argument about defining the sub-discipline, its method and purpose. In fact, Mallinson, the first after Hans to publish a textbook of comparative education, in 1957, had already presented a clear definition of its nature and purpose:

> By the expression 'comparative study of education' we mean a systematic examination of other cultures and other systems of education deriving from those cultures in order to discover resemblances and differences and why variant solutions have been attempted (and with what result) to problems that are often common to all. To identify the problems of education thus becomes the most important preliminary task of the research worker in the subject. To become familiar with what is being done in some other countries than their own, and why it is done is a necessary part of the training of all serious students of educational issues of the day. Only in that way will they be properly fitted to study and understand their own systems and to plan intelligently for the future which is one where we are thrown together into ever closer contact with other peoples and other cultures (Mallinson 1957, pp. 10–11).

This remarkably prescient statement was made in the context of a committed European, but serves also to recognize the cultural bases of educational activities and the fact that if one has no knowledge of education in other cultures and countries, it is impossible to understand and evaluate one's own. That is the prime function of comparative and international education, but Mallinson gave little indication as to what methods of study and research would be appropriate. However, these aspects were the core of Bereday's book in 1964. Mindful of the cultures influencing educational activities and decisions and the range of factors that inform them, he proposed a method of comparative analysis that is straightforward and still popular in the twenty-first century. He saw the function of comparative education as academic and informative: to educate policy and decision-makers as to all the factors involved and, therefore, the sub-disciplines relevant for their further examination. To some extent, he was supported by Edmund King, whose best-selling *'Other Schools and Ours'* ran into five editions by 1979. More eclectic in his view of methodology, King did, however, set out a number of functions for comparative education in 1968, which Jones (1971) interpreted as a sequence of actions: (a) to be an informative analytical aid; (b) to be a repository of techniques; (c) to provide criteria for specific enquiries like international surveys and (d) to help secure effective implementation of decisions (p. 123).

In Scotland, around this time, Nigel Grant had begun to develop a strong profile in the field with three rather different initiatives. Grant was one of the few in the field to take a detailed interest in education in the Soviet Union (1964) and in Eastern Europe (1969), then mostly Soviet 'satellites' behind the 'iron curtain'. With Robert Bell (1977), he also looked inside the British Isles to compare the systems of the four components of the United Kingdom and that of the Irish Republic. Nigel Grant also pioneered the comparative and collaborative study of Celtic language-medium education in Ireland, Scotland and Wales and took the lead in establishing the first Gallic-medium higher education facility in Scotland, on the Isle of Skye. In short, he was one of the first to operate at different scales of analysis and innovation. Grant also took a keen interest in adult education, a somewhat neglected area within comparative education. It had been pioneered in the United Kingdom by Peers (1958) and Fordham (1980) and was greatly strengthened at Glasgow by the appointment of Lalage Bown (2000b). An important early contribution to international perspectives on adult education was also made by Coles (1969).

So far, so good, in that what are sometimes called the 'Sadlerian principles' of the founding fathers had been recognized by at least some of the second generation. Others of this generation, though, were seeking something more scientific, leading to social science 'laws' that could be predictive. Such was the aim of Brian Holmes (1965), who developed what he termed 'the problem approach' as the way forward, against other, more inductive, approaches:

> Holmes' method of analysis, deductive and anti-positivist, is based on a combination of Popper's critical dualism and Dewey's stages of reflective thinking and change/no change theory of causation. A structure involving

normative patterns, institutional patterns and environmental patterns is used to apply only the aspects of the contributing disciplines (i.e. factors) relevant to the problem. The approach seeks to establish general laws for a science of education of the same order as those operating in the natural sciences (Brock 1988, p. 29).

He was supported in his quest for a 'science of education' by Noah and Eckstein (1969), though not in respect of his somewhat convoluted method. Also in the United States of America, Barber (1972) and Farrell (1979) saw a comparative approach as a necessary plank of any scientific enquiry following systematic analysis of a problem and the assembly of relevant data. Like Halls (1977), both were critical of what Barber called 'methodologism masquerading as science' (p. 9). Farrell's objection was that of inadequate data on education, in any case, too much concerned with observables, such as gender and age, and not enough on concepts such as socio-economic status and ethnicity. He was nonetheless of the view that '. . .there can be no generalising scientific study of education which is not the comparative study of education' (p. 10).

At this stage, it is worth pointing out that much of the argument contesting the identity, method and purpose of comparative education was now appearing in the specialist journals of this and related fields that had been founded as part of the identity of the 'tribe' that Becher (1989) termed 'patterns of communication'. The leading academic journals in English, all of which are still published, are: *International Review of Education* (IRE) (1955); *Comparative Education Review* (CER) (1957); *Comparative Education* (CE) (1964); *Compare* (1970) and *The International Journal of Educational Development* (IJED) (1980). Some regional journals developed that were related to the field, such as *The European Journal of Education* and others that were thematic, such as *Gender and Education and Language and Education*.

What Becher refers to as 'aspects of community life' within academic tribes include the creation of learned societies that also developed at this time, some of which founded journals. The main examples in the Anglophone world are: The Comparative and International Education Society of North America (CIES 1956 – CER); The Comparative Education Society in Europe (CESE – 1961); The British Association of International and Comparative Education (BAICE 1965 – *Compare*). As societies in this field began to multiply across the world, The World Council of Comparative Education Societies (WCCES) was founded in 1970 (Maseman et al. 2007). It operates as an NGO in relation to UNESCO and organizes a 'World Congress of Comparative Education' of which there have been fourteen between 1970 and 2010.

Within the United Kingdom, different strands of the broader activities of cross-national co-operation and international educational development have come together to form the UK Forum for Education and Training (UKFIET). This is a Consortium of a range of players including, not only individual academics – a few of whom enjoy specialist centres – but also societies, consultancies, publishers and the Department for International Development (DfID) of the UK government. UKFIET now convenes a bi-annual comparative and international education conference in Oxford, colloquially known as 'The Oxford Conference', initially established in the early 1990s by David Phillips and Colin Brock of the Centre for Comparative Education at the University's Department of Education.

These networks lead on to discussion of the further development of comparative, and especially international, education under what we might call the third generation of scholars and practitioners in this field in the United Kingdom. Similar 'successions' of academic progeny have occurred in the United States of America, Europe and elsewhere. So, Becher's 'tribe' is now truly global, with over 40 comparative education societies due to meet at the fifteenth session of the WCCES in Buenos Aires in 2013.

Comparative and international education today

Progress towards this global networked community across the turn of the millennium has obviously been made possible by the revolution in ICT, which has had its effect on the nature of the field and, especially, on the relationship between its comparative and international strands. The majority of practitioners now either work in both or are in an institution, department or centre where colleagues in both strands interact. However, since about 1990 and the high profile given to Education for All (EFA), and other aspects of international educational development, this is now a more prominent dimension of the field. This does not mean that the range of contributing disciplines discussed above are any less important. Indeed, the opposite is the case, since the economic dimension of development has become the fixation of governments and the multilateral and bilateral agencies. Application of initiatives seeking to promote economic development have often been less than successful because of failures to take due account of other factors.

In the United Kingdom, the original 1927 Colonial Education Department of the Institute of Education in London has progressed through several stages to its present designation as 'Education and International Development'. The University of Leeds has had a sizeable Overseas Education Unit for at least 45 years and at the University of Sussex, Department of Education, Keith Lewin, Fiona Leach and others have developed an outstanding Centre for International Education over the decades straddling the millennium. The Institute for Development Studies (IDS) includes education and development and is located on the campus of the University of Sussex. It houses the British Library for Development Studies, the largest of its kind in Europe. The educational dimension of the IDS was led for many years by Chris Colclough, now Commonwealth Professor of Education at Cambridge, where there is an active Centre for Education and International Development. Other concentrations of international educational development in Britain are at the University of Birmingham's Centre for International Educational Research led by Michele Schweisfurth, the Research Centre for International and Comparative Education at the Graduate School of Education, University of Bristol, led by Michael Crossley and the UNESCO Chair Centre of the Political Economy of Education at the University of Nottingham led by John Morgan.

In these hubs of significant activity as well as in the United States of America, Europe and Hong Kong (developed by Mark Bray), there tends to be a much greater focus on themes rather than countries or even regions, themes such as: globalization, neo colonialism, policy and planning, funding, public versus private provision, aid and education, literacy, teachers, assessment and qualifications, gender and education, basic education and higher education. The prominence of the last-named area has been especially well served by the establishment by Phillip Altbach of 'The Boston College Center for International Higher Education'. Its quarterly newsletter, *International Higher Education,* now has over 70 editions and is invaluable.

Education and conflict (Davies 2004 and 2005; Brock 2011a and b; Paulson 2011b) has become a growing concern, so much so that it was the theme of the 2011 EFA Global Monitoring Report (UNESCO). This issue, its resolution and reconciliation (Paulson 2011a) is a significant component of 'Education in Emergencies' (Sinclair 2001), an emergent sub-field that involves education in response to dislocation (refugees, asylum seekers, internally displaced peoples); neglected minorities; disadvantaged children and young people; education, malnutrition and famine; health and disease; natural and man-made disasters. The necessarily holistic nature of urgent responses to the educational needs inherent in such situations has been termed 'Education as a Humanitarian Response' by Colin Brock (2011a), who has occupied a UNESCO Chair under that title at Oxford since 2006. Another UK-based UNESCO Chair in this field is that of Alan Smith in 'Pluralism, Human Rights and Democracy' at the University of Ulster, where he has established a Centre for Research on Children and Youth.

Since the late 1990s, the field has seen the re-emergence of higher education as a key focus of international educational development, following its relative neglect after Jomtien in 1990 and the increasing dominance of EFA. Leading the way has been Philip Altbach's aforementioned Center for International Higher Education at Boston College and its quarterly newsletter. The most recent edition at the time of writing (No. 66, Winter 2012) is looking at branch campuses and cross-border themes. Indeed, the exponential expansion of the tertiary sector, involving large numbers of private universities, outreach campuses and cross-border online studies is a serious concern for UNESCO in its attempts to provide a framework for the maintenance of good and comparable standards, leading to genuine equivalence of qualifications and standards. The fundamental role of universities in securing sustainable development and survival has been highlighted by Pyle and Forrant (2002) and Brock (2012).

Does this expansion of more applied and developmental work in the field exclude or replace the efforts of the previous generation to undertake individual country studies, to seek to understand the identity of comparative education and to be concerned with methodology? No, it does not. In fact, the opposite is the case. Is the evident growth and popularity of the field in terms of centres and societies a sign of its intellectual development? No, not necessarily. It could be a sign of superficiality (Bray 2007). Does the increased interest of governments in international surveys of certain aspects of educational achievements in schools or the international rankings of universities mean that sound methods of comparison are being used and the hitherto scant recognition of its existence has been reversed? No, it does not.

A turning point became evident by the last two decades of the twentieth century, as observed by Altbach and Kelly as early as 1986 when they say:

> We do not ask here how the social sciences can guide research; rather our intent is to draw attention to the new and diverse currents of thought about comparative education, the use of the field, regional variation and world systems analysis, the theories undergirding comparative studies and paradigm shifts, and the debates over ideology and scholarship that give the field vitality and strength (p. 1).

Such new perspectives are certainly welcome and, indeed, inevitable in a globalized world, but as Raivola (1986) observes in the same volume: 'Comparison is not always used for the purpose of constructing an explanatory theory. Often it is used in creating a frame of reference to which varying observations can be related. . . . Not all comparative research, then, seeks general explanations, but all research that seeks to offer general explanations must be comparative' (p. 262). This is a direct reflection of the view of Farrell, referred to above. It may not be coincidental that innovative ways of working in this field at that time were emanating from the United States of America.

A particularly interesting perspective fostered by Paulston (1996) of the University of Pittsburgh was that of social cartography. With obvious allusions to the spatial dimension and, therefore, the geographical factor, social cartography can accommodate the incidence and dynamic interaction of other social sciences in relation to themes of educational importance in comparative perspective. Stromquist (1996) makes imaginative and telling use of this tool with reference to 'gendered spaces' (pp. 223–47).

From the 1980s, in company with the social sciences in general and educational studies in particular, the field of comparative and international education has been concerned with research and the development of theory. In part, this has been driven by national and international rankings of universities and their departments. Consequently, significant publications in this field have considered the role of research in addressing major influences on educational activity and policy, such as Alexander et al. (2000) in their two volumes: *Learning from Comparing*. This arose from a collaborative seminar by three centres of comparative and international education at the universities of Bristol, Oxford and Warwick.

Crossley and Watson (2003) made a further substantive contribution to the debate with *Comparative and International Research in Education: Globalisation, Context and Difference*. The inclusion here of the issue of context reflected an ongoing argument by a number of comparatists over the years that context must not be overlooked in the interests of generalization and prediction.

This brings us back to the issues of scale, community and units or levels of analysis (Bray and Thomas 1995). They proposed a framework for comparative educational analyses on three axes: (a) geographic location levels (from individuals to world regions/continents); (b) non-locational demographic groups (such as age, ethnicity and gender) and (c) aspects of education and society (such as teaching methods, curriculum and finance). It was unfortunate that their geographic axis, apart from individuals at one end, was based mainly on the formal and political, but the general idea of multilevel analysis is important. It resonates with the units of analysis discussed by Wirt (1986). If units of analysis differ in a cross-national or global study, then any potential value of comparative analysis is inevitably compromised.

Bray et al. (2007) devote nearly two-thirds of the text of their book on *Comparative Education Research* to 'Units of Comparison'. There are chapters on eleven such units: places, systems, times, cultures, values, educational achievements, policies, curricula, educational organizations, ways of learning and pedagogical innovation. Clearly, they range across a mixture of some units allied to the factors discussed in detail earlier. In the penultimate chapter of this book, Mark Bray picks up on Becher's notion of academic tribes and territories, including the differentiation between urban and rural societies in terms of communities, cultures and competitiveness and how this has affected the nature of researches into their educational profiles and problems. He suggests that 'If it is doubtful that the whole domain of education could be considered a discipline, it is even more doubtful whether comparative education could be considered one' (p. 345). This is explained by the dependence of both on the contributing disciplines of the social sciences, which is why they have been discussed in some detail above.

This is a strength rather than a weakness of comparative and international education, to which the term 'areas of study' may be preferable, and just as honourable.

Conclusion

The very necessary balance in the identities of units of comparison illustrates the continued significance of comparative and international perspectives on education. It cautions against a total rejection of the idea of examining national units, their seemingly similar systems but idiosyncratic cultures of operation and localized mediations. Theory and method in this field have to be mindful of context and, especially, have to remember the majority contribution to learning made by non-formal and informal education. This is not a textbook of comparative education, but an historical, contextual and illustrative introduction, and for those who would wish to delve further into the intellectual and methodological dimensions, recourse is recommended to Bray, Adamson and Mason (2007) and Phillips and Schweisfurth (2008), as well as the journals listed above.

3

A Global Overview: Legacies and Inertias

Having discussed the disciplines that feed into the study of education, in this chapter we shall review some of the key issues and institutions that these disciplines are concerned with. In doing so, we shall also attempt to establish links between institutions and localities and, at times, provide explanations for the shape that education systems (or parts of them) have come to adopt.

Education institutions and complexity

Education in recent years has become a very central and visible field of policy and politics. It is at the root of big reform programmes of the economy and the civil society, both in developed and developing countries. Governments and international organizations are increasingly talking about 'learning' (or lifelong learning) as opposed to education, often linked to the ultimate political objective of creating the 'knowledge economy' and the 'knowledge society' of the future. These have become dominant discourses in nation states all over the world, disseminated through powerful international organizations, such as the World Bank, the UN and the European Union, and they provide the arguments for the re-design of whole systems of schooling. There is lively debate across not only the various areas of education but also sociology and political science on how to understand and how to research these developments and their implications for the millions of young people (and, increasingly, adults) involved in the process. But, of course, developments in education cannot be understood unless we review them against a wider historical, economic and social framework (see Phillips and Ochs 2004; Steiner-Khamsi 2004; Sultana 2008b).

In the more industrialized parts of the world, the developments in the forms but also to some extent content of schooling have followed social and demographic changes that relate to occupational structures and the economy at large. In addition to the economy, the institutions of the family and, indeed, the state remain as fundamental today to the study of education as they were a 100 years ago. In the past, the Church had a very powerful role in designing and providing education. This is certainly no longer the case to the same degree, but 'faith', more broadly, is still an influence in many national education contexts, and the relationship between organized religion, the state and education is still present and mostly settled, across different national contexts. All these institutions, in their interplay with local cultures and local economies, produce diverse and often distinct education outcomes that relate to major aspects of social organization and the creation of individual and social identities.

Education, through the process of assessment and certification, strongly contributes to the distribution of labour market positions, challenges (sometimes) and reproduces (usually) inequalities defined by socio-economic background, ethnicity or gender of students. While doing this, education institutions legitimate the stratification of the labour market through the distribution of rewards (credentials, access to elite, mass, vocational sectors of post-compulsory education, etc.). Mass education is inherently unequal (Shavit 2007) and one of the main roles of the school is to grade students and sort them out through differentiated school tracks and curricula, according to their ability/performance. This is something that employers want (to filter and sort out workers), professional groups expect (to maintain occupational closure and control of selection) and teachers practice as the system's gatekeepers (ibid.). But, we live in an age where discourses of 'inclusion' are linked to education participation and where all are supposed to have the same opportunity to be successful. In a recent European Council and Commission Joint Report (2012), we read the statement "To emerge stronger from the crisis, Europe needs to generate economic growth based on knowledge and innovation" (Joint Report on the Implementation of the Strategic Framework for European cooperation in education and training, 2012/C 70/05). Beyond this, there is little consistency across countries on how education and training systems connect to the labour market, how and when systems differentiate their education provision and select pupils – other than the fact they all do all these things. The role of the state and the role of the market in the production of these relationships are highly contentious issues and viewed very differently in states with different national social welfare models.

But, the role of education is not only defined by its function to allocate young people to various places in the occupational structure. It has distinct cultural dimensions that relate to issues of socialization and citizenship and these shape, in their own way, boundaries around opportunity and life chances in relation to gender, class, ethnicity and disability. Education institutions from pre-school to higher education, intentionally through the curriculum and unintentionally through their social organization and practice mediate, construct and reconstruct what it means to be a male/female, ethnic/religious/linguistic minority or majority, middle class or poor, heterosexual/homosexual citizen and what expectations and possibilities are available to these various identities and their intersections. Creating and negotiating meaning is one of the core activities of the school, which, of course, is on its own a complex cultural and social institution. The outcomes of these negotiations are not predetermined, nor are they completely open. Individuals tend to construct their response to the institution of the school not only in terms of values, beliefs and tastes, but also symbolic dimensions of language codes and patterns of 'acceptable' behaviour that they draw from their membership to family, community and class groups – what Bourdieu has called 'habitus'.

Schools are also sites that reflect the agency of teachers and the school's institutional/local history. Teachers are not just civil servants (in most countries), instrumentally performing a teaching task. They need to be seen as embodying identities, experiences and norms and bringing these to the organization of the school/university that shapes behaviours, perceptions and understandings of what is the right way of doing things. In shaping the subjectivities of their students, schools and universities mediate and often contest or silently re-shape the official or dominant ideology or policy designs that come from the 'top'. The implementation of large education reform projects is heavily mediated by education spaces where values, meanings and purposes are debated (Jones et al. 2008) and where not only 'reforms change schools', but also 'schools change reforms' (Sultana 2008a, p. 10).

In the European rooted liberal thought, the institution of the school was tasked with preparing young people for adult life without significant interference from other institutions (family, state, economy, religion) (Crouch 1999). But, this has clearly not been the case for any of these institutions although the school has had relative autonomy to exercise control of some of its functions, mainly through the (quasi-)professionalization of teachers. The relationships between church and state have been resolved in one way or another around the end of the nineteenth and early twentieth centuries in Europe and north America, with smaller 'battles' still fought over issues of control and influence of the curriculum and faith practices (Brock 2010; Watson 2010; Zambeta 2003). Faith still plays a central role in the education systems in many other parts of the world, where there are continuous negotiations between 'modernization' reforms (entailing a strong secularization element) and tradition (see, for example, Findlow (2008), in relation to the Arab education systems). The relationship between the economy and the school goes through cycles of looser and tighter couplings. As we shall see later in the book, we are in a period of fairly strong connections, and the relationship between the state and the schools is changing dramatically with fast changing roles of the state in an era of rapid globalization. We shall examine issues of the 'changing state' and the economy in relation to education in this and the following chapters in more detail.

In differentiating and mediating schooling structures, pedagogy and curricula, we should also take into account the role of the family. The place of the family within schools has been almost unchanged throughout most of the twentieth century, when all industrialized countries established free and compulsory systems of schooling. Even though the modern European model of the school is meritocratic, there is evidence from all over the world that the institution of the family plays a very strong role in shaping the outcomes of schooling for children, which of course is connected to the allocation of young people to positions in the job market. In countries where social and economic inequalities are steep and the welfare state is limited, the outcomes of schools seem to be more sharply differentiated by socio-economic background of the students. Education systems have not managed to successfully 'neutralize' the influences of the family in the achievement of children; on the contrary, they seem to be reproducing social inequalities (Shavit and Blossfeld 1993). In the first two decades of the new millennium, the trend seems to be intensifying. The latest OECD report, *Education at a Glance* (2011), shows similar patterns today, with children from low socio-economic and immigrant background being particularly disadvantaged:

> PISA results show that some countries have been more successful than others in mitigating the impact of socio-economic background on students' performance in reading. In general, students with an immigrant background are socio-economically disadvantaged, and this explains part of the performance disadvantage among these students.[1] (OECD 2011, p. 88)

The institution of the family has always been instrumental in the life chances of children. What seems to be distinct today, as opposed to 60 years ago, is that the ever expanding education systems provide *more opportunities* to *all* children (most of the institutional barriers that would privilege almost explicitly the upper classes have been eliminated by national reforms, by the 1970s, in most places). But, education is a positional good, so selectivity and stratification have been reinforced in different ways. Expansion and selectivity go hand in hand, and many studies have shown that as inequalities in education opportunity decline at the bottom end of the educational trajectory, they are becoming more stable or they increase at the top end (Shavit et al. 2007). Florencia Torche (2010) found that, in four Latin American countries (Brazil, Chile, Colombia and Mexico), there is a decline in inequality in the lower educational transitions (explained by the universalization of education and the reduced advantage of males). At the same time, she observes a marked increase in socio-economic inequality at the secondary and post-secondary levels, especially in the cohorts particularly hit by the recent economic crisis. Contemporary discourse around the knowledge economy emphasizes the importance of continuing education and inclusion to all children more than ever. But, this is done against a background of globalization, higher urban mobility and segregation more than ever in the past and economic and cultural competition that Van Zanten (2005) suggests provide 'new routes to social advantage or disadvantage for all social groups' (p. 166).

In addition to all this institutional complexity, 'education' as an instrumental, social, moral and cultural endeavour is not a singular project. The meaning of education, the purposes of it and the specific functions it performs in relation to economic exigencies, political circumstances and cultural and social imperatives are highly variable in space, time and across national and local cultures and sub-cultures, as we have noted already in Chapter 2. We also know that the site of educational institutions is fertile ground for challenge and contestation. Individuals and groups (teachers, students, parents, local government education officials, local communities and many other stakeholders) often redefine the tasks they are given and attribute the meanings that make sense to them in relation to their particular student population, local circumstances and personal experiences. This is, by no means, a necessarily progressive or empowering process, although it has the potential to be (see, for instance Jones et al. 2008; Van Zanten 2005).

Given the great complexity in origins of education systems, actors, sites and their interactions that constitute 'education', how can we explain the striking similarities of organization, forms and curricula across most education systems in the globe? And what do these similarities consist of? To even attempt a response to this question, we need to move our lenses beyond the national state boundaries, and view world-wide changes in education.

Global convergence of education policies and practices

Political and economic agents and structures that operate beyond the nation state have, over the last part of the twentieth century, framed and steered education systems by promoting particular policy options as available, desirable or 'fundable'. This does not necessarily mean that nation states are forced to take certain directions although, as we shall see later, this also happens in cases of countries that receive international financial assistance. In most cases, the process is much more subtle than that. Education directions often followed shifts in wider policies that aimed to respond better to imminent problems of the economy, within the remits of what was politically feasible (see Dale 1999). Political expediency, but also policy borrowing and following 'suggestions' or 'best practices' promoted by international and transnational organizations have led to a situation of internalized policy processes, with remarkable degrees of convergence in policy articulations and often structures, if not necessarily practice (Grek 2009; Moutsios 2010; Ozga and Lingard 2007). Neo-liberal assumptions about the economy and the role of the state have a significant role to play in the way education is understood. Such assumptions often underpin the construction of 'education spaces' beyond the nation state (for instance, the European education space), while international organizations, such as the World Bank, the OECD and the WTO, among others, act as agents for the dissemination of such ideas, often without reference to national/local contexts. Alexiadou and Jones (2001) argue that the processes of globalization have supported the emergence of a global 'travelling discourse' around education policies that cross national boundaries. These travelling discourses and policies come into contact with local education spaces that carry their own cultures and values in terms of how education is understood. The interaction between the two produces varied and unpredictable outcomes sometimes, but the homogenizing effect of such travelling policies cannot be denied. So, we observe that:

1. At international level, and through the work of international and inter-governmental organizations, there has emerged a coherent set of travelling policy themes that policy makers have sought to translate into projects for the re-design of national schooling systems.
2. There is a second kind of 'travelling policy', one that crosses boundaries between different disciplines and social practices. Arguments from management theory and economic research come to be deployed in the field of education.

These policy themes refer to agendas that intend to reshape how we conceptualize education purposes, but also what are the 'right' forms of governance to effect successful reshaping of education systems. International organizations are very much at the centre of formulating these agendas, which have a distinct and direct correspondence to education as an economic strategy. Questions of 'competitiveness', economy and efficiency in the use of resources, and the development of human capital of a kind appropriate to an information age are central to these agendas and discourses. So too are issues of social inclusion, even if their relationship to economic agendas is problematic. This kind of travelling policy serves both as a reference point for national policy development and as a legitimization for national level changes whose implementation may be controversial. It is embedded not just in the practice of international organizations, but also in the positions of national governments and policy elites. We are aware of the dangers of reductionist

approaches that over-simplify complex policy changes, but a certain degree
of summation is necessary in an introductory volume such as this. Drawing
on Ball (1998) and Meyer and Rowan (2006), we can point towards such a
set of policy themes that underpin global education tendencies of the last
20–25 years.

The first refers to 'new institutional economics' that conceptualize social
actors as rational and calculating while pursuing their interests in various
social and economic spheres. Economic markets are seen as institutionally
embedded and, thus, affected by the ways in which the state and civil society
regulate contracts and modes of operation. In redesigning the institutions
of education, these assumptions lead to the replacement of bureaucratic
forms of organization, by market-modelled forms of schooling that combine
institutional devolution and target-setting that provide incentives for all actors
involved (parents, teachers, schools, local authorities, etc.) to pursue their own
self-interest. The faith in the force of 'choice' for consumers who can 'voice'
their complaints, or 'exit' the system, is paramount. Neo-liberal assumptions
about social behaviour and institutional adaptation underpin all these policy
themes and are organically connected to the idea of the 'knowledge economy'
and the 'learning society' (Hatcher and Jones 2011).

The second policy orthodoxy relates to the state no longer being the monopoly
provider of education. The dominance of the discourse of 'governance' has
seen the state reduce its own roles in (but not control of) education, and bring
in new practices of regulation and new public or private actors into schooling.
This type of governance relies on a set of principles and ideologies, such as:
(a) managerialism as an alternative to bureaucracy, that aims to bring to
the public sector, innovation and empowerment; (b) steering mechanisms
of benchmarking and setting targets for the purposes of accountability and
comparisons and (c) a multitude of actors that participate in the setting but
also monitoring of education standards. These actors include professionals,
administrative personnel and political actors in the sector, but also a wider
group of experts, think tanks, advocacy groups and unions. But, education
is not just 'big politics' but also 'big business', with many private and quasi-
public organizations that are in the business of providing technical services
and products to schools, as well as research and evaluation services, training,
textbooks, etc. (ibid.). This is all too familiar in many national contexts,

certainly within the United States and Europe, where privatization in various forms has been taking place quite aggressively and systematically (see Lundahl et al. 2010 in relation to Sweden; Ball 2007 in relation to the United Kingdom). All this, of course, did not just affect structures and forms of organization, but also pedagogies and curricula. Schools are expected to foster entrepreneurship and equip young people with relevant skills and attitudes for the market place. But, schools are also expected to develop social capital and to act as core agents that promote social cohesion.

Interestingly, these are not discourses and policies that one can only find in the so-called 'developed' world. In Africa, Samoff (2003) talks of a discourse of 'African education in crisis', with international organizations consistently offering the same 'remedies' for any, and all, local contexts in this huge and extremely diverse continent: reduction of involvement of the central government in the provision of education, the expansion of private schooling, decentralization, introduction of multi-grade classrooms, favouring of in-service over pre-service teacher education. In the early 1990s, the countries that formed the USSR became independent states, with responsibility for developing their own education systems, and with education again being seen as a 'significant level in responding to the demands of the new national context and also the pressures of globalisation' (Seddon 2005, p. 1). The education reform initiatives in these post-socialist contexts, often supported by the World Bank or the Asian Development Bank, conform to a similar pattern to that described by Samoff for many African contexts. National governments are required to adopt foreign education solutions to local problems, often against long histories of institutional contexts that were organized on very different logics of practice shaped by Soviet models of organization. Local policy makers and practitioners may have different ideas to those of the 'donors' in terms of curricula, textbooks and pedagogies (see Bahry 2005 in relation to Tajikistan) or the dissemination of 'best policy practices' that do not always translate to 'best practices' under different 'political constellations' (see Steiner-Khamsi and Stolpe 2005, p. 31 in relation to Mongolia). In Latin America, the World Bank assistance relied on a development model based on privatization, deregulation and trade liberalization and, in education, promoted amongst other things, decentralization, greater school autonomy and putting more importance on 'outcomes' (Bonal 2004). In higher education, Latin American institutions have been facing pressure for institutional change towards an 'Americanized' model, one which is now very familiar to all of us, characterized by reduced state funding and higher reliance on private sources, closer links with business and industry, a decline in institutional autonomy to accommodate market demands and pressures for accountability and performativity (Torres and Schugurensky 2002).

In all these developing economies and societies, despite their differences in pretty much everything (state and nature of the economy, political system, social, family and cultural organization and education infrastructure and traditions), international financial assistance for the development of education for a modern knowledge economy comes with conditions. And these conditions tend to promote solutions that are remarkably similar in emphasizing discourses, policies and agendas that are, in effect, identical in all developing countries. We should still make a note of caution at this stage. We are not claiming that there is no institutional diversity in education across the globe. This is clearly not the case. We observe a very complex picture of conflicting trends and practices, within diverse systems and institutions. But, even though this diversity defies easy categorization, there is a strong tendency to what Samoff (op. cit) has called a process of 'institutionalization' of international influence.

How can this be explained?

Explanation is notoriously difficult in social science! But, depending on the theoretical perspectives of different researchers, there have been substantial accounts that have, over the last 30 years, attempted to interpret this remarkable trend of increasing convergence in the forms, structures and, often, content of schooling across the globe.

From the perspective of early institutional theory, organizations (including schools and school districts) follow a process of 'isomorphism' during which they standardize their responses to political influence that comes from the 'top', in order to maintain legitimacy. In addition to complying with dictates from governments, organizations standardize their practices through: (a) mimetic processes, in which competition with other similar organizations leads to imitation, but also (b) through the professionalization of teachers (DiMaggio and Powell 1983). Institutional historians, such as Samuel Bowles and Herbert Gintis, and Jerome Karabel, among others, have charted the sociological and comparative dimensions to the process of formation of school systems throughout the twentieth century, which culminated (by the 1980s) into a heavily bureaucratized, state-regulated, funded and controlled system, run by a professionalized administration. One of the key arguments that emerged from this body of work was that education institutions (in industrialized contexts) had, as their most important function, 'legitimacy' – 'the need to maintain the trust and confidence of the public at large' (Meyer and Rowan 2006, p. 5).

More recent analysis within this tradition shifts the focus from the bureaucratized schooling system to the quasi-market one, and the changes that this has made to schools in terms of their relationships with the economy, the state and their constituencies (communities, business and industry, parents, etc.). But, theoretically, there has also been a shift of research focus after the 1990s to: the socially constructed nature of institutions and the significance of building shared beliefs and norms in 'building institutions'; the importance of questions of power and network building in forming alliances and effecting change in institutional settings; as also, the power of 'history' in allowing for a limited range of possible actions for the future. So, from within an institutional perspective, Ramirez (2006) analyses the process by which the American 'model' of a university has become an almost dominant world model for higher education. He argues that the relative strength of the 'national' versus the 'global' models of education differs across nations, with significant differences between countries with weak versus strong academic traditions. Despite the strong and historically nationalized model of the European university that has kept its distances from society and the economy, the Bologna process now provides an interesting experiment of bringing universities closer to the labour market, as happens in the US system. Developing countries, depending on their colonial links, have emulated the university structures and curricula of their former colonial masters. Differentiation, of course, is strong – both in types of institutions and their aspirations – and the Bologna process is likely to further this as elite institutions across Europe are likely to loosely follow the Bologna recommendations or even resist them and offer a more traditional, old fashioned and elitist education, with 'mass' universities homogenizing their structures, curricula and operations at the other end of the scale.

Institutional theories have tended to focus more on stability of organizational forms and 'isomorphic' change. Power, politics and conflict have not been very central dimensions in most institutional perspectives (with notable exceptions, as discussed in Meyer and Rowan 2006). Starting with theories of the capitalist state, Bowles and Gintis argued in the mid-1970s that the state is never a neutral coordinator of disinterested parties, but it is controlled by the capitalist class (in industrial nations) and by the local elites, together with former colonial groups, in developing countries. The aim of these groups is not democratic rule or equitable distribution of resources and opportunities – this is just the necessary rhetoric to legitimate their rule. Rather, it is to achieve economic stability and advantage to themselves. In that system, education is viewed as an instrument of the state and aims at producing workers for the capitalist economy in terms of the technical but also social skills necessary for the smooth functioning of the society and the economy. When markets are introduced in previously bureaucratic systems, the state is not merely the regulator ensuring fair play, but, because it represents the vested interests of the ruling classes, it makes sure that deregulation, decentralization, institutional competition and individual choice are all working for their benefit. So do the particular sets of knowledge and social meanings that schools, as cultural institutions, embody and transmit. Marxist and neo-Marxist analysts view school knowledge not as technical and deriving purely from scientific discovery, but as linked to the ideological dominance of powerful groups in society.[2] Such accounts view the role of the school as not just repressive, but also potentially progressive in dispelling the myths propagated by the ruling class (ex. the myth of 'meritocracy') and carrying the seeds for emancipation.

World-system and postcolonial analysts have taken the neo-Marxist critique to the international arena and have given a distinctly global and non-state bound reading of education. They argue that education in national contexts is often shaped by forces beyond the nation state more than by domestic/internal politics. Martin Carnoy's 1974 book, *Education and Cultural Imperialism*, was the first of its kind in this genre, followed by many subsequent analyses that examined the relationships between elite groups, classes, regions and nations and how these affect schooling and its economic, social and political outcomes (Altbach and Kelly 1986; Carnoy and Samoff 1990). Despite the variations in focus or research methodology and field of application, all these theorists view national schooling systems as existing within the context of unequal power relations among nations. Nations such as the United States, Great Britain and France exercise their power or/and colonial links to export their education systems and to distribute particular types of knowledge in developing countries. In this paradigm, the similarity in schooling structures and contents across the world is the product of these relations of dependence between the industrialized and non-industrialized countries. Despite the numerous critiques to this model (Altbach and Kelly, op. cit), the appeal of this analysis is still strong, but it has, of course, developed over the last 40 years to include more nuanced and sophisticated analysis of the links between the global North and the global South and their implications for education (Tickly 2011). This is something we shall pick up again in Chapter 5.

Acknowledging the pressures that operate beyond the remit of the 'national', nation states still matter and control the international discourses and resources to their capacity. There is a lot of commonality in the world stage in how education is organized. But, we share Lingard and Rawolle's (2011) observation that there is a 'global education policy field' that has distinct effects on national education policy and policy processes. This is of relevance to both developed and developing countries. The OECD performs this function of homogenizing what is articulated as problematic and as valuable to pursue in education – to a large extent, by the very process of measuring certain aspects of education systems and not others (Pereyra et al. 2011). In developing countries, multilateral organizations, such as the World Bank and the IMF, shape education policy through sometimes coercive measures (through structural adjustment policies in education or lending) and, often, through 'softer' processes similar to those of the OECD and the EU, such as setting policy agendas, benchmarks and indicators.

Policy reception and selective adaptation

So, how do these travelling policies and agendas get 'embedded' in the local contexts? The answer is never straightforward and the outcomes are not always predictable. They tend to interact with traditions, ideologies, forms of organization and cultures of practice that have developed locally, although of course these have themselves, in part, been shaped by international contexts and influences. Education spaces at the level of the school, city, region and nation mediate the global policy themes through established practices, identities and priorities that may or may not be compatible with those coming from the floating global space. As the brief examples earlier suggest, institutions and practices that were established during social democratic or national-statist reforms may be at odds with market-oriented or managerial agendas. So, the outcomes of the 'travelling policies' in education, in combination with the changing ideas about the governance and role of education, are increasingly embedded within national policy elites that tend to adopt such policies in responding to local problems. They are the ones that carry Samoff's 'institutionalization' task and integrate the global themes with the national agenda for reform. At the level of local policy communities, however (to include, trades unions, academic practitioners, student organizations), there is often a degree of local policy 'inflectedness', where the global discourses get recontextualized (adapted, resisted or silently transformed from original intentions) – what Ball (1998) has expressed as 'big policies' operating in a 'small world'. So, the process is one where politics is as important as policies, where nothing is neutral in the technical reports that present national 'remedies' for educational change. For example, drawing on the cases of Kazakhstan, Tajikistan and Turkmenistan, Silova (2005) shows how travelling policies from international financial institutions, multilateral donor agencies and various NGOs interact with the legacies of Soviet centralist traditions and, in the process, become 'hijacked' by local policy makers to use for their own local/political purposes: 'travelling policies have not always been imposed, copied and reproduced locally, but, given the centrality of local agency, have been infused with new meanings reflecting a dynamic interplay between the global and the local' (p. 57).

The international policy problem of 'inclusion'

We want to devote the rest of this chapter to one of the biggest issues that affects education everywhere – the problem of 'inclusion'. In subsequent chapters, we shall examine in more depth the problem of poverty and disadvantage in relation to education in developing countries, and the policy responses that have been designed over the last 40 years from international and national organizations. In this chapter, we highlight some more general issues in relation to 'inclusion' and how these affect the more industrialized parts of the world, and we shall draw on the situation in Europe to illustrate the main points.

We view 'inclusion', in rather broad terms, to include economic, social, political and cultural elements. Being included in a society is about having good possibilities and prospects for fully participating in all aspects of economic, social and cultural life of that society and about having as many chances as all other citizens to fully experience what that society has to offer. So, we view inclusion as a valuable concept when it has a strong equality dimension to it, rather than a minimal legal connotation of having a 'right' to participate (but not necessarily the means).

In this stronger definition of inclusion, there are many barriers to access and to participation that would place young people from particular backgrounds at a disadvantage early on in their lives. Such barriers relate to conditions of relative and absolute poverty and disability, but also a range of other dimensions that may combine with poverty or disability to produce even further disadvantage in particular societies, such as faith, ethnicity, language and gender (see Rogers 2007; Shain 2012). Education is clearly fundamental to achieving an inclusive society, but it is by no means the only, or even the main, institution to make this a reality. Education is at the root of providing the necessary skills to young people so that they can get employment, and is important in equipping citizens with social and cultural attributes that can help them 'fit' in whatever society they live. But, as we have discussed already in earlier parts of the book and this chapter, education is never free or apolitical, and is often used by groups in the population to maximize the advantage of their children (by minimizing the advantages of other children). So, how can we think of inclusion and exclusion in relation to education?

Discourses around 'social inclusion', 'social exclusion' and their relationship to public services have been in circulation across Europe and beyond for about 30 years. The terms have been applied to attempts by governments and academics to define the relationship between society, the economy and institutions, in times of deep economic and social transformations. The versatility of the term 'inclusion' (and, by association, 'exclusion') has resulted in evolving frameworks of understanding around the concept that have placed different emphasis on the definition of an 'inclusive' society, the relationship of such a society to the state and to the institutions of the market (Lindblad and Popkewitz 2000). In a seminal paper, Silver (1994) elaborated three different 'paradigms of social exclusion' according to their intellectual origins and national applications:

a. A paradigm based on the French political philosophy of solidarity, where exclusion occurs when the social bonds between the individual and the organic whole of society ruptures. In this paradigm, the inverse of exclusion is not 'inclusion' but 'integration', which refers to a process of insertion and assimilation of the individual into the dominant national culture;

b. In the second paradigm that is widely accepted in the Anglo-Saxon world (driven by policies in the United States of America, but also in Britain and Australia), exclusion is the result of an inadequate separation of the various social spheres where autonomous individuals are free to enter into networks of voluntary exchanges. Pluralism is celebrated in this paradigm of specialization since it protects individual liberties and can be efficient as long as individuals can move freely between the boundaries of various social spheres. The assumption here is that social differentiation can be horizontal and does not necessarily imply inequality between individuals and social groups. When group affiliations create boundaries that are not permeable to 'outsiders', then the role of the state is to protect individual rights of participation and to stop the operation of discrimination. Inclusion, in this case, refers to the ability of individuals to exercise their 'right to participate', but this is closer to Isaiah Berlin's 'negative freedom' and the removal of obstacles to free action, rather than a more 'positive freedom' that would allow people the capacity to act (including the right level of resources);

c. The third paradigm is described by Silver as a 'monopoly'. Social differentiation here is primarily conceived along the lines of vertical social structures and, so, characterized by unequal levels of resources (material and cultural) distributed to various social groups. This inequality would result in groups that possess fewer resources facing constraints in their capacity for action, participation and, hence, full social inclusion. Drawing on ideas of 'closure', prestigious institutions and privileged groups construct boundaries around themselves in order to exclude less desirable social groups from participation and, thus, (deliberately or not) perpetuate inequality. For instance, access to elite secondary and tertiary education institutions across Europe from less privileged social groups has been seriously constrained by their more limited material resources, or possession of the 'wrong' types of cultural, linguistic or social capital (Öhrn 2011).

The monopoly paradigm has been empirically confirmed by various large-scale research studies across Europe, which suggest that countries with strong social welfare traditions view the school as a core institution to the creation of an ideal 'inclusive' society, where policies of redistribution of opportunities are given priority over policies for high diversification and specialization. But, education is also an institution that, since the 1980s, 'feels' the tension from the pressures of an increasingly competitive labour market where privileged social groups try to use it as a means of maximizing advantage for their own children and as a mechanism of legitimation of this transmission of privilege through the award of credentials. The potential of the school to bring together social groups with homogeneous characteristics (in terms of socio-economic, cultural, linguistic and religious capital), which are then in a position to reproduce the group through an exclusion of less desirable individuals, exchanges with institutions of similar features and the careful guarding of institutional boundaries from the infiltration of undesirables, are all issues that have been explored in research across Europe, which draws implicitly or explicitly on such monopoly paradigms (Daly and Silver 2008).

When the institution of the secondary school is 'located' in a policy context that promotes a strong social democratic agenda, then a lot of these tendencies to forms of exclusion are under control. This kind of policy and educational context is found primarily in the Nordic countries in Europe. But, when the policy context is one of retrenchment of welfare provision and the increase of privatization of aspects of public services, then the role of school seems to be changing accordingly. This is overwhelmingly the paradigm that one observes in North America and many European countries, as well as Australia and New Zealand. In principle and in policy rhetoric, the application of the principles and practices of 'the market' on the organization of schooling results in horizontal differentiation of institutions – since the freedom of parental choice requires diversity of institutional provision. But, research across many countries has shown that differentiation of schools in the education marketplace soon becomes vertical. Parents interpret 'choice' to the best interests of their child in a process that is inherently one of 'closure', since achieving this 'choice' for their own child necessarily involves depriving this choice from another child (Arreman-Erixon and Holm 2011; Gewirtz and Cribb 2009). Rather, the institutional goals that take primacy in a marketized system are those of accountability and responsiveness to consumer demands (even when these are about social distinction), pluralism of provision, efficient use of resources and reducing costs and improved quality of provision – a necessary requirement to remain competitive.

Not achieving your choice of school or not performing at the top throughout your educational career does not, of course, suggest that a young person will be socially 'excluded'. What we are suggesting is that, in a highly competitive, stratified and differentiated system of education, young people who come from particular groups in the population are much more likely to underachieve and, subsequently, more vulnerable to the harsh realities of the labour market. Young people who have grown up in relative, or even in some cases absolute, poverty may find that the education system has done very little to break the cycle of disadvantage they find themselves in.

Policy responses to the problem of 'exclusion'

Individual governments have not been idle in response to some of these problems. France was one of the first countries to talk about social exclusion as early as the 1970s, concerned about people who fell through the net of social protection and were potentially also a threat to social cohesion. Poverty, disaffection and disability were core problems to be dealt with by the state. But, the term took a more Europeanized dimension when the European Commission set up in 1990 the Observatory on National Policies for Combating Social Exclusion. Defining inclusion and exclusion primarily on the basis of citizenship rights, the concept began changing from its original French definition. When the UK government, in 1997, set up a Social Exclusion Unit, there was a further emphasis on defining social inclusion in terms of employment. As many critics have pointed out, this emphasis tended to marginalize or even ignore issues of equality and emphasize the much more 'safe' and un-threatening (to the governments) concept of social inclusion

(Alexiadou 2002 and 2005b). Twenty years on, combating social exclusion has become a standard item for concern within the European Union that has designed a strategy for 'sustainable and inclusive growth', with the reduction of poverty as a target for the first time (EU leaders have pledged to bring at least 20 million people out of poverty and exclusion by 2020). The situation in the year 2011–12 is dire:

- 80 million people in the EU – 16 per cent of the population – live on less than 60 per cent of their country's average household income
- 19 per cent of children in the EU are also currently in, or at risk of, poverty
- 17 per cent of Europeans suffer from material deprivation, i.e., their living conditions are severely affected by a lack of resources
- Welfare systems reduce the risk of poverty by 38 per cent on average in the EU, but this impact varies from less than 10 per cent to nearly 60 per cent across the EU.

(http://ec.europa.eu/social/main.jsp?catId=750&langId=en)

The problem is a difficult one and not likely to be successfully addressed soon. Despite the policy attention to it over the last 20 years, there is increasing polarization in the opportunities and life chances of young people from different backgrounds (Lundahl 2011). Young people from ethnic or racial minority backgrounds are particularly vulnerable to falling behind in the various transitions within the education system, and from school to work and so are young people with a disability. This highlights the problem of exclusion to be not just linked to economic poverty but also to cultural practices and understandings, as well as institutional arrangements of welfare within and around the school. In times of economic crises, the institutional and social barriers to job opportunities and to further education are likely to exacerbate the problem. In a recent report by the Council of Europe, it was highlighted that even when jobs exist, many young people have to accept poor wages and poor conditions of work with lack of good quality training opportunities and, often, discrimination on the basis of race, gender and socio-economic background:

> Racism, xenophobia, and gender-related discrimination and violence are major contributing factors to social exclusion. Evidence suggests that they are endemic in the education system, and that attempts to challenge them

on an individual basis are ineffective without broader efforts to eradicate institutional discrimination. Attention also needs to be paid to the barriers they present to equitable labour market access (*Social inclusion for young people: Breaking down the barriers*, 2007, p. 200).

Young people with a disability are in an even more precarious situation. The debate around inclusion of children with special needs within mainstream classrooms is still going strong, and even after many years of research and (positive overall) policy developments in this field, there is a huge problem, in terms of satisfactorily addressing the educational and further needs of these children. In many instances, class and ethnicity intersect with issues of ability/disability to produce particularly nasty outcomes for certain population groups, such as the example of Roma children who have been found, by the European Court of Human Rights in 2007, as unjustifiably designated to special schools in the Czech Republic. This may seem extreme, but Roma children are found in extreme disadvantage (and often identified within the special needs category in schools) in several countries in Europe (Allan 2010). UNESCO states that the inclusion of children who would otherwise be perceived as 'different' means 'changing the attitudes and practices of individuals, organisations, and associations so that they can fully and equally participate in and contribute to the life of their community and culture'. The 2006 United Nations Convention on the Rights of Persons with Disabilities recommends that inclusive education (i.e., children with special needs to be taught together with other children of their age group) as the norm (UNICEF 2007). But, creating a barrier-free and child-focused learning environment would require resources (in terms of infrastructure and expertise) as well as a change in public perceptions and attitudes that seem to be still far from sight.

What is the extent of the problem worldwide? According to the WHO, around 10 per cent of the world's children and young people (some 200 million) have a sensory, intellectual or mental health impairment and about 80 per cent of them live in developing countries. The World Bank estimates that persons with disability account for up to one-fifth of the world's poorest people, with poverty being a key contributor to disability, as well as resulting in very limited ways of addressing it (ibid.). Any account of 'education around the world' needs to consider this very vulnerable and, often, marginalized category of young people who, by their very weak political status, have no voice in the struggle for resources, especially in financially difficult times and in a climate of creating global policy convergence around 'high performance' in the future knowledge economy. We shall close this section with a quote from Julie Allan (2010), who has extensively discussed the problems around inclusion in mainstream schooling systems:

> The economically driven imperative to raise achievement along with the fragmentation of provision threatens to undermine inclusion, whilst the emphasis on individualisation and the continued dominance of 'special needs' and, in some parts of Europe, defectology discourage approaches to inclusive practice which are about all children. At the same time, the power of legal frameworks, particularly the European Convention on Human Rights, to challenge exclusion and discrimination and the mandate for children's participation and inclusion set by the UN Convention on the Rights of the Child provides some grounds for optimism (p. 206).

Notes

1 On average across OECD countries, 14 per cent of variation in students' reading performance can be explained by their socio-economic backgrounds. In some countries, this is much higher (20 per cent in Hungary, Bulgaria, Peru and Uruguay). By contrast, in Iceland, Hong Kong, Qatar, Macao and China, less than 7 per cent of the variation of student performance is explained by socio-economic background. In the countries with the highest reading performance (Shanghai, China, Korea, Finland and Hong Kong), the link between student background and performance is weaker than on average (OECD 2011).

2 See Michael Apple (1986) *Ideology and the curriculum*, Michael Young (1971) *Knowledge and control*.

4

Scale, Space and Place with Reference to The United States of America and The World of Small States

Introduction

Everything educational takes place somewhere and sometime. Examples may range from a 40-minute lesson in a school classroom to the global transmission of a lecture on the internet. It does not have to be formal and could just as well be a two-minute advertisement on TV, followed by a global transmission of a violent conflict at a distant place on a news channel. Temporal and spatial scales were introduced in Chapter 2. Here, we aim to illustrate their relevance to comparative and international education, with examples from one of the largest countries (certainly the most influential country in the world) and some of the smallest. First though, some theoretical and conceptual background will be discussed under the overarching label of scale.

Scale and comparative education enquiry

In everyday life, we are well aware that matters relating to educational activity, and the factors and disciplines that influence them, operate at different geographical and historical scales. Yet, despite the cautionary comments of founding fathers, such as Sadler and Kandel, it is only relatively recently that comparativists have embraced their advice. Such awareness has been encouraged, for example, by the multi-level analytical contribution of Bray and Murray Thomas (1995) and the conceptual concern with context of Crossley and Watson (2011). Both were in part, reactions not only to the fixation on national scale, but also to the so-called 'scientific' approach to comparative education seeking social science laws, leading to predictions of policy outcomes. As physicists Cox and Forshaw (2009) point out: 'science is a discipline that celebrates uncertainty', a sentiment long ago outlined by Edmund King in his 1979 inaugural lecture, *Education for Uncertainty,* as Chair of Comparative Education at King's College, London. The contribution of Bray and Murray Thomas has become a canon in the literature of the field. It proposes the virtues of multi-level analysis on three axes: (a) geographical/locational levels, (b) aspects of education and society and (c) non-locational demographic groups. The geographical axis is largely based on regulated space, from classrooms to countries, which means that it relates mostly to politically delivered formal education. In reality, education is culturally embedded as well, and this is accommodated by the conceptual framework developed by Griffin and Brock (Griffin 2001), illustrated as Fig. 4.1.

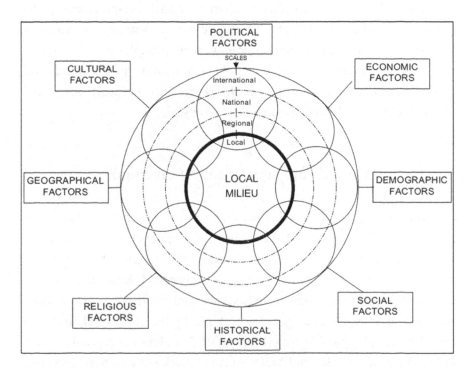

Figure 4.1 Spatial scales and factors affecting education in any location

This framework is based on four geographical scales and eight factors, all bearing on education – in this case, schooling in three particular locales. It was developed for the purpose of comparing the mediation of market-oriented (i.e., school choice) reforms at the local level in England, Ireland and the United States of America. The way the four scales relate to the seven in Murray and Thomas is shown in Fig. 4.2.

The area outlined boldly in black in both diagrams accommodates the essential issues of culture and context at the local level. It embraces the concepts

BRAY and MURRAY THOMAS (1995)	GRIFFIN (2001)	
World Regions / Continents	Supranational space within which discourse influencing policy on educational provision disseminates.	Global / International
Countries	National units within which unitary or multiple systems of formal educational provision operate according to enacted policy.	National
States / Provinces	Sub-national units responsible for the provision of public education in different degrees of authority in different countries within which enacted policy is mediated.	Regional
Districts		
Schools	Local cultural milieu within which public education is delivered according to policy filtered down from national and regional levels, and further mediated at the point of provision by principals, management bodies and teams, interest groups and individuals all contributing to the milieu which is an organic combination of the residual and the dynamic.	Local / Locale
Classrooms		
Individuals		

Figure 4.2 Bray/Murray Thomas and Griffin Scales
Source: Griffin (2001, p. 25)

of place and space at the only level at which learning and teaching actually takes place – the individual. This is the geography of educational reality.

> '... is not education in reality one of the most individual of human acquisitions? One that is ultimately effective only at the smallest scale, in operational terms almost totally client controlled. That is to say, that the individual – child, student and parent – have both a clear perception of their learning needs and a related level of motivation that may be negative or positive in expression. It is not, however, to say that such individual perceptions are either accurate, or in the best interests, however defined, either of the client or the various human groups, local national or international of which he or she forms a part (Brock 1984b, p. 3).

This reality has become intensified by the direct connection between the global and local scales through ICT. It does not nullify the influence of regional, national or sub-national operations on education but it compromises and complicates them. What Arnove and Torres (1999) called 'the dialectic of the global and local' is not always positive in nature, and has given rise to tendencies of fragmentation as well as conformity (Barber 1996).

Apart from those who are stateless, we are all citizens of one or more countries and subject to the formal educational regulations of the country in which we reside. In this sense, the national scale does matter, especially to those in power at that level. Policies are formulated, enacted and enforced, but their relationship to scale may be complex. For example, at the time of writing, the Secretary of State for Education in England is in the process of enabling maintained (i.e., state) schools to opt out of Local Authority jurisdiction. The rhetoric is one of enabling individual or collective choice at the local scale. The reality is that they are ultimately subject only to national centralized political authority. Such a situation makes for difficulties of cross-national comparison if the realities are not perceived. These are not the communities of the Bray and Murray Thomas scale but a complex web of interest groups, *de facto* 'free' but publicly funded and, therefore, *de jure* under national centralized control, albeit remote.

Other factors are fortifying the national scale, especially in the more economically advanced nations, and they are international surveys of a partial nature. The longstanding International Evaluation of Achievement (IEA) studies have a relatively respectable history in terms of comparative education

(Postlethwaite 1999). They covered a wide range of curricular fields that related to the ideal of a liberal education. The Trends in International and Science Study (TIMMS) surveys operated periodically since 1999 and the Programme for International Student Assessment (PISA), operated likewise since 2000, are partial in that they concentrate only on a limited range of related subjects that are assumed to relate more than others (and all other forms of education at all ages) to national economic growth prospects. Whatever the pros and cons of these surveys, the main concerns here are their methodological validity in comparative terms and, even more so, their ability to fixate politicians at national level on the so-called 'league tables' that result. A similar trend has arisen in higher education in the form of national and international rankings of universities, resulting in some countries in the directing of resources into their leading institutions at the expense of the tertiary sector as a whole. The criteria employed relate mainly to only one of the three functions of a university, conducting research. The other two, the teaching of students and, especially, making a contribution to the well-being and development of the communities in which they are located, are virtually ignored. The national scale of reference is gaining ground.

The current global complement of over 200 'national' political units, comprising mostly states but also many dependent territories, covers an enormous range of scales in terms of population totals, physical area and economic status. These units have come into being at different times in the past. Some, for example, England and France, emerged around the time of the first millennium; others, for example, South Sudan, only after the turn of the second millennium. Some have come, gone and returned, with related and, sometimes, considerable adjustments to their territory, as seen in Central and Eastern Europe. Some have moved from being colonies to independent states. What defines a state, a country or a province is a complicated issue (Hurst 1986), but the educational 'DNA' of each and every one bears traces of its unique history. If, when comparing educational systems and issues cross-nationally, the temporal scale is not taken into account, then the quality of the exercise will be poor.

Whether a country, or territory, has a unitary, centralized system or a decentralized arrangement, there will still be multiple educational disparities: between political sub-divisions; between urban, peri-urban and rural areas;

Table 4.1 Hierarchy of countries and territories by population

Over 1 Billion:	PRC China 1.35 bn
	India 1.21 bn
Over 200 Million	USA 313.5 m
	Indonesia 237.6 m
100–200 Million (seven countries)	Brazil 192.4m
	to Mexico 112.3m
50–100 Million (12 countries)	Philippines 92.3m
	South Africa 50.6m
25–50 Million (20 countries)	South Korea 48.6m
	to Afghanistan 25.5m
3–25 Million (87 countries)	Yemen 24.5m
	to Lithuania 3.1m
Less than 3 Million (The World of the Small States)	(102 Small States and Dependent Territories) Albania 2.8m
	Pitcairn 66 people

Abstracted from official UN Statistics based on the most recent census/estimate.

between ethnic and linguistic groups; between core and periphery. Issues of scale, space and place will be evident within, and between, all these disparities.

For any particular educational enquiry, including comparative and international, if the most appropriate scale or combination of scales, is not employed, then the necessary evidence on which to base conclusions will not be found. Before moving on to exemplify some of the issues raised above with recourse to the United States of America and the world of small states, it is necessary to place them in the hierarchy of countries and dependent territories in terms of population. This is illustrated in Table 4.1.

The case of the USA

Two caveats are necessary at the outset. First, the prior settlement of the mainland territory of what is now the United States of America was first colonized by Amerindian communities, who are, therefore, the indigenous population. They had their own forms of education and were subject to what Altbach and Kelly (1978) have called 'internal colonialism' (see Iverson 1979). Second, the section that follows is not an account of contemporary education in the United States of America, but a reaching into a number of legacies from the history of that country that inform and help to explain issues of scale there at the present day.

As well as having by far the greatest international outreach of any country in terms of educational influence, the United States of America also exhibits the most intense degree of local control of formal public schooling. The early nineteenth century model of 'the common school', that is to say, the neighbourhood school, has become that of the majority of public systems in the world. The creator of the 'common school', Horace Mann, was not slow to praise it, proclaiming in 1840 that: 'This institution is the greatest discovery ever made by man: we repeat it, *the common school is the greatest discovery ever made by man*' (quoted in Perkinson 1976, p. 59). He made this claim in defiance of criticisms laid against him when he was Secretary of the State Board of Education in Massachusetts.

The origins of highly localized control of public schooling long predate the founding of the United States of America itself, and derive from its early colonial identity. This began with colonization itself, at least in terms of European settlement, and proceeded through over 150 years of colonialism, before the founding of the nation in 1776 and the proclamation of its laconic and distinctive Constitution in 1787.

McPartland (1979) begins his analysis of formative features of public schooling in the American colonies of Britain by considering the adaptation of 'Old World practices', notably: (a) widespread zeal for formal education; (b) strong community support, including general taxation and (c) democratization in the form of devolution of decision-making to full town meetings and, further, to local districts (p. 120). He is referring to the earlier New England colonies and their towns. The 'town' in those early colonial days was often a considerable area of land surrounding the main settlement itself. In *The Connecticut Town 1635–1790*, Daniels (1979) describes the types of meetings held to effect local democracy. What were known as 'societies' populated the area of a 'town', which would be mainly rural. Consequently, spatial and locational issues governed the operation of schooling. According to Daniels:

'In the first few decades of the eighteenth century, many societies had just one or two schools and almost all of the school locations were rotated. Pomfret First Society voted to have the schools in session "eight weeks at the

north, seven at the west, seven at the south, and four at Wappaquasset"... as
the population of the colony increased, the number of schools per society
increased accordingly, and by the mid-eighteenth century all but the lightly
populated societies stopped rotating their schools and instead established
many permanent ones to serve the various areas' (p. 109).

Such locational decisions were made and reviewed at the annual town meeting,
where the allocation of funds from local taxation to school buildings, teachers
and the minister would be debated and decided in open session with public
participation.

The neighbouring colony of Massachusetts was the first to develop a proto
system as such (King 1965), taking over from the Massachusetts Bay Company
and deriving patterns of schooling that had emerged in Tudor England, a
period of educational expansion. The Massachusetts Act of 1647 was designed
to bring into line a variety of approaches being transferred from the Old World,
as colonization gathered pace. The Act 'made the provision of town schools
mandatory upon the attainment of a certain level of population' (McPartland
p. 122).

The gaining of independence from Britain led to the formulation of the
Constitution of the United States of America. Few nations have had the
benefit, in their establishment, of a range of founding fathers with public
education high on their list of priorities (Pangle and Pangle 1993). In creating
a federal nation, they were mindful to preserve local democracy and, thus, the
provision of public education was excluded from the Constitution, becoming
the responsibility of each state and the school districts therein. James Madison,
Fourth President of the United States of America and generally acknowledged
as the 'Father of the Constitution' proclaimed: 'The error ... seems to
owe its rise and prevalence chiefly to the confounding of a republic with a
democracy ... A democracy ... will be confined to a small spot. A republic
may be extended over a large region' Madison 1787/2011. With schooling and
higher education already developing for nearly 200 years, the connections
between democracy and learning were already well established by the time of
Madison's Presidency (1809–17). With growing urbanization, the environment
was developing in ways in which the young Horace Mann's idea of the common
school would come to fruition. As internal colonization proceeded to the west
and south, new states were created in addition to the original 13 and the States

of the Union eventually numbered 50, with the promotion of Hawaii in 1959. Most states followed the template created by Mann in Massachusetts for their systems of public schooling.

Another spatial feature of the states of the United States of America as they developed was the 'land grant', illustrating the complex interaction of federal, state and local in public education. Indeed, this also involved a regional scale. In the expansion of the infant nation westwards, a 'Northwest Territory' was identified, comprising Illinois, Indiana, Michigan, Ohio and Wisconsin.

> Following the adoption of the Constitution of the USA, a federal ordinance decreed that 'section sixteen' of each township established in the Northwest Territory be earmarked for the use of schools, and that one town in each land district be reserved for the use of a 'seminary of learning'. In the event, Indiana, Illinois and Michigan each subsequently received one of these seminary townships. Three interrelated problems arose from this approach: political, locational and economic, and the emergence of Michigan with the best deal of the five states in the region, had to do with politics and economics in particular, with the enhancement of educational prospects manifest in the locational outcome. Unlike the other four emergent states in the region, Michigan secured the agreement of the Congress of the USA that the school lands constituting section sixteen of all townships be granted directly to the State, and not to individual local community townships (Brock 1992, p. 87).

As urbanization proceeded in the emergent United States of America in relation to industrialization in Britain – still the main source of immigrants then – some towns became industrial, again beginning in New England and often using water power. There were some direct links, such as between the brass makers of Birmingham, England and Waterbury, Connecticut, which became the 'brass capital' of the United States of America. With urbanization (migration from countryside to towns) came urban growth, in part expansion in the form of suburbs. In association with this, a city/suburban administrative division came into being that had significance in terms of regulated space and public schooling provision. There were exceptions, but as Johnston (1981) describes, in general, five forms of local government have resulted: (a) counties (subdivisions of states), (b) townships, (c) municipalities (with elected governments), (d) school districts (providing for the compulsory phase of formal public schooling) and (e) special districts (single-purpose units e.g. for drainage or fire protection). Although only school districts provide for public schooling as such, funded by local taxation, they interact with the other local units in various ways. School districts exist in both metropolitan and suburban areas, since many predate the rapid urbanization of the past 150 years. Due to the intensely localized origins of public schools, described by McPartland (1979) and Daniels (1979), the number of school districts overall, as the convention spread with the number of states, became enormous. Consolidation over time has reduced their number overall, but in municipalities, they have increased due to higher population densities in the inner zones of cities, often associated with industrialization and immigration.

The abolition of slavery following the American Civil War (1861–65) led to a mass migration of black Americans from the southern states to northern industrializing cities (Hummel and Nagle 1973) at a time when increased immigration to the United States of Ameica from various parts of a troubled Europe was also gathering pace. The result was a mosaic of ethnic diversity, especially in metropolitan areas (inner cities) and, to a lesser extent, in the suburbs. After World War II, the shortage of labour led to increased immigration, legal and illegal, from Latin America and, so, a major Hispanic dimension was added to the so-called 'melting pot'. The outcome has been what Peach (1975) has termed urban social segregation. This is, of course, *de facto* segregation and not *de jure* segregation, which survived in some of the southern states until the mid-1950s. Despite the creation, by consolidation, of some massive metropolitan school districts in major cities, including Boston, Chicago, Los Angeles, New York and Philadelphia, the reality on the ground was a kaleidoscope of shifting neighbourhood locales, with their common schools and ethnic identities. Spring (1978) conducted a study in 1976 relating to high educational aspirations of a black suburban community and the resultant migration. He found that:

> The population moving into Black Suburbia was primarily in the middle-income range and very concerned about the quality of the education system. When income figures for the 1960 and 1970 censuses for this suburban area are compared, and 1960 dollars are adjusted to 1970 dollars, it is revealed that the black population moving into Black Suburbia in the 1960s had slightly higher incomes than the whites moving out of the community.

The bulk of the black population moving into the area during this period were in what one would call the middle-income range and could be viewed as a group interested in upward mobility (p. 52).

The situation of ethnic diversity in urban America had become highly complex and shifting, with local educational opportunity and quality being a key factor. Ethnic intermarriage had also become another issue related to scale and space. Peach (1980) found that the degrees of intermarriage between ethnic groups in American cities correlated with the degree to which they were separated spatially.

Cultures of local financial independence led many counties on the fringe of large cities to favour incorporation rather than annexation by the neighbouring metropolitan area. In practice, this applied to the more affluent suburbanites, and 'meant that they could avoid "subsidising" provision for the relatively poor who remained in the central cities' (Johnston p. 291). For the same reason:

'. . . by creating separate school districts (irrespective of whether they were incorporated as municipalities, schooling had to be provided) they avoided, through the property tax, subsidising education finance for the less affluent (including the large stream of immigrants – plus blacks – flooding the central cities). Most of the large cities at the heart of metropolitan areas provide education as part of the city government service: most of the suburban municipalities do not, and instead the area beyond the city boundary is served by a mosaic of school districts, most of whose boundaries are not co-terminous with those of the independent municipalities. Thus administrative separateness from the central city brought financial advantages; the suburban residents paid only for what they themselves wanted' (ibid.).

We can clearly see that issues of scale, space and place are crucial to understanding the realities of educational provision and activity in the United States of America. We can also see how the range of factors determining this – historical, political, social, cultural and economic – all operate at the very local level, creating the milieu outlined in Figs 4.1 and 4.2. As mentioned, these two figures come from Griffin (2001), a study that will now be used to illustrate the next phase of local educational development in the United States of America – the implementation of school choice, a major departure from the community-based common school of Horace Mann that had survived for 150 years.

The issue of school choice is probably the main outcome of neo-liberal economic and political policies in the field of education. Neo-liberal theory emerged in the 1960s, mainly in the United States of America, but did not gain much traction with leading politicians until the more austere economic climate following the creation of The Organization of Petroleum Exporting Countries (OPEC) in 1973. The Republican Reagan Presidency in the USA (1981–89) was receptive to the leading supporters of marketization of public schooling in American educational academia, such as Chubb and Moe (1990). However, for reasons already explained, the federal government had no direct power to legislate in favour. Such power resides with the governments of individual states and many preferred to remain with the traditional system of neighbourhood public schools. The state of Massachusetts, however, encouraged by the take up of neo-liberal policies for public education in England and Wales, as legislated for in the Education Reform Act of 1988, enacted 'The 1993 Education Reform Act for the Commonwealth of Massachusetts'.

> The Act required school districts to move towards participatory school-based management systems. It empowered the board to publish profiles of achievement at institutional and district level, as well as to declare situations of under-performance and act accordingly. An open enrolment policy allowed for movement between catchments and districts. This was subject to certain regulations and limitations, including the flow of public funding. Districts had the option to withdraw from this arrangement. (Griffin 2001, p. 54).

Issues of scale, place and space were, and still are, all at work here in the changes that have resulted. Some school districts retained their right not to allow cross-border enrolments with their neighbours, others allowed only movement out, while a third group only movement in. All had to accept open enrolment (i.e., school choice) within. Ethnicity was a clear issue in a significant number of districts where, for example, a broad band of affluent outer suburban districts to the west of metropolitan Boston declined to permit movement in from a band of mainly ethnic minority districts to the east. Within any one district, of course, school choice is dependent on excess capacity being available in individual schools and, if this is not evidently available, then in some cases, it was engineered by the creation of charter schools. These are public schools set up by interest groups through a time-bound charter agreement with the superintendent and government of the school district as well as the state authorities. The charter provides public funding from local taxation for students and teachers but not for buildings. Premises have to be sought in empty buildings, such as old empty schools, or hired from business or churches. In the main case study undertaken in Massachusetts by Griffin, the school district was the core of a medium-sized city in the west of the state. The population was predominantly of Hispanic (mainly Puerto Rican) origin. This largely removed ethnicity from the 'equation'. The superintendent embraced the open enrolment policy with some vigour, encouraging the creation of several charter schools in order to engender more enterprise and competition on the part of the five public high schools serving the city. Once this was achieved, it was of no concern to the district if the charter schools declined, as they tended to do anyway when the children of the interest group had passed through. In such cases, and there are many, we can see the changing geography of educational reality with the political factor to the fore.

Mention was made above of the transatlantic common ground between the Republican administration of Ronald Regan and the Conservative government of Margaret Thatcher. Given the largely American origins of modern neo-liberal philosophy and economics, plus the much greater global power of the United States of America, how was it that at a national level, in the Thatcher case, education in England and Wales, open enrolment measures were enacted earlier than in the United States of America, and totally? The explanation involves further and wider issues of scale and comparison.

Finegold et al. (1993) chart the transatlantic flow of influence on education and training policy from the 1970s to the early 1990s. They show clearly that, for the first decade of the two, the flow was entirely from the United States of America to the United Kingdom. The Regan administration gives voice to neo-liberal concerns in its survey *A Nation at Risk* (1983) and there follows a stream of visits from leading UK politicians to the United States of America. What is learnt contributes to the 1988 Education Reform Act in England and Wales.

'The convening of the educational summit, as it was known, by President George Herbert Walker Bush in Virginia in September 1989 marked the belated beginnings of concerted efforts by the federal government to respond to the challenge thrown down in *A Nation at Risk* six years earlier, and by the nation's Governors thereafter. It ushered in a new phase in the development of federal educational policy, one emphasising goals and standards. The passage and signing into law of *Goals 2000: Educate America Act* by President Clinton in March of 1994 represents at least a partial culmination of these efforts. It also provides a reference point for considering continuity and change in federal educational policy in the period and the role of Presidency therein' (Mulcahy 2001, p. 1).

American initiatives at local and state levels continued to influence further market-oriented reforms in England and Wales, but were followed by the reverse in the early 1990s, including influencing of the Massachusetts Act of 1993. This shows the international scale of American educational influence – part of its strong global outreach – but also the inability of the federal government to enact nationwide legislation due to the continued restrictions of the Constitution. This is unlikely to change because of the strongly democratic, that is to say, local traditions of control that are embedded in the culture. No such traditions existed in England and Wales to prevent the Thatcher administration from imposing a centralized national policy by emasculating the local authorities that had been responsible for education in their areas for less than a 100 years. With the establishment of the Welsh Assembly in 2003, that country acquired the freedom to rescind the 1988 reforms and did so, there being a different culture of education in the principality.

The Bush Snr. and Clinton initiatives mentioned above are part of the consistent pressure of federal administrations to inject a national-level policy into public sector schooling and diminish local control. They are also designed to influence the large parochial schooling component. In part, such pressures are a reaction to the rise of international surveys of educational achievement that reflect status at the national level in a competitive mode. Direct federal funding is not permitted, but project funds are created that can be competed for by individual school and districts. This trend was taken further by President George W. Bush with the national *No Child Left Behind Act* of 2001, effective from January 2002. This requires individual states to develop their own standards, tested through annual assessments. Non-participation means no federal funding at all. Through the first decade of the twenty-first century, this has proven to be a tough challenge at individual school and school district levels due to the diminishing of the ability to respond differentially to spatial, economic and ethnic disparities. The role of school choice has been enhanced. So, schooling in the United States of America continues to exhibit greater diversity than most other countries while, at the same time, becoming subject to increased federal pressures of conformity. The three scales – local, state and federal – continue their struggle in the face of a tradition of local democracy challenged by international pressures to compete and conform.

Not least among these pressures are cross-national comparisons of grade level achievements where, as Dalton (2012) illustrates, methods of comparison are not necessarily helpful. Students at secondary schools may be compared according to age level or grade level. Some surveys use age, some use grade.

> In the United States, 15 year olds score lower than the OECD mean at every grade level and US 15 year olds in higher grades receive fewer benefits from their high-grade membership than similarly placed peers in many other OECD countries. However, the negative effect on US achievement of such grade level differences is more than offset by the advantage that US fifteen year-olds in higher grades, and fewer in lower grades, than most other OECD countries. The US scores would actually decline if they had a similar grade distribution and grade effect profile as an average developed nation (ibid., p. 148).

It is clear that the concern of the Presidency and federal government of the United States of America, with the nation's place in international league tables, is gradually shifting the balance of influence and power over public schooling as between the three levels of scales: local, state and national.

The educational influence of the United States of America also operates on a global scale, through the export of its formal output, especially, but not exclusively, in higher education. The research and entrepreneurial influence of many of its universities is profound, influencing the policies and developments of many countries. Possibly the most influential and perhaps invidious global influence is that of international university rankings. Unlike the example of public schooling, this influence does not come with the 'health warning' of local democratic control. The initial international ranking system and criteria came from the United States of America, the 'US News and World Report' survey dating from the early 1980s. Although this is now one of four global surveys, its credibility has declined due to changes in the criteria used. The other USA-based world ranking, the 'QS World University Rankings', is also regarded as suspect due to its over reliance of reputational image as provided by peers (Altbach 2011). Although the remaining two rankings, 'The Academic Ranking of World Universities' (Shanghai) and 'The Times Higher Education World University Rankings' (UK) are now more respected, both rely heavily on criteria that favour universities in the United States of America. Publishing in a limited range of academic journals recognized by American agencies and operating mainly in the medium of English is a key factor. The criteria favour universities with strong research concentrations in the STEM disciplines (science, technology, engineering and mathematics), which can attract industrial and commercial as well as governmental funding for research. The result is that about 60 per cent of the top 100 universities are in the United States of America and about 25 per cent in the United Kingdom. In so far as other institutions are gaining places in the top 100, it is because they are adopting the American model of 'the university'. As Altbach (2011) rightly comments: 'Most of these rankings have little validity but are nonetheless taken with some seriousness by the public' (p. 2). More to the point, they are taken very seriously by governments of most countries and are, therefore, massively influential on a global scale. The spread of English as a *Lingua Franca*, leading to the 'Internationalization of Academe' (Rostan 2011) is also a prime factor in the global outreach and influence of American education.

The world of the small states

Although international statistics used above recognize over 100 states and territories with less than 3 million inhabitants, the list compiled by Martin and Bray (2011) gives only 89. This is because they include only: (a) full member states of UNESCO below this threshold, (b) associate members and (c) certain others. They explain: 'Certain non-sovereign territories are excluded because their populations are below 1,000 and/or their constitutional arrangements do not fit the classification adopted for the table' (p. 27). The table to which they refer usefully places the 89 small states and territories in eight regions, which are: Africa (11 cases), Arab States (4), Atlantic (6), Caribbean (21), Europe (18), Indian Ocean (4), South Pacific (20) and Asia (5).

In identifying these 89 as 'small', Martin and Bray use the premier criterion of smallness – that of population. Other criteria that generally come into the

Table 4.2 Matrix of small states and territories by population and region

Region	<100K	100–250K	250K–1m	1–2m	2–3m	Total
Africa	0	1	3	5	2	11
Arab States	0	0	2	0	2	4
Atlantic	5	0	1	0	0	6
Caribbean	8	6	5	1	1	21
Europe	7	1	5	1	4	18
Indian Ocean	1	0	2	0	1	4
South Pacific	11	6	3	0	0	20
Asia	0	0	3	1	1	5
Total	32	14	24	8	11	89

Derived from United Nations Statistics Division, 1988 (Martin and Bray 2011)

equation are: geographical area, economic status and the degree of completeness of the education system. These are discussed further below. For now, we can use further demographic information provided to create Table 4.2, which is a matrix according to five categories of smallness and the eight regions.

Recognition of, and interest in, small states may be traced back to works in fields other than education, or to island studies. Examples include: geography (Fosberg 1963), sociology (Benedict 1967), economics (Selwyn 1975), politics (Clarke and Payne 1987) and sustainable development (Beller et al. 1990). These, of course, detail factors that directly affect education, but as far as education itself is concerned, both the Commonwealth Secretariat and the Pacific Commission acted in 1980, resulting in two significant publications (Brock 1984; Thomas and Postlethwaite 1984).

The main focus of these early publications was on islands, but in fact, small states come in four territorial forms: landlocked, littoral, single islands and archipelagos (Brock 1980b). The spatial significance of these categories for education can be considerable. As far as the eight regional groups in Table 4.2 are concerned, the number of small landlocked states is: Africa (3), Europe (7) and Asia (2). Another geographical factor is that of isolation, which has to do with location relative to other states. This can apply to landlocked states if they do not have positive relationships with their surrounding neighbours, but is more commonly a condition arising from remoteness in oceanic terms. The Bahamas, for example – clearly a small archipelago state – is so close to

Florida in the United States of America as not to be remote at all. The others in the Caribbean, mostly islands, are all much more favourably located than their counterparts in the South Pacific, many of which are obviously much more isolated.

While the total population is the main criterion of smallness, territorial area is also a measure. Very small territorial scale has implications for education that can be positive as well as negative, while some states with small populations have massive territories, such as Guyana (0.75m), Botswana (1.9m), Namibia (2.1m) and Mongolia (2.6m). Within these vast territories, populations are clustered into what geographers term 'land islands', which share some of the problems of their maritime counterparts. Such 'land islands' occur, of course, in large nations such as Canada and Russia, but do at least have access to much greater resources. So, unlike the population threshold of 3 million people, there is no precise figure for territorial area. However, this dimension obviously becomes more critical in places that are genuinely spatially small by any standards. Shand (1980), with reference to the small island states of the Indian and Pacific Oceans suggested three categories: 'Small States' (10,000–30,000 sq. km.) – e.g. Fiji, Vanuatu; 'Very Small States' (500–10,000 sq. km.) – e.g. Mauritius, Tonga; and ' Micro States' (less than 500 sq. km.) – e.g. Seychelles, Maldives, Tuvalu and Nauru.

In addition to population and territorial size, another criterion of smallness is economic in nature. Shand (1980) suggested another version of his three categories on the basis of GDP. The thresholds suggested would be meaningless today. What is most important is the degree of concentration of the economy of the small state. Most such states exhibit highly concentrated economies, meaning that they depend almost entirely on one or two key exports. In a minority of cases, a key export may be extremely profitable, such as oil for Brunei Darussalam and Kuwait. In another minority of cases, a diversified economy has been made possible by entrepot functions, such as for Fiji and Barbados. Most small states are in neither of these positions and, so, achieving a correspondence between the curriculum and the economy is problematic, for a number of reasons (Brock and Smawfield 1988). The school curriculum in most of the small island states reflects the conventions of the metropole at the time of colonial control. The same is true of the structure of schooling and the mode of progression from primary to secondary level. In the former

'British West Indies', for example, only a minority could proceed to academic secondary schools by way of examinations, based on either the eleven plus or common entrance examination models in England. The majority received only primary schooling until the 1970s, when a compulsory junior secondary sector was introduced as in larger states (Brock 1984). This enabled an opportunity to create a curriculum that corresponded to the needs of the economy by relating content to local ecological and economic reality, though this opportunity was not often taken.

Despite their small scale, such states tend to be highly idiosyncratic for a number of reasons: territorial compactness or otherwise, cultural diversity – linguistic and religious – and; particular historical experiences. For example, Barbados has a high degree of compactness. Its lack of mountains meant that sugarcane virtually covered it in colonial times so that when slaves were emancipated, they mostly remained working on the plantations and, as schooling developed, were able to participate. This, in turn, led to a high proportion of literate adults who were able to gain employment in the diversified economy, itself a product of Barbados being an entrepot for the Eastern Caribbean. The diversified economy arising from the value-added processing, manufacturing and regional exporting typical of entrepots meant that the liberal curriculum derived from the metropole provided the type of educated workforce the country needed. As Lowenthal (1957) put it: 'almost everyone is accessible to the dissemination of ideas as well as of goods and services' (p. 495). By contrast, the nearby Windward Islands, recipients of the value-added products of Barbados, with their concentrated economies dependent mainly on banana exports, found their derived curricula not in correspondence with their economies at all.

One of the outcomes of smallness of scale, especially in the developing country situation that applies to the majority, has been regional or metropolitan emigration of the educated. In small states, there is a greater risk in this regard than in larger ones. Bray (2011, p. 52) quotes Cammish (1985, p. 25) with regard to Seychelles: 'Of three students sent (abroad) to train as physics teachers, for instance, one may elect to stay overseas, the second may change to electronic engineering and the third may fail his examinations: no physics teacher for Seychelles'. Such problems make educational planning in small states problematic and different from other states, as Bray (1992) and

Baldacchino and Farugia (2002) discuss in some detail, the latter with regard to a large number of national cases. One of the key problems is the capacity of small ministries, where education is often under the same authority as culture, sport and/or even health. The multiple expertise required of a minister and permanent secretary is something not experienced by their counterparts in large countries. On the other hand, close proximity of politicians to the public in small contexts can be advantageous to both parties (Brock and Parker 1985).

> Smallness, especially when allied with compactness, provides a degree of proximity and accessibility in respect of involvement and management that is simply not available to larger systems of education. The ability to communicate rapidly with (say), the Director of Education, the Minister of Education, the Principal of the Teachers College, a Head teacher and an individual class teacher on the same day, perhaps even in the same street, obviously provides these compact systems with advantages in terms of responsiveness to the community's point of view. By the same token, it makes the community very much more aware of the realities of what is going on within the system and in the curriculum (pp. 44–5).

Bray and Fergus (1986) also mention such advantages with reference to Montserrat, one of the smallest states. Small scale and, where it also obtains, compactness, proved advantageous in the past, when primary schooling for all was an objective. Such states achieved this relatively quickly because of the small number of schools and people involved. Likewise, at the present day, curriculum and other staff professional development programmes can be relatively easily discussed with all involved and implemented rapidly.

Over the past 40 years or so, the gaining of independent nationhood by the majority of small, mostly island, states that were former colonies of Britain has afforded them further political status. This includes membership of bodies with keen educational interests, such as the agencies of the United Nations and the Commonwealth. Both are sources of limited additional funding as well as ideas and expertise. Independence also confers the same level of power and influence as larger states enjoy predatory advances of strong commercial corporations, as well as the ability to make deals that are to their advantage. Some small states in quite remote locations have been able to benefit from their special geographical situations in respect of technical aspects of global ICT networks. This makes up, to some extent, for their physical remoteness. Others have benefited from so-called 'offshore universities', both in terms of income and of enhanced chances for their own citizens (Brock 2008).

The issue of independent, internationally recognized, qualifications can be problematic for small states. Whereas, for example, in the Caribbean region, former French colonies became a part of France in every respect, the former British colonies did not, for better or for worse, have such an option. After a failed attempt at federation (1958–62), some became independent immediately, others over time, and the smallest remain 'dependent territories' (i.e., colonies) to this day. After early discussions, as far back as 1946, with a view to a regional examinations system, the issue became prominent again after the collapse of the federation, as use of external bodies proved problematic. Eventually, in 1973, the Caribbean Examinations Council (CXC) was formed and the first examinations sat in 1979 (Augier and Irvine 1998). A rather more complex model emerged in the South Pacific (Rees and Singh 1998) due to the more widely diffused territories and more diversified cultural situation (indigenous as well as derived) as compared with the Caribbean. The South Pacific Board for Educational Assessment (SPBEA) 'did not originally operate a regional examination. Rather, its principal role, which it still plays today, was to support the national examinations of its member states' (ibid., p. 162). Over the years, a wide range of local, regional and international examinations have been accommodated.

As the last few decades have passed, the advance of globalization, including increasing sophistication of ICT, has fundamentally changed the educational prospects of small states for the better. This is just as well as, at the same time, some severe environmental challenges face those that are island states (Crossley et al. 2011): sea level rise, pressure on water resources, threats to marine biodiversity, constraints on subsistence agriculture and adverse effects of tourism are listed (pp. 15–16). At the same time, the pressures of the global economy are reaching out to those small states on the periphery (p. 18). Higher education is going to be a key factor in combating and overcoming environmental and economic challenges, with the special cybernetic link between the global and the local in the vanguard (Pyle and Forrant 2002; Brock 2012).

Tertiary education provision is an especially difficult challenge for many small states. As Bray (2011) points out, for all countries, large or small, this sector requires more resources per head than do primary and secondary schooling. Unit costs are disproportionately high for all resources required in all sectors of education, especially for maritime and landlocked small states that are remote to different degrees. Bray (ibid.) notes five strategies that are being differentially employed by small states in response to the tertiary challenge: creating multi-level programmes; creating multi-faceted tertiary sectors; engaging in international outreach; creating regional cooperation and engaging in distance learning (ibid., p. 54). These are all issues of scale and space. Such cooperative initiatives potentially enable all small states to contribute to the global knowledge economy and also benefit from it. In the smaller states, especially, the third function of any university, after teaching and research, that is to say contribution to its own locality, can be national in effect. Things have changed remarkably, as Bray describes:

> In that connection it is worth noting the World Bank's declaration (2002, p. 116) that states with populations below 1 million 'can rarely marshal sufficient resources to establish and sustain even one national university'. Even in 2002 the statement was of questionable validity. At that time universities existed in well over a dozen countries with populations below 1 million, and since then institutions have been established in additional countries as distant from each other as Aruba, Equatorial Guinea, Luxembourg, Djibouti and Fiji (pp. 62–3).

ICT has enabled students and the general population, in many small states, to engage in and benefit from the international knowledge economy. A particularly special innovation is The Virtual University for the Small States of the Commonwealth (VUSSC), enabled by the Commonwealth of Learning, which complements the work of existing national and regional institutions (Crossley et al. 2011, p. 47). For example, VUSSC is available to connect the community colleges of the small Caribbean states and the regional University of the West Indies. This helps students of all ages to undertake post-secondary studies without having to leave their home countries unless and until they reach final degree years. Previously, having to go to one of the three campus locations for the entire programme resulted in the loss of the most able through emigration, as employment on graduation was more likely in the diversified economies of the regional centres – Bridgetown, Kingston and Port of Spain. Contributors to Martin and Bray (2011) detail a range of tertiary innovations in some of the small states of the South Pacific, Mediterranean, Gulf States and Caucasia.

Such a range of opportunities and innovations involving many of the small states of the world does not mean that all of the inevitable constraints of scale, isolation and dependence outlined above have been overcome. But, the element of globalization that is ICT does enable the essential feature of education as a space-reducing mechanism to be optimized.

Conclusion

In this chapter, the fundamental importance of the issue of scale has been illustrated with reference to both temporal and spatial dimensions to help to explain selected features of education in the world's most influential, and third largest, state and also with reference to the worlds of the numerous small states that exist. Scale is one of the fundamental, yet oft forgotten, of the key methodological issues of comparative and international education. It applies just as much to all those systems and forms of education in between, such as in the various regions and nations discussed in the following chapters.

5

National and International Educational Development

Introduction

In this chapter, we shall approach education in relation to national and international development historically, but also in terms of the significant contemporary issues that have framed the debate. In doing so, we inevitably focus on the economic dimensions of education and the perceived significance of education in the development of economic (primarily) growth. This does not reflect our understanding of development as being driven solely by economic definitions; it clearly is not. But, this has been the dominant approach to education in relation to national and international development over the last few decades and so it deserves our attention in reviewing the debates as these have shaped the field of development.

Before we begin this review, we need to briefly outline our position in relation to the term *development*. In 1990, the Human Development Report published by the United Nations Development Programme (UNDP) opened up with the statement 'people are the real wealth of a nation'. This is important as a statement for policy, in that it calls governments and international organizations to consider 'brains', knowledge and information as part of the productive forces in the economy, when, in more conventional older approaches, 'wealth' was seen to be created by the interaction between natural resources, labour and technology applications. The idea of course is not new, neither is it that innovative. Since World War II, there has been a surge of research and policy that looked at human capital as a source of wealth and production. The debate is, however, shifting. Development is no longer defined solely on the basis of economic growth, even though this seems to be an important dimension to it. Depending on the organization that defines the concept, development can refer to primarily economic growth or have much wider connotations. In the 2010 Human Development Report, the UNDP widened the terms of reference to 'human development' that is viewed as a dynamic process that builds on the principles of equity, sustainability and respect for human rights. The report defines human development as:

> The expansion of people's freedoms to live long, healthy and creative lives, to advance other goals they have reason to value, and to engage actively in shaping development equitably and sustainably on a shared planet. People are both the beneficiaries and the drivers of human development as individuals and in groups.
>
> What is new in the way that the UN is approaching the issue is the way that people and human capital are re-positioned in the debate about development, where the goal is to create 'an enabling environment for people to enjoy long, healthy and creative lives' (MahbubulHaq, Founder of the Human Development Report, 2011).

In this book, we adopt such a definition of development that views economic growth and prosperity as necessary but not sufficient, unless they take place within a sustainable environment and are distributed in a fairly equitable way in populations within and across national borders. In this respect, development has economic but also social and environmental dimensions and, of course, a political strand, since political will is necessary to enact such a multifaceted notion of development. But, even though this and other similar definitions of development are gaining ascendance, we see far too often national debates around the role of education that draw primarily, or even exclusively, on the rates of return to investing in schooling. Such indicators of the contribution of education to the economy are also drivers of the formation of policies of powerful international organizations, such as the World Bank and the IMF, and this then has significant implications for the development 'paths' that are available to developing countries.

So, we shall begin by exploring the concept of human capital as one of the fundamental building blocks around the role that education can play in development. Human capital theory and research have, over the last few decades, provided evidence for the investment in, expansion or reform of all sectors of education in countries across the globe, and still underpin strongly the approach of international organizations to aid and development.

Human capital theory

This is a theory that has made a first appearance as far back as the eighteenth century, with the publication of the works of Adam Smith, who observed that human effort is at the root of wealth. This referred not merely to effort as work on natural resources, but also to human competencies, abilities and skills that are acquired through forms of training and education, and that add value to what human labour can produce. Since then, a number of important contributions to that original formulation turned human capital into a more pluralistic and inclusive concept that accounted for personal wealth (abilities as agents of wealth production and human participation in the production process) as capital. But, it was in the 1950s that human capital theory began its development in full, and became part of economic theory (Sweetland 1996). The core idea is that investing in education and training is like investing in any other form of capital in order to produce growth and returns in the future. As with other forms of investment, individuals, firms and the state will acquire education if they expect to benefit from it in the longer term, and the benefit has to be higher than the investment. What seems to be a common-sense idea – that a higher educated/skilled workforce will produce higher economic growth – needed to be accounted for, i.e., how can it be proved that it is the skills and knowledge that have produced the higher growth and not some other form of investment?

This question led to the work of economists such as Gary Becker and Theodore Schultz, who began measuring the contribution to the US national income of a number of factors. Schultz found that there was a total growth in income that could not be accounted for by the combined amount of other traditionally understood wealth generation factors (land, man-hours worked and reproducible capital). He estimated that, during the same period, the education across the (US) workforce had grown twice the rate of other forms of capital. Attributing the national income growth to the increased levels of education in the population got Schultz in 1979 a Nobel Prize in economics. Gary Becker (1962) viewed post-compulsory education as a key form of investment that affects future earnings by improving the physical and mental abilities of people and, so, raising their real income prospects. His research also showed that education (as well as on-the-job training) is related to the earning profiles over an individual's working life. So, investment in the younger ages reduces earnings at the time, but increases them later in life. These calculations also take into account the initial cost of education, i.e., cost of infrastructure (buildings, human resources, technology, etc. – a cost usually borne upfront by the state), possible tuition fees (a cost that is usually borne by states, but, increasingly, at higher levels of education by a combination of state and individual contributions) and reduced or complete lack of earning capacity while studying. So, when individuals or states decide to invest further in education/training, they have to be convinced that the additional skills they get will produce significantly higher earnings than they would have got otherwise. In terms of private returns (to individuals), research has shown that the link is clear. In developed western economies, evidence suggests a rate of return to one year's additional education ranges between 5 and 15 per cent (with differences by sex, ethnicity, type and level of qualification etc.). In less-developed economies, the returns to education seem to be higher in low income countries (Bassanini and Scarpetta 2001), but, these figures are highly variable. In 2010, the estimated private rate of return to education in advanced economies, including East Asia and the Pacific and South Asia was 13.3 per cent, 6.6 per cent in Sub-Saharan Africa and 6.5 per cent in Latin America (Barro and Lee 2011). According to Psacharopoulos and Patrinos (2002), the average rates of return to schooling have declined in the 1990s compared to the previous decade, while the supply of education has increased and so have the average levels of schooling.

The links between individual investment in education and national economic growth are less conclusive; still, the relationship is a positive one and this constitutes a major incentive for individuals as well as nations to invest in developing their human capital. What is, of course, more difficult to do is to convince people that investment in education is a good thing (that *it is* actually an investment), when the economy is in crisis and highly qualified people are out of employment, or in low paid employment.

Economists have identified a number of methodological problems with calculating the causal relations between education/training and individual earnings. One of these difficulties relates to the so called 'screening' effect. Individuals with higher levels of skills (as reflected in qualifications) are usually receiving higher wages compared to the less educated. But, is this because they are truly more productive or the result of employers' perceptions that education is positively correlated with productivity? Earnings may get higher for highly educated individuals not because these people are really better workers, but simply because their higher level of education is seen as a signal of increased productivity (Chevalier et al. 2004). At the same time, it could very well be the case that individuals with greater earning ability are the ones that most likely will choose to acquire more education/training.

One major other institution that has been central in the research around education and investment is that of family. In that respect, a lot of the debates within economics have overlaps/similarities with research in the field of sociology of education that explores the connection between family and investments in education. The previous chapter has reviewed some of the important sociological debates in the role that the institution of the family plays in education. Here, we shall review the role of the family, as it features in economics research in relation to human capital.

Human capital, the family and inequality

The family is one of the most important institutions that affect decisions about education. There is research of over 50 years that shows the very strong connections between family characteristics and the education and career trajectories of offsprings. Even though these are not *determining* the future of children, they tend to be very strong in *shaping* this future. And, of course, as we have briefly seen already, other institutions, such as the welfare state and the education system, mediate the family influences and produce variable results, depending on the particular social and political context.

Researchers from various disciplines have linked family characteristics to participation and success in education and training in developed countries. The general observation is that children from poorer backgrounds generally achieve lower levels of schooling (in terms both of years of participation and levels of attainment) and overall lower outcomes later in life. Research from within the field of economics suggests that this is because, in general terms, families from poorer backgrounds are less likely to invest in education. The human capital literature identifies two main strands that contribute to this tendency (Lanot and Chevalier 2002): (a) the first refers purely to financial constraints that place obstacles to human capital investment (lack of money to purchase materials that directly or indirectly contribute to the advancement of education, but also, unaffordability to defer earnings in the present while a young adult studies in a post-compulsory sector); (b) the second strand refers to family background characteristics that may affect attitudes and motivation, but also information necessary to make educational decisions. What is interesting is the relationship between (a) and (b). Economists point out that even though income is linked to post-compulsory education participation, what seems to have a stronger impact on the decision of young individuals to invest in their own human capital is other family characteristics – in particular, the level of education of the parents (and, more specifically, the education of the mother) (ibid.). This research concludes that a direct financial transfer to young people is not going to be as effective or efficient in increasing education participation – in other words, investing resources in 16-year-old young people from poor backgrounds is too late to make a significant difference. In economics terms, 'early interventions are estimated to have high benefit-cost ratios and rates of return' (Heckman 2008) and, so, investment in much earlier stages of life is a better strategy by governments that wish to increase their population's levels of education.

There are some strong critics of the human capital approach, as we shall see later. But, the message from this strand of research is clear: education is not just good for the development of individual attributes and the expansion of one's horizons and critical thinking. It is primarily good because these very characteristics of education, as well as the more technical training it provides, benefit individuals and the economy, but also lead towards the creation of a less unequal society.

Education – technology and human capital

In their book, *Race between education and technology*, Goldin and Katz (2008) call the twentieth century 'The Human Capital Century', a century that was dominated by American economic success. The two authors provide a causal link between the two, i.e., they attribute the American per capita income, which was the highest in the world during parts of the twentieth century, to the investments in education that the country made when it was critically important for economic growth. In their book, they view education and technology in a relationship of a 'race'. Technological advances produce growth only if there is sufficient supply of skilled workers in the population to make that happen. So, this is a race between a growing demand for skills as these are shaped by technological advances, and the supply of skills that reflects education investment, immigration as well as demographics. Goldin and Katz suggest that when progress in educational investment slows down, economic and social inequality rise. The openness and accessibility of the US education system (with the notable exception for a large part of the twentieth century of the education of the African American population) resulted in a mass education and, gradually, higher education system, that the middle decades of the century meant not just high economic growth, but also no large increases in inequality. They observe a reversing of education trends in the 1970s (where high school graduate rates stopped rising and college completion rates stalled or slumped) and they argue that, as a consequence, productivity of national growth has been reduced and inequality spiked. Between the 1970s and today, even though the demand for highly educated workers is as high as it has ever been, the supply is not there. Technological change, at the same time, is advancing rapidly and, as a result, it widens the wage gap in the population since it pays a much higher premium to the qualified few (or fewer). Similar to other research in this tradition, the policy message seems clear and straightforward – improving and extending mass education at a high level is imperative, both for economic growth and for closing the gap between the top and the bottom earners in society.

But. . .

There are many critiques of research around human capital investment; more often than not, these apply to the narrow uses of that research by governments and international organizations but, in some cases, they also apply to the theoretical assumptions that lie behind the research. The critics come from a critical theoretical orientation, who question the very assumption that the education system is neutral in the process of economic and social reproduction or that equality is, in any way, part of the design of the system. On the contrary, in that analysis, the main role education is seen to play is the maintenance of inequality of economic and social privileges, while retaining the belief of the population to a meritocratic system where social mobility is possible for all. Bowles and Gintis (1975) argued that the human capital approach, in its very functionalist and technicist understanding of schooling and of labour, makes the mistake of abstracting from the issue of social reproduction. The various repressive ideologies that play out within schools (sexism, racism and elitism) are seen by the economists as distortions of the system that need to be addressed,[1] whereas according to critical theorists, they are an essential mechanism of reproducing the capitalist order. This role of schools is quite inseparable from their capacity to produce 'good' workers. In that respect, the human capital research framework in seen to provide a legitimacy to the system of maintaining the unequal status quo, by attributing failings to individuals and their families, or to technical aspects of a process that can (and should) be repaired. The critiques of the human capital approach have evolved since the 1970s, particularly from within research in the sociology of education that applies a structural analysis to curriculum and pedagogic practice and their relationships to wider relations of power, as well as the role of individual agency in mediating these in their educational careers.

Both human capital theories and their critiques have been important in understanding the evolving theories of modernization, development and education. So, now we turn our attention to the wider debates around development and its relationship to education that draw from these perspectives.

Modernization and development

Human capital research is central in understanding the models of development that have dominated the thinking of national governments in relation to education policy in most economically advanced countries. It is also at the root of a lot of the policies designed by international organizations that tell less-developed countries how to develop. It is part of the core understanding of a key factor that contributes to the modernization process of a country and, so, we shall briefly review the main approaches to development that have appeared in the last 60 years.

Some countries are rich **and**. . .*other countries can get rich*

The story begins with the establishment of the principles of economic and political multi-lateralism that found their expression in the so called Bretton Woods institutions in 1944 (the International Monetary Fund and the International Bank for Reconstruction and Development – the 'World Bank'). Straight after World War II, the United States of America was anxious to establish a set of economic and political ideas about how best to organize the post-war political order, while at the same time safeguard against communism, and be at the driving seat of these 'international' organizations. Economic and social progress and development were part of the mission of the IMF and the Bank, initially guiding the reconstruction in Europe, and soon underpinning aid programmes to the world's poorer countries. The dominant economic ideas at the time were those of Maynard Keynes, who advocated an interventionist role for governments that needed to manage the market economy and to protect their populations against risk when the economy turns bad. This Keynesian approach in the aftermath of the war led to a new kind of capitalist world in the so-called western countries, where full employment, welfare, education and healthcare came to be expected as the normal functioning of state provisions. In terms of the US international affairs, a lot of resources and effort were expended within Europe in the reconstruction process, which of course had also a strong political aim: not to allow countries such as Greece and Italy to elect communist governments. The decade straight after the war saw the US and the Bretton Woods (US-led) institutions define the meaning of development, which was promoted along the lines of western Europe and US economic and political reconstruction (Jones 2006). This particular path of development was used as a model for the nation building of many newly established states that emerged after a wave of decolonization throughout the world in the 1950s and 1960s. The United Nations, as well as the IMF and the World Bank, promoted to these 'new' nations the ideas of human rights together with a design for modernization. But, modernization had very distinct connotations and values that were underpinning assumptions about economic growth and social progress. The idea in the 1940s was that poor countries could develop along the same lines as rich ones if they followed certain prescriptions for internal reform and organization. Famous works, such as those by Arthur Lewis, *The Theory of Economic Growth* (1955) and Walt Rostow's *The Stages of Economic Growth: A Non-Communist Manifesto* (1960), identified factors that impeded economic growth, such as tradition and old-fashioned cultural belief systems, an agrarian-based economy and social organization, lack of technical infrastructure and the scientific knowhow that could turn natural resources into secondary products and lack of institutions that would support industrialization and trade. They then advocated the necessary actions to help underdeveloped nations to make the transition from tradition to modernity. Modernization theory had profound implications for education. Investing in education and the building of human capital was expected not only to equip populations in underdeveloped countries with skills and technical knowledge, but also to transform cultures and value systems, and inculcate positive attitudes towards social change, entrepreneurship, flexibility and risk taking.

The United Nations included education as part of its 1948 Universal Declaration of Human Rights due to its perceived centrality to economic and social development but also as a fundamental human right. This had important implications for making education a priority area of action. But, selecting and promoting particular education priorities for funding and for projects is a deeply political exercise that reflects the values and political commitments and bargaining between governments, civil service elites and international development organizations. Sharp divisions over setting education priorities were apparent between new national governments from developing countries and UNESCO's programmes for education. Questions over the purposes of formal education beyond primary schooling, selectivity of post-primary education and the involvement of stakeholders (national governments, local communities, parents, international funders, etc.) proved to be not only deeply political in terms of choice and financing, but also raised tensions between what was seen as the developed North versus the developing South. Formal education, a universal primary education followed by selective secondary, vocational and higher education sectors (the classic 'western' model) were seen on one hand as desirable by developing countries, but were also seen by the critics of the UN and its organizations as a westernizing tendency that ignored the particularities of local traditions. The World Bank approved education lending only in 1962, in a decade that became the first 'development decade', with the emergence of many postcolonial 'new' nations in Asia and Africa. Education for nation building would, of course, need to include many dimensions of education contributions but, in the 1960s, the dominant views came from a fairly narrow application of human capital theories. It was expected to provide literacy to 20–40 per cent of the male population and a smaller pool of higher educated elite. Theodore Schultz was instrumental in these debates through published work on human capital, showing why the industrially developed North enjoyed sustained economic growth. Cost–benefit analysis and calculating rates of return from education had profound impacts on how the World Bank approached education policy priorities (Robertson et al. 2007; Mundy 2006).

Consistent with modernization theory, such education growth was not just aiming at developing the individual productive skills of citizens, but also of changing their attitudes to all aspects of life. Modernity, as a state of mind, was seen as an important outcome of the process of education. The modern person would effect a rapture with tradition in favour of a rational (western) and scientific form of thinking that would underpin social organization of knowledge, economic skills and technology. This huge project of modernizing economies, individuals and whole communities was partly seen as the job of the school that should develop in these newly established nations in similar ways as it did during the industrialization stage of the developed nations. These ideas were very much supported not only from international organizations, but also from the new postcolonial governments, who embraced the rapid expansion of formal education systems along western lines, in what Jones (2006) saw as 'an ironic expression of newly-acquired freedom from colonial rule' (p. 36). More 'peripheral' areas of education included functional literacy projects for the mass of the population not benefiting from the formal education systems in place. But, these were projects that were not seen as dominant by the World Bank or even by the governments of many of the developing countries throughout the 1960s and 1970s. The narrow views of formal human capital investment of a western style dominated those decades of prioritizing and financing education for development. But, the voices of critiques that came from the South began raising the questions about the emerging development models that went far beyond the technicist assumptions of education for growth.

*Some countries are rich **because** other countries are poor*

Modernization theory focuses on the internal/domestic factors that can lead to development, from building industrial and trade infrastructure, to investing in human capital and changing individual attitudes, skills and social relations. It does rely very much on liberal/neo-liberal economic assumptions about the nature of progress and about the values that are seen as desirable in any social and economic system and it does try to export the 'successful' western style of social and economic progress to the rest of the world. In that paradigm, all countries can become successful if they follow and implement these models well.

During the 1960s, modernization theory (still developing then), was challenged by (mainly) academic thinkers who focused on uneven power relationships on the world stage. They formulated 'dependency theory' that argued that it is external forces that shape the path of development for countries and that these forces are shaped by the economic, neo-colonial interests of the powerful western world. In this paradigm, not all countries can be equally successful. Rather, the developing countries are, at the outset, placed in relations of dependency towards the North. In this view, the main interest that the wealthy North has is in keeping low-income countries in a subservient role, since they can provide them with cheap exports of raw materials, low paid labour and less regulated industrial sites. Classic works by the so-called Latin American school of thought were triggered by Paul Prebisch's *The Economic Development of Latin America and its Principal Problems* (1950) and further expanded by Andre Gunder Frank's *Capitalism and Underdevelopment in Latin America* (1967) and Samir Amin's *Neo-colonialism in West Africa* (1973). The idea of a core–periphery world structure was challenged by Immanuel Wallerstein (1974 and 2004) who argued that the world is an integrated global system that, since the sixteenth century, has an organized world economy '*not bounded by a unitary political structure*' (2004, p. 23). The various political units inside this economy include states and markets but are not limited to them, and the unifying feature of this structure is the division of labour that constitutes it. 'World-systems' theory moves away from the dualities of the core–periphery approach, and introduces a polity thesis that looks at globalization as a particular manifestation of unequal power relationships between the developed North and the developing South. This approach provides explanations for the exceptions that are observed in terms of national economic growth (e.g., why certain previously underdeveloped economies have thrived in the globalized context, such as South Korea, parts of India, now belonging to a 'semi-periphery'). But, still, at the core of this thesis is the belief that this integrated world system is built on power structures that are designed to maintain global inequality and to maintain the strong position of the wealthy North.

In education, arguments similar to those from within critical theory that saw unequal power relations playing out within industrialized countries were extended to the world stage. So, within national borders, education was seen to serve the interests of the capitalist class, with inequality as an in-built design of the system. The purpose of this system is to select and allocate individual students for labour market positions and their corresponding economic and social status while, at the same time, legitimate the unequal distribution of rewards through meritocratic mechanisms. In other words, the system is designed to fail students from lower socio-economic groups, but it does so in a way that is beyond reproach through public examinations and through also rewarding few 'exceptional' individuals from the lower socio-economic groups. The economic and social elite within the industrialized countries needs a substantial group of the population to underachieve in schools and eventually to take up positions in the labour market that will feed into the kind of industrial or other work that is low paid and precarious.

Dependence and world-system theorists saw similar relations between the 'core' developed nations and the 'periphery' and 'semi-periphery' countries that aspired to development and followed the prescriptions of organizations such as the World Bank and the IMF. In terms of education, they view human capital theories as serving a similar function to that of the idea of meritocracy, i.e., as a means of control of populations in the (semi-)periphery that serves both to legitimize the superiority of the core and to exploit the resources that the (semi-)periphery produces in a post/neo colonial style of relations. The role of the state and national governments is seen as important both for modernists (governments as key to implementing the modernization project) and for dependency theorists (governments representing the interests of the national elites and being instrumental in reproducing inequalities within and between national boundaries), even though world-system advocates have a much less state-centric approach to their analysis. In Latin America, Paulo Freire was advocating the rejection of irrelevant western models of education and curricula in favour of authentic local knowledge that could be built on and developed in an organic way towards cultural and social liberation-driven projects. UNICEF's adult literacy programmes and campaigns for attention to the masses of dispossessed and their basic education and health needs, were akin to the Freire initiatives but, as Jones (1990) suggests, these were of rather limited political significance and were seen as attracting resources away from more mainstream concerns of building formal schooling.

The Washington Consensus

Post-1970s, a revived set of economic and political ideas – those of neo-liberalism – became political orthodoxy, and dominated the approach to development and the perceptions of education's role in it. The governments of Reagan in the United States and of Thatcher in the United Kingdom were instrumental in marginalizing (or rejecting) a lot of the fiscal policies that were based on Keynesian assumptions in favour of radical alternatives drawing on classic liberal economic thought. At the core of these ideas rests the assumption that markets and trade should be supported by states but not controlled or regulated by them. The expanded welfare states of the wealthy North were increasingly seen as constraints on the free operation of markets and as giving the wrong incentives to the population in terms of generating economic growth. The impact of these ideas and these administrations on development and its relationship to poverty and education was significant. Economic globalization (often referred to as the global capitalist approach) became hegemonic, although with strong contestation from social movements (e.g., the World Social Forum, which symbolically represents 'movement of movements' of resistance to globalization – but with the impact on cultural, rather than economic, spheres).

In the sphere of aid and development to poorer countries, these shifts took an institutional form through the Stabilization and Structural Adjustment Policies (SAPs) that were designed by the IMF and the World Bank as policy prescriptions to debtor countries. These prescriptions came to be known collectively as the 'Washington Consensus', after a term used by John Williamson to summarize what he called the 'conventional wisdom of the day among the economically influential bits of Washington' (1993, p. 1329). The financial crisis of the post-1973 period saw many low income countries having huge debts and having to accept SAPs.[2] The rolling out of these policies to the world's most vulnerable economies meant widespread privatization of key sectors of the economy and infrastructure, reduced protection of local production, the freeing of trade and the insertion of these economies in a world market. There is more or less consensus today that this forced liberalization of weak economies and vulnerable states in Latin America and Africa has led to deep recessions and a backward trajectory throughout the 1980s and 1990s (Klees 2010; Samoff 2007). By contrast, the so called Tiger Economies (including China and India), who followed alternative economic policies with a market orientation but controlled by a strong state, saw different and better paths towards development (Stiglitz 2001; Anand et al. 2011). The issue of the role of the state in regulating the market and in pursuing some form of redistribution strategy in alleviating poverty and inequality continues to be central in debates around development. In the field of education, the impact of SAPs was not direct and straightforward, and produced different outcomes, depending on the national context of implementation. But, overall, governments under the guidance (or imposition) of SAPs were following two main education policy directions: (a) an increased emphasis on viewing education as human capital investment based on rates-of-return analyses and (b) a move towards increasing decentralization[3] that was seen as necessary for the successful operation of markets in education, as the alternative model to state planning (Robertson et al. 2007). Both of these policy frameworks were operated within a context of cost reductions for education due to reduced international aid levels in the 1990s, privatization of higher education and policies of teacher accountability across the developing world. The combination of these factors has produced a depressing picture in terms of education investment and development. Declining GDP in countries undergoing economic restructuring was accompanied by reduction in education budgets, as a result of the failure of SAPs to generate economic growth (Mundy 2006). These changes also meant in many cases, changing patterns of access to education, with the poorest parts of the populations in developing countries suffering the worst of the negative implications of the cuts and of structural adjustment. The poorest parents would withdraw children from school in order for them to contribute to family income, and also because of their inability to cover the increasing costs of schooling that were no longer supported by the World Bank's funds – books, transportation to school and school fees (Robertson et al. 2007, p. 45). In summary, the gains in terms of education access, provision and quality, made through the 1960s and 1970s, were reversed or undermined by the austerity and the market-driven reforms of the 1980s and 1990s.

Post Washington Consensus

In their review of the post-1990 developments in the World Bank/IMF policies, Robertson et al. (2007) identify a number of factors that led to a shift in international thinking, from the hard austerity measures of the earlier decades to a period of the *good governance agenda* that introduced social concerns to the market driven approach to development. The criticisms against the structural adjustment policies (SAPs) that dominated the 1980s were harsh since these were seen to undermine the capacity of countries for social spending without, at the same time, leading to economic recovery. As a result, education as well as health and other social spending was reduced since low income countries were prioritizing debt repayment over investment in the future (as it happens, this is the main fear expressed in 2012 about the situation of Greece and its acceptance of the debt relief from the EU). Governance was identified as a big problem in the implementation of aid programmes and in the failure of SAPs to bring about positive change. Identifying problems of corruption, poor institutions, lack of accountability and disrespect for the rule of law in many of the poor countries receiving aid, the World Bank promoted the good governance agenda 'as both an explanation of and solution to the deficiencies of the Washington Consensus development model' (ibid., p. 55).

According to Mundy (2007), the theoretical roots of the development of the concept of governance in this period can be found in shifts in academic thinking from the 'bipolar power politics', which dominated international relations during the cold war period, towards a new approach to account for big changes in the world system. The transformation of state capacities through processes of 'globalization' and the increasing power of transnational organizations (such and the Bank and the IMF) that operated outside the traditional nation state territories gave rise to the concept of 'global governance' as a new tool to understand emerging world relationships. At the same time, international politics was changing. The collapse of communism and the changing geopolitical scene meant that the United States changed its priorities in terms of financial support to regimes in particular regions (see Latin America), and brought countries in the European 'eastern bloc' into the mainstream capitalist/liberal democratic paradigm of the rest of Europe. Against this context, the failure of SAPs to lift countries out of poverty was acknowledged even by the World Bank (Jones 2006), while the economic success of the Asian Tigers who followed alternative paths to progress raised questions about the effectiveness of the market-driven model of development (ibid.). So, in the period post-1990, the role of the state and its capacity to facilitate better government has been revisited, while a new actor came to the scene – the 'civil society' as a major mediating force between markets and states. Economic policies on their own were no longer seen to be the only requirement for successful reform; there was recognition that society and states mattered.

These ideas gave rise to a set of policies that Joseph Stiglitz (2011) refers to as the post-Washington consensus that viewed 'the state' and 'the market' as complementary, with the former in the role of balancing and redressing market imperfections. This consensus, under the governments of Clinton in the United States and Blair in the United Kingdom found concrete formulations in ideas about the role of education in economic growth. Two important developments need to be addressed here. First, the introduction of a new agenda on Education for All (launched in the World Conference on Education for All in Jomtien, Thailand 1990, and reaffirmed at the World Education Forum in Dakar, Senegal in 2000). The spread of basic education through the agenda, Education for All (EFA), became the symbol of the post-Washington Consensus in education, and includes a strong dimension of education as a human right, as we have already seen in Chapter 1.

The situation with regard to primary school attendance has been changing. The numbers of children attending (at least) primary education worldwide has been rising steadily since the 1950s, but the North–South gap is not closing. The number of out-of-school children of primary school age fell from 106 million in 1999, to 68 million in 2008. In 2010, the world population aged 15 and over had an average 7.8 years of schooling, increasing steadily from 3.2 years in 1950 to 5.3 years in 1980. The rise in average years of schooling from 1950 to 2010 was from 6.2 to 11.0 years in high-income countries and from 2.1 to 7.1 years in low-income countries (Barro and Lee 2011). Thus, in 2010, the gap between rich and poor countries in average years of schooling remained at four years, having narrowed by less than one year since 1960. In 2010, the level and distribution of educational attainment in developing countries are comparable to those of the advanced countries in the late 1960s. Within the governance debate, EFA was important and its effects long-lasting:

a. It relied not only on states to implement top-down reforms, but explicitly wanted to 'ensure the engagement and participation of civil society in the formulation, implementation and monitoring of strategies for educational development' (World Bank 2011a, p. 8). NGOs, together with governments, community leaders, parents and learners, are seen to be involved in more democratic processes that will incorporate EFA into wider poverty reduction and development frameworks;

b. It placed emphasis on organizing aid on the basis of 'sectors' as opposed to 'projects'. In terms of education, that meant that the whole sector of education in a country would be examined to identify and meet the greatest need. The new emphasis on the reform of 'education systems' is still strong, as can be seen in the World Bank's *2020 Strategy* that approaches education systems as including 'the full range of learning opportunities available in a country, whether they are provided or financed by the public or private sector. . .This more inclusive concept of the education system allows the Bank Group and its partner countries to seize opportunities and address barriers that lie outside the bounds of the system as it is traditionally defined' (ibid., p. 5).

c. EFA incorporated a range of mechanisms for the monitoring of success of the goals, such as the development of national action plans and performance indicators, benchmarking and periodic assessments of progress. All of these instruments were to dominate the international scene for comparative and international education, and they represented a 'coming together' of international organizations (IMF, World Bank, OECD, UN in the 2000 joint Declaration entitled 'A Better World for All') in the coordination and monitoring of the progress of countries towards the selected priorities. And, of course the problem with targets is that, however necessary, they are always the outcome of negotiation and bargaining between different actors, as well as constantly in need of revision (Lewin 2011). As we shall also see in Chapter 6, the beginning of the new millennium signals a new form of transnational and international governance framework for education (and other policy areas) that sees non-state actors select national priorities for reform, commit to assisting national governments into their implementation, and devise detailed monitoring instruments to evaluate their development.

The second important, and closely connected development in the 1990s is the setting up of the MDGs. As a result of a resolution adopted by the General Assembly of the UN, the United Nations Millennium Declaration made strong commitments to a new global partnership to reduce world poverty by 2015, emphasizing good governance both within countries and at the international level. The targets set to achieve this ambitious project have become known as the Millennium Development Goals (MDGs, see Table 1.1).

Following the Jomtien Conference, the Bank funded some goals more than others, reflecting a wide range of interpretations of 'basic education'. So, while the MDGs covered young people and adults, the Bank financed primarily formal primary schooling for children, and this is something that was also strongly reflected in the preferences of other donors (UNICEF, UNESCO, etc). But, despite the disagreements about the specifics, the literature views the development of the MDGs as politically significant because they 'aligned the United Nation (and its agencies), the Bretton Woods institutions and OECD governments behind a unifying substantive framework' (Mundy 2006, p. 24). This was heralded as a consensus around aid to combat poverty that brought the 'left' and 'right' closer together – with the UN agencies accepting a greater role for markets and the Bretton Woods institutions acknowledging the importance of the social dimensions to development.

Problems and issues

What seem to still be the main issues in relation to education and development? The big issue that frames this question of course is poverty. According to World Bank (2011a) figures, in the year 2005, huge numbers of people were still living on very low incomes and, in some cases, this represents two-thirds of the population (Table 5.1):

Table 5.1 Poverty headcount ratio at US$2 a day (PPP) (% of population), 2005

East Asia & Pacific	38.7%
Europe & Central Asia	8.8%
Latin America & Caribbean	17.2%
Middle East & North Africa	17.2%
South Asia	73.9%
Sub-Saharan Africa	72.9%

Source: Ravi and Sumner (2011).

In 1990, 93 per cent of the world's poor lived in low-income countries. Now, more than 70 per cent – up to a billion of the world's poorest people or a 'new bottom billion' – live in middle-income countries and most of them in stable, non-fragile countries. So, there is a high concentration of the world's poor in relatively few countries: about 60 per cent of the world's poor now live in just five middle income countries – China, Pakistan, India, Nigeria and Indonesia (ibid.).

In terms of education, the number of children that are out of school worldwide has dropped from 106 million in 1999 to 68 million in 2008 (World Bank 2011a). This still presents a huge challenge for development, compounded by difficulties of extreme poverty, conflict situations and fragile states in a lot of poor countries. The distribution of these out-of-school children is also not linear. Most of them are concentrated in 'hot spots' of sub-Saharan Africa and South Asia. Girls are still less likely to attend school, even though the situation is slowly improving as the figures below suggest. In 1999, almost 61 million (58%) of out-of-school children in the world were girls, compared to 45 million (42%) boys. In 2009, around 35 million girls were still out of school, compared to 31 million boys. Almost half of the world's out-of-school girls are in sub-Saharan Africa. Around a quarter are in South Asia. In South Asia, the region's total number of out-of-school girls dropped from 23 million girls to 9.5 million since 1999. In sub-Saharan Africa, the number of out-of-school girls has decreased more slowly, from 25 million in 1999 to 17 million in 2008. In Latin America and East Asia, girls have reached parity with boys; however, more boys complete primary school than girls in all other regions. So, overall, although the gap in gender parity has decreased substantially, there are still many more girls out of primary school than boys (UNESCO, Institute for Statistics in Education, 2011).

So, will the consensus described above make a difference? In some quarters, this 'consensus' on what 'good governance' is and what a 'good education' is has also been seen as a revival of modernization theory, with powerful transnational organizations defining the desirable outcomes of education for countries that only have ownership of the detailed means to achieve the goals set by others: 'good' education is what the Bank (and other donors) define as 'good' (Jones 2006; Mundy 2007; Samoff 2007).

At the same time, and while consensus would seem to be the best strategy to achieve the MDGs and EFA, there have been concerns that universal access to primary schools by 2015 is not realistic, while the goals of equality and quality look certain not to be achieved. In addition to the many resource-related problems that impede progress, Kosack (2009) identified 'political will' as a prerequisite for development, and Davies (2011) highlights issues around 'capacity' for education development in 'fragile' states.[4] The organization and management of human and financial resources, the setting up of efficient information systems and the building of trust are seen as necessary to support the selection of skilled individuals who will implement education reform at different levels (from classroom teaching to local, regional or national administrative units). Significant here is customary change that includes the normative frameworks that govern communities (from families to states) and very much provide the context for the successful implementation of reform of schooling. Finally, the political dimension is important, not just in terms of top-down political will, but the whole 'enabling environment' that, in fragile contexts, can make the difference between success and failure: 'Many fragile states are organised into networks of social and religious organisations, families, clans and enterprises based on clientelism and patronage. Angola and Afghanistan are characterised by clientelism in different ways, Angola by oil clientelism and Afghanistan by dependent client relations' (ibid., p. 167). What donors and international organizations need to do, according to Davies, is to stop using the monolithic Western language and models of development and pay attention to the local contexts and cultures and their significance in making aid successful.

Two important reports have been published in 2011. One is the UNDP's Human Development Report (*Sustainability and Equity: A Better Future for All*).

This report explicitly draws on the work of Amartya Sen and Sudhir Anand, who made the case for considering sustainability and equity together, as well as the Brundtland Commission (1987) report and subsequent declarations on sustainability. The report's main argument is that human development and the expansion of peoples' choices builds on shared natural resources. Equity, empowerment and capacity development for progress are not possible without sustainable growth. The UNDP constructed the Multidimensional Poverty Index (MPI) that measures serious deficits in health, education and living standards, looking at both the numbers of deprived people across the world and also at the intensity of their deprivations. Exploring the complex interplay between environmental deprivation and living conditions, education is identified as severely affected. For instance, girls are more likely to be adversely affected where poor environmental contexts (for example, lack of access to clean water and poor sanitation) means that they are the ones, more often, to combine schooling with resource collection.

In spring 2011, the World Bank published its *Education Strategy 2020*, where it reaffirms its commitment to help support all countries to achieve EFA and the education MDGs. This is placed within the wider multilateral commitment, in the language of international organizations, to reduce poverty within an increasing convergence of the UN and Bretton Woods on the means to achieve this. What are the ongoing issues?

The *Education Strategy 2020* continues to draw heavily on the rates-of-return approach to the investment in education. But, it is also broadening the remit of the discussion, both in terms of setting priorities and in terms of the actors that are needed to make education reforms successful. Universalizing primary schooling and improving gender equality are still among the core priorities, but there is a new recognition that 'growth, development, and poverty reduction depend on the knowledge and skills that people acquire', something that moves the debate beyond the primary level of formal schooling and out of the boundaries of classrooms (although these still seem to be at the top of the agenda). The new strategy also emphasizes accountability and quality control and reinforces the earlier commitment to monitoring the progress of education reforms through 'new tools and benchmarking' for assessing the outcomes of aid. Ideas of policy learning and providing internationally comparable information about education systems aim to identify strong and weak performers, as also to 'facilitate South–South learning'. For that purpose, the Bank is developing performance, outcome and impact indicators under the System Assessment and Benchmarking for Education Results (SABER) Program.

In this strong elaboration of the good governance agenda, the Bank has certainly endorsed the managerial tools that many wealthy states in the North have developed over the last 20 years to assess the progress against education reforms. Together with the other UN organizations, and through the emerging consensus on the role of states, markets, civil actors and the role of donors in defining the priorities and roles for education, there seems to emerge a very powerful transnational system for the global governance of education that fits well with the discussions around the effects of globalization on education and the convergence of education discourses about what good education consists of.

The North–South debate seems to be taking different directions – at least on the surface. The North is no longer merely represented by one or two powerful states and their agencies, but is made up of many and more diverse actors who, despite disagreements and competition over areas of influence, have come to a 'consensus' about education priorities as well as instruments. At the same time, the South is (supposedly) made up of more than the elites running national governments; rather, it includes (in principle) a larger set of interests and representatives through the operationalization of 'civic society' in developing countries.

Is this real or, is this just a changing discourse crafted by the powerful North in order to gain legitimacy over the development debate? Only time will tell, although past experience would suggest caution in being over-optimistic.

Notes

1 Economics research today recognizes the role of many education systems in increasing, rather than decreasing, income inequalities, but it is still seen as a 'perverse effect' due to the positive correlation between level of education and level of lifetime earnings (Todaro and Smith 2008, p. 388)

2 We are not claiming that the financial crisis generated these debts. The debts arose largely because of the oil price hikes of 1973 and 1979 and major droughts (in various parts of Africa). Oil-importing countries and those that also had

to import food racked up foreign debt to finance imports. The crisis was made worse by the world recession of 1979–81, largely brought about by neo-liberal policies to shrink the state. Then, developing countries with large debts were forced into SAPs in order to get import support. We are grateful to Professor Peter Lawrence (University of Keele) for this clarification.

3 The term 'decentralization' has been usefully discussed in terms of shifts of political authority and re-organization of roles from the centre to the local–regional levels, in terms of its political rationales (liberal, democratic, localist), but also in relation to shifting the cost of services from the state to the private sector (see Lauglo 1995).

4 The World Bank has published the World Development Report 2011: *Conflict, Security and Development*, where it defines fragility on the basis of conflict, violence, security and volatility. In combination with the African Development Bank and the Asian Development Bank Country Policy and Institutional Assessment, countries are given a rating of 'fragility' – a characterization that can be formally also assigned on the grounds of peace-keeping or building missions operating in a country.

6

Europe: Issues and Comparisons

Introduction

Europe as a continent comprises countries of great diversity in terms of size, history, political economy and wealth, with education systems that have been in significant ways, very different from each other. After World War II, we have the emergence of the two political 'blocks' within Europe that have divided the continent in political and economic terms, with education following distinctly different trajectories in the countries of the 'eastern' and 'western' block. In the west, most countries followed some similar trends straight after 1945, which included big investment in infrastructure, with even the poorer countries of the south establishing universal and free schooling for all. Welfare states were created – in some countries very comprehensive, while in others more residual, but still present everywhere, and certainly better resourced than in most other parts of the world in the 1950s.

In all countries of Western Europe, education was seen as a big force for modernization and followed significant expansion (mainly in the form of higher participation of young people in higher education) throughout the 1960s and 1970s. In terms of organization, some countries (e.g., Germany, United Kingdom) created highly diversified secondary sectors, while in others (such as France, Sweden), selection would come at a later stage. Progressive movements in these decades influenced curricula but also schooling and university organization that tended to become less rigid and authoritarian, and more open to participation from staff and students. Still, there were countries experiencing authoritarian regimes (Greece, Portugal, Spain) that emphasized hierarchy and tradition (in content and process), but they were affected to different degrees by progressive ideas once these regimes collapsed. These trends seemed to be overhauled in most places over the last 20 years by the emergence of new and very powerful discourses that, as we saw in Chapter 3, seemed to be travelling across national and disciplinary boundaries. These discourses tended to emerge as a result of governments' and international organizations' reactions to global economic changes and recessions, and they emphasized a more utilitarian and narrow role for education. The economic context of the post-1970s Europe articulated discourses of globalization as a threat or an opportunity (depending on the particular national situation), but always as an undisputed reality. This 'reality' gave the impetus in most European governments to reduce their welfare spending and to introduce the principles and (selective) practices of quasi-markets in education systems. Teachers and schools began being evaluated and held accountable in very systematic ways, both for higher standards and learning outputs but also for the spending of resources. Parents and students began being treated as consumers of education and given more choice over schooling and university, and the principle of competition between institutions and individuals underpinned almost every aspect of education policy and practice.

The former 'Eastern' block of countries saw different developments in the period since World War II. Education systems were successful in achieving almost complete population literacy, and basic education extended to 8 years, followed by technical schools, while vocational studies were closely linked to the industrial and agrarian organization. These were systems that were well organized, and characterized by deeply (and explicitly) ideological principles. The 'transition' to democracy, civil society and liberal market economy throughout the 1990s was not smooth for all of these countries. The experiences of social and political conflicts as well as, in some places, war, represented huge upheavals that, in parts of the south-east Europe, delayed progress in education reforms. By the end of the 1990s, the most difficult period seemed to have been over, and the road to accession to the European Union opened for many of these countries. Education has been a fundamental part of social reconstruction as well as democratizing tool (Zgaga 2005).

More recently, and certainly post-2000, we observe a greater convergence in education goals and discourses across Europe than ever before. Lifelong learning, the expansion of education to all ages and all people has become a dominant discourse in almost all national contexts of Europe, but it is taking place in a new economic, social and political context characterized by deep economic restructuring, whose 'coherence' can be encapsulated within the term of 'neo-liberalism' (Jones et al. 2008). The implementation of the quasi-markets in education systems seems to be a key underpinning reform that most countries have adopted in one form or another. Education is linked more than ever in the post-war period to the needs of the economy, while expansion of education through almost mass systems of higher education has led to a huge increase in certification (mainly at post-compulsory but pre-university levels), but also an increasing differentiation in the forms and types of schooling and higher education establishments. Many of these more recent developments can be usefully explored through the project of European integration and its consequences for education across Europe. So, in this chapter, we shall focus on education in the EU and we shall illustrate some of the core themes of the book through the developments that have been taking place in this part of the world over the last few decades.

We view the EU as part of an economic, political and cultural globalization process, with effects on education policy and practice. The member states have voluntarily given up some of their national sovereignty to be partially replaced by the 'complex transnational networks' of the EU (Held et al. 1999, p. 9). This process, which the EU member states themselves have initiated and negotiated, has led to the creation of a network of states that have invited and accepted an additional political authority within their own national borders. This authority impinges on economic, but also political and cultural, aspects of state organization and functions, such as creating a common identity, constructing cultural symbols and educating citizens (Alexiadou 2005a). But, the EU has also, throughout the 1990s, attempted to deal with some of the social problems that are seen as impeding growth, social cohesion and prosperity (social exclusion, poverty, racism and discrimination), and has made some (fairly limited) efforts to construct a response to them. Even though social policy and education do not, strictly speaking, fall within the remit of the EU, it can be said that there is a distinct social dimension to the EU actions. We should remember, of course, that education as well as social policy in Europe are not, and should not be, approached in a way similar to these areas in national policies. But, education has been increasingly considered as an important part of wider strategies to ensure competitiveness, contribute to economic growth and combat social exclusion (Daly 2006). As such, we can observe over the last

20 years a deepening and widening of EU functions in relation to education that have challenged the monopoly of the state to decide the direction and shape of education systems.

The European and the national in education

This was certainly not the case in the early periods of European history in education.[1] The early establishment of the European Community in 1957 was based purely on the free movement of workers, goods and services, and the Treaty of Rome had just one article (art.128) on vocational training and another one (art.57) on the recognition of University qualifications across the (then) six member states. This began to change slowly throughout the 1970s and 1980s. The Union expanded its membership and, in response to remarkable worldwide and European events (the recessions in the 1970s, the German unification, the collapse of the Soviet Union), it began to strengthen the ties between the member states and to work towards establishing structures (economic and political) that would give it a higher profile on the international stage. In the field of education, this period saw the first Resolution on cooperation in education that announced an 'action programme' based on research and study visits across member states, as well as the beginnings of compiling education statistics in many education fields (Hingel 2001). Despite the success of this cooperation, which led to the establishment of the first Socrates programme in 1995, the sensitive nature of education soon became apparent. The attempts to articulate a more integrated policy in education that would link to a European identity touched the very core of a nation: history, culture and language, and created tensions between the Community and member states (Pépin 2006).

Since the middle 1980s, the efforts to establish an internal market brought education more into the centre of political and economic agendas. The intention to create a big internal market where no national barriers would impede trade and mobility, as well as the need to improve competitiveness at a world stage, meant that education became an area of some significance, in relation to: (a) continuing and intensifying the focus on creating a European identity for citizens and (b) increasing considerably the activities around education exchange and mobility programmes. In that respect, we can view the increasing activity in education as part of a wider Europeanization process, and the advances in the integration project that brought the economy, labour markets and some areas of social policy closer together. The most important development for education in those years was the signing of the Maastricht Treaty in 1992, which identified the three pillars of the EU (social cohesion, economic and monetary union and the single market). The Treaty set for the member states an ambitious programme that included, among other things, the introduction of European citizenship, the goal of monetary union (to be achieved by 1999), the aim to bring aspects of social policy within the remit of the Union and limited competence of the EU over education.

This Treaty was very important not only for the particular areas of action that it introduced, but because it signals officially the end of an era of absolute national sovereignty. The political and ideological consensus of the 1990s was that only by joining forces can European nations compete at a world stage, and deal with the major economic and social problems facing them. The problems of balancing the diversity of European nations and the creation of this more integrated Europe were certainly acknowledged. There has been significant debate since the 1990s on the best ways to manage such a big entity democratically, but also with respect for national diversity while, at the same time, achieving this gradual coming together. The Maastricht Treaty placed education for the first time under Union authority, but strictly under the principle of 'subsidiarity'. Article 126 of the Treaty of the Union defines the competence of the European Commission in education as limited, and extending only to general 'quality issues':

> (the Community) shall contribute to the development of quality education, particularly by encouraging cooperation between Member States and, if necessary, by supporting and supplementing their action, while fully respecting the responsibility of the Member States for the content of teaching and the organisation of education systems and their cultural and linguistic diversity.

So, the twelve member states (in 1992) of the European Communities agreed on building an economic, political and monetary union, and fundamental to this new political nature of EU was the concept of 'European citizenship'. Promoting the image of Europe and the project of European integration in order to gain political support and legitimacy, the EU saw education programmes and forms of educational cooperation as core to this mission. Citizenship is a very interesting example here of how national concerns with building nationhood have parallels in the European project of building 'a sense of belonging'. Even though the main activities of the Community were driven by concerns with economic integration, the construction of a 'European identity' was emphasized as essential, as early as 1973 and the Copenhagen summit. Since then, the themes of 'European identity' and 'citizenship' have been recurrent and formalized in later Treaties (Lewicka-Grisdale and McLaughlin 2002).

But, in the Maastricht Treaty, the emphasis on the definition of 'citizenship' is still primarily on the economic dimensions of citizens within a free(er) labour market, which reflects and reinforces 'the continuing prioritisation of economic rights in the European Union' (Douglas-Scott 2002, p. 491). The political aspect of citizenship is widely acknowledged to be fairly underdeveloped in the EU context, while 'social citizenship' is vaguely defined and seems to be all-encompassing (ibid.). But, article 126 of the third chapter of the Maastricht Treaty considerably expands the competence of the EU in actions that develop the 'European dimension' in education, mainly through the teaching of languages and the exchange of education participants (Tulasiewicz and Brock 2000). The goals for Community action on education by the 1990s were summarized by Karlsen (2002) as falling into three central aims, all of which feed into both the economic mobility and 'identity'-related functions of education: (i) promoting mobility, exchange and cooperation in education and training through student and teacher exchange programmes, (ii) developing a European dimension as part of a wider attempt to create a European identity and (iii) encouraging academic recognition of qualifications and study and exchange of information. The creation of a European identity, of course, has been also linked to the issue of the 'discursive construction of Europe', a process that goes beyond merely aggregating particular features of the member states' economies' (Dale 2005, p. 9; Nóvoa and deJong-Lambert 2003). Seen from that perspective, this aspect of EU policies with regard to the key functions of education is similar to that of nation states' building and the techniques used to forge a sense of a national identity. The publication of documents such as the White Paper, *Growth, Competitiveness, Employment* (1993), discussed education as one of the core conditions for the development of a European model of economic growth, while urging the adaptation of education and training systems to meet the social and economic challenges facing the Community. The so-called 'mainstreaming' of education in policies related to employment, economic growth and in the late 1990s, social cohesion, continued treating education very much as part of economic policy of the EU, rather than a policy area on its own (Brine 2002). By 1999, a *Rolling Agenda* was agreed by education ministers in order to create more efficient and effective education policy making.

Building a European area of education

All those activities throughout the 1980s and 1990s certainly point to an ever-increasing cooperation in education matters in the EU, but more radical developments were to follow.[2] In 2000, the Heads of State and Government met in Lisbon and initiated the so-called 'Lisbon strategy' that aimed to make the EU the 'most competitive and dynamic knowledge-based economy in the world capable of sustainable economic growth, with more and better jobs and greater social cohesion' (European Council 2000). The strategy aimed to 'modernize' education systems and provided what Robertson (2010) calls a 'mandate for extending the reach of Europe's policy responsibility deeper into national territory – education – and ultimately outwards to the rest of the world' (p. 27). Education was given a central role to play in this ambitious goal, and member states were invited to agree on common objectives for European education systems. In a context where respect for diversity was always paramount in such a culturally and politically sensitive area, this was an unprecedented move that has serious implications for national education. In paragraph 27 of the Conclusions, the Education Council was invited to reflect 'on the concrete future objectives of education systems, focusing on common concerns and priorities while respecting national diversity. . . '. A year later, the ministers of education agreed on 3 overall objectives (and their operational sub-objectives):

Objective 1: Increasing the quality and effectiveness of Education and
Training (ET) systems
Objective 2: Facilitating the access of all to ET systems
Objective 3: Opening up ET systems to the world

Throughout the next few years, the 'Work programme on the future objectives of the education systems' (known also as 'Education and Training 2010' or E and T 2010) brought education as a field to a much higher visibility at European level, but also tied it even more closely to policy areas such as the European Employment Strategy and the integrated guidelines for the economy (Lange and Alexiadou 2007). The 'tools' used for the implementation of this European project were provided by a new governance mechanism, known as the Open Method of Coordination (OMC). This was applied to many sensitive areas of social policy, such as education, where European action is limited by the principle of subsidiarity. Within the framework of the OMC, the education ministers adopted five 'benchmarks' (or, 'reference levels of European average performance'), supported by indicators. These were not intended to provide national objectives to be attained, rather as averages across Europe, and they covered mainly school education (areas of failure and key competencies). Even though some of these were not achieved by the year 2010, their aim was to secure what Pépin (2011) called a 'collective effort towards the realisation of the benchmark as an "ideal" ' (p. 28). New benchmarks have recently been agreed for the year 2020 (European Council 2009):

- By the year 2020, at least 95 per cent of children between the age of four and the age for starting compulsory primary education should participate in early childhood education;
- By the year 2020, the share of 15-year-olds with insufficient abilities in reading, mathematics and science should be less than 15 per cent;
- By the year 2020, the share of early leavers from education and training should be less than 10 per cent;
- By the year 2020, the share of 30 to 34-year-olds with tertiary educational attainment should be at least 40 per cent;
- By the year 2020, an average of at least 15 per cent of adults should participate in lifelong learning

The developments in achieving close cooperation in education matters across the EU have been very many since the original Lisbon strategy was announced in 2001. Through the method of the OMC, a number of instruments have been devised to define what is the minimum required for all young people leaving school, to recognize qualifications and key competencies[3] in the areas of not just vocational education but also lifelong learning[4] across the EU. The OMC has also facilitated the design of 'Common European Frameworks' on other aspects of the E and T 2010 programme to cover quality assurance, guidance, non-formal education and training and mobility, which aim to 'offer Member States and stakeholders commonly defined principles, references and tools to support national reforms and give them a European dimension' (Pépin 2011, p. 28).

Issues of implementation and criticisms

What have been the successes of this strategy in education? This, of course, depends on our definition of 'success' and the extent to which we view the Europeanization of education as a positive development or not. Starting with the issue of effectiveness of the strategy, it is certainly the case that EU countries are participating in this cooperation process and take part in the exercises of benchmarking, measuring success against indicators and feeding to the various organizations the statistics needed to compile the progress reports. Member states have to publish biannual progress reports (since 2005) on the implementation of the Education and Training 2010/20 work programme. Following that, the Commission produces an annual progress report with analysis and national statistics for each of the areas identified by the indicators and benchmarks while, every two years, there is a joint report on the overall progress by the European Council and the Commission. According to the latest Commission report (European Commission 2011a), education performance improved since 2000 in all five areas of the benchmarks that were agreed by education ministers for 2010 (early school leavers; low achievement in reading; upper secondary completion; maths, science and technology graduates; adult lifelong learning). But, despite the improvement, the benchmarks have not been achieved (with the exception of the maths, science and technology graduates). The new benchmarks for 2020 are seen as 'achievable', even though some of them will require significant effort. But, of course, the political and economic climate in 2010 was not as optimistic and promising as the climate of 2000 when all these ambitious objectives were agreed. The economic crisis has put a substantial pressure on the Lisbon agenda. In the latest *Joint Report by the European Council and the Commission,* and in the context of this economic downturn, the role of education and training in achieving the Lisbon objectives is reaffirmed:

> Education and training are central to the Lisbon agenda for growth and jobs and a key element for its follow-up with the 2020 perspective. Creating a well-functioning 'knowledge triangle' of education, research and innovation and helping all citizens to be better skilled are crucial for growth and jobs, as well as for equity and social inclusion. The economic downturn puts these long-term challenges even more into the spotlight. Public and private budgets are under strong pressure, existing jobs are disappearing, and new ones often require different and higher level skills. Education and training systems should therefore become much more open and relevant to the needs of citizens, and to those of the labour market and society at large (Council of the European Union 2010a).

In terms of the responses by the member states, this is a more difficult assessment to make. In most cases, it is very difficult to establish whether a national reform of an education system (or part of a system) is due to the pressures from the Education and Training 2010 work programme, or have a different origin (Lange and Alexiadou 2007 and 2010), such as for instance, PISA. In some cases, we can observe a more or less direct influence of these developments on national education policies. In Austria and the Netherlands, European benchmarks have been set as targets for national policy, while in Flanders, comparative information and policy learning are used to 're-orient education policy and optimise its performance' (Simons 2007, p. 540). For the 'new' member states from the former 'eastern' Europe that joined in 2004, the situation is even more interesting, since a political 'choice' about whether to accept the OMC was not an option (a voluntary process for everyone else). While older EU members were active in the development of EU policies – though often against the background of some resistance to the EU project – the new central and eastern member states had to incorporate EU policies and adapt their institutions before having any say in their formation (Halász 2006).

Overall, however, there seems to be the case that despite the continuing and strengthening cooperation in education and training, and the distinct improvement of the monitoring of progress against the agreed objectives (through the OMC instruments), member states, in most cases, have proved quite reluctant to take ownership of the European framework and invest the resources that would have been necessary for the achievement of the European objectives. This was made apparent in the mid-term review of the overall Lisbon strategy that took place in 2004–05. More specifically, in education, there is increasing evidence that member states are not as systematically involved in the process or politically committed to make it a success (Alexiadou and Lange 2013). The 'E and T 2010/20' programme very much relies on a range of social actors (not just government officials and experts) to participate in the 'mutual learning' processes and in the dissemination of activities and information to all levels of their own education systems. Without such commitment and participation, 'the Lisbon Strategy (and "EU 2020") would be condemned to inefficiency and remain the prerogative of a limited circle of actors' (Pépin 2011 p. 30).

Creating the new knowledge economy

In the years since 2008, Europe, as well as the rest of the world, is facing an economic recession of unprecedented severity in the post-war period. When governments and the EU itself make announcements about the necessity for states to reduce their budgets and cut social spending, the fear is that the social welfare provision of many nation states is going to suffer, with grave implications for the most vulnerable parts of the population. In 2010, average unemployment across the EU was at 9.1 per cent and the projection for 2011/12 is that it could reach 10.3 per cent. These figures hit certain groups in the EU population harder than others – the rate of unemployment is more than double for young workers (20.7%) and for migrants (19.1%) – and there are also big differences across countries (average unemployment ranging from 3.9 per cent in some countries to 20.9 per cent in others) (Council of the European Union 2010b). Since the 1990s, the EU has progressively built an agenda for an economic policy that emphasized 'economic growth', the 'creation of more and better jobs' and 'improving social cohesion'. The first phase of the Lisbon strategy (2000–05) had social objectives that occupied, if not a core, certainly an important place. Constructing a European response to issues of global economic shifts meant creating a knowledge-based economy where cultural diversity and social cohesion were seen as necessary, and the preservation of good welfare systems as paramount. For many (particularly in the political centre-left), the project of European integration was seen as not just a project of economic progress, but also as providing protection to European countries from the extreme effects of neo-liberal globalization. In a speech that Commissioner Diamantopoulou gave in 2002, she argued that:

> The 'European social model' is threatened by globalization, which is forcing societies to converge around an American-style model of capitalism characterized by radical deregulation, labour market flexibility and welfare retrenchment. The only way for Member States to preserve the cherished 'European social model' is to invest further in the EU (Diamantopoulou 2002).

Oskar Lafontaine (former German Finance Minister, Social Democratic party), in a recent speech, attributed the current financial, economic and social crisis, and the resulting destruction of democracy and end of welfare states, directly to the 'neoliberal globalized capitalism' as a hegemonic project led by the United States. He argues for a reversal of all European Union policies that link education, and in particular universities, to 'the logic of the market', and promotes a European project of integration that constructs an EU of social and ecological responsibility where the market economy is regulated and the themes of neo liberalism (privatization of public services, deregulation of wages and financial services and 'flexisecurity') curtailed (Lafontaine 2009). But, these voices are by no means dominant or even very loud in the contemporary period of economic recession.

By the middle of the decade, the Lisbon strategy was seen to be in crisis. The economic objectives around growth and competitiveness were not realized, comparisons to other major economies in the United States and Asia were not favourable to the EU, and the Mid-Term Review chaired by WimKok pushed a more aggressive economic agenda to the fore, through the launching of a 'new Lisbon' (Kok 2004). The re-launch of Lisbon represents a discursive break with the softer, more socially sensitive, original Lisbon strategy, towards a more intense, freer-market integration project, that put education (and in particular higher education) at the centre of human capital investment strategies (Robertson 2010). Education is key to knowledge and innovation that will produce value in the market place, hence a much stronger and explicit emphasis than ever before on supporting research and development in the 'hard sciences'. The idea permeating the first phase of Lisbon was that a strong economic performance and social cohesion are not competing against each other; rather, they are mutually strengthening. In other words, economic competitiveness is the imperative without which job creation or fighting poverty are not possible. But, this has been significantly weakened over the last 7 years, with a distinct shift that sees social protection as a dimension of the productive economic forces, and not as a right based on solidarity.

Strong criticisms have been voiced against the EU and, in particular, the Lisbon agenda of creating the future 'knowledge economy', which refer to the connections of the process of Europeanization to globalization and the neo-liberal forces of 'Anglo-American capitalism'. These criticisms view Europeanization as fundamentally contributing to the wider globalization and to furthering the goals of neo liberalism. Wolfgang Streeck (1999) and Fritz Sharpf (2001) are typical of this pessimistic/critical view that, even before 2000, saw the European Monetary Union (EMU) project as driven by the political 'right' and a strong business agenda that promoted reduced social protection, further deregulation of labour markets, wage differentiation and other supply-side strategies that seem to be the only political options freely available amongst the countries of the single market. National governments are seen as weaker (or unwilling) to influence economic growth and employment in their territories due largely to European legal constraints (ibid.). The effect of such policy direction on issues of social justice and education is a political discourse that is shifting towards 'investment in collective means of production, that is, infrastructures of all sorts' and, particularly, towards investing in human capital, through education, as a 'productive asset of the community' (Streeck 1999, p. 5). The argument here is that the drive within the EU to deregulate labour markets even further will result (or indeed require) an unequal educational and social pool and, in that case, concerns with 'social exclusion' of individuals, groups and whole regions across Europe will become even sharper (ibid.).

More specifically, in education, this reading of the EU integration project resonates with the symbolic refocusing of political attention from 'education' to 'learning' (often 'lifelong learning') that is primarily about investment in human capital to respond to the rapidly changing requirements of a globalized economy. The EU discourse on education, through the OMC, is all about employability, i.e., the acquisition of the right skills for the new knowledge economy and the right personal attributes as well as knowledge on how to use such skills throughout one's lifetime. The OECD and the World Bank use the same kind of discourse to encourage (or impose) the radical re-design of the institutions of schooling and higher education, in order to equip future citizens with employability skills. But, of course, this imagined future knowledge economy is not going to be made up entirely of high-end, highly specialized technical jobs that only well trained specialized workers can manage. Already, the OECD recognizes that there are, among its member countries, high levels of mismatch between skills and occupational shortages: a large number of people seem to be under-qualified for the work they do, but an even larger number are over-qualified (OECD 2011c and e). One of the solutions offered for this mismatch is drawing on the lifelong learning discourse:

> opportunities for retraining in high-growth occupations and pathways back into the education system could play a crucial role in addressing skill mismatch and shortages. The availability of accessible retraining options would also allow workers who have qualified in fields in which labour demand is limited and who face the prospect of over-qualification to retrain in a different area. Some features could make the return to learning easier for adults: (i) a modular structure allowing learners to take only the parts of a course they need to re-qualify; (ii) high quality RNFIL (Recognition of Non-Formal and Informal Learning) systems to provide learning credits for skills that are transferable between two fields/occupations; and (iii) part-time learning opportunities for those wanting to continue working (OECD 2011e, p. 218)

The 'fault-lines' in the idea of a knowledge-economy are recognized by organizations, such as the OECD, that acknowledge that the most vital characteristic of such a knowledge economy is flexibility and adaptability, rather than high levels of education and entrepreneurship (Halász and Michel 2011; Mahieu 2006). Only certain sectors of the economy will require workers with high quality education. For the rest, 'education' is likely to be about re-training in an attempt to be adaptable to changing demand for skills in a precarious labour market. So, greater specialization in the vocational and training fields, but also greater flexibility and transferability of learning experiences, are likely to dominate both the vocational and the university sectors. Some of the OECD suggestions are already well underway as part of the developments in higher education and the Bologna process.

In the next section, we shall provide a very brief account of developments in higher education. This account does not aim to be comprehensive; rather, it gives a selection of issues of interest that we consider significant in thinking about education in Europe in relation to the wider world.

Higher education in Europe

Even though higher education was acknowledged throughout the 1980s and 1990s in relation to its contribution to economic mobility and social coherence across Europe, it was outside the institutional structure of the EU that systematic cooperation to harmonize higher education began. In 1998, the education ministers of four countries (France, Germany, Italy and the United Kingdom) signed at the Sorbonne a Joint Declaration on *Harmonisation of the Architecture of the European Higher Education System*. Since then, six ministerial conferences have taken place, which mapped out the so called 'Bologna process'[5] that aims to create the European Higher Education Area (EHEA). Today, there are 47 participating countries that are, in principle, committed to (a) implementing a system of 3 cycles of higher education that are based on system of credits, (b) promoting mobility of students and staff, (c) promoting cooperation in quality assurance and (d) promoting the European dimension in higher education.

The narrative of 'lifelong learning' and its contribution to the future knowledge economy finds its most comprehensive manifestation in the development of a European Higher Education Area that includes Russia and former USSR republics, thus extending far beyond the political entity of the EU. The development of the knowledge economy in Europe was seen to be a necessary condition for economic growth, but it was also seen very much as a way universities could actively contribute to making Europe an attractive education market that would rival the dominance of the United States (Corbett 2011).

After the launch of the 'new' Lisbon strategy in 2005, the EU set out several globally targeted higher education projects, in an attempt to attract leading European researchers back to Europe (from mainly US institutions) and to attract more Chinese and Indian students to EU universities. Collaboration in higher education was being pursued with countries in Latin America (through initiatives such as the ALFA programme), the western Balkans, Eastern Europe and Central Asia and neighbouring Mediterranean countries (through the development of the Tempus cooperation programme) since the 1990s. But, this was not done in a very systematic or coordinated way and things changed, with the Lisbon process and its successful incorporation of the Bologna process. Robertson (2010) identifies a complex set of more recent relationships between the EU and Asia (funded by the EU's development agency EuropeAid), with higher education in the EU as an attractive new market for Asian students, as an opportunity to recruit 'Asian talent' by developing research collaborations and synchronizing Asian university structures with those of Bologna. Ultimately, these strategic moves are seen as using higher education as an instrument of furthering Europe's global reach while at the same time rivaling the United States:

> Under the banner of this 'new economy', higher education policies, programmes and practices have been increasingly co-opted and shaped by wider geo-strategic political and economic interests . . . the growing range of educational initiatives at the European level has affected – both directly and indirectly – American and Australian policymaking in higher education. The European higher education project, which is increasingly perceived as having some significance to the global economy, has set off a series of dynamic reactions in both Australia and the United States, which is leading to multiple new logics and new imaginaries about the global higher education landscape. (Robertson and Keeling 2008, p. 221).

In short, even though the Bologna process began as an intergovernmental process, there is a growing convergence with EU processes that aim to strengthen cooperation in higher education (Zgaga 2003). The European Commission is one of the Bologna Process members, and is driving, to a large extent, the process through the commitments to the Lisbon objectives. Since the mid-2000s, the process is no longer voluntary for the member states of the EU (as it is, of course, for the participating countries beyond) and follows the monitoring instruments of the OMC and the concrete future objectives of education and training systems.

In May 2010, the Council published its Conclusions on *The Internationalisation of Higher Education*, where it reaffirms its commitment to supporting the Bologna process in making the degree structure 'more compatible and comparable' through tools such as the European Qualifications Framework.[6] In improving the quality and comparability of degrees, there is a commitment to increase the attractiveness of European higher education institutions as places of study. The Commission recently published a new agenda for the modernization of Europe's higher education systems, in order to support member states to reform their systems and meet the goals of 'Europe 2020' (European Commission 2011b). This document emphasizes the core position of higher education in the achievement of a knowledge economy and identifies four areas for reform in order to make this successful: (i) an increase in the number of higher education graduates, (ii) the gearing of teaching and research towards producing transferable competencies for high skill occupations, (iii) a strengthening of links between education, research and business and (iv) the creation of governance and funding mechanisms to support 'excellence'.

These developments leave little space for alternative paths in higher education. The discourse of economic competitiveness and the construction of education and, more so, higher education, as core to a European global/ regional economic strategy, position universities as market players with limited space for professional judgement of academics or for autonomous action where priorities may be different (see Jones et al. 2008). Developments such as the EQF and the emphasis of the Lisbon agenda as well as the European Higher Education Area on specialized and transferable knowledge for innovation and economic growth are likely to have serious impacts on higher education departments and subject areas that do not easily fit this paradigm. A political economy of higher education that is highly specialized and diversified even further than it is today into elite and mass, looms large. And, in the context of a recession, governments across Europe have given clear signals that education (and, especially, the non-compulsory sectors) is going to face serious cuts in funding. These combined pressures, and the political commitment of national governments as well as the EU to a neo-liberal ideology underpinning the role and functions of higher education, will lead to a radical re-design and re-shaping of higher education with implications for our traditional understanding of what universities 'do'. To quote Giroux (2010) in his critique of development in higher education in the United States, 'there is little interest in understanding the pedagogic foundation of higher education as a deeply civic and political project that provides the conditions for individual autonomy and takes liberation and the practice of freedom as a collective good' (p. 336). But, other than the pedagogic function of higher education, the developments described above through the Bologna and the Lisbon processes are likely to have very serious impacts on the most vulnerable groups of the population that may find access and participation in higher education as difficult as that of their grandparents' generation. This, of course, may be politically rectified by the revamping of the 'mass', less prestigious new higher education institutions with a distinct vocational orientation, which will provide the majority of the population with the transferable skills they need for a life of changing occupations.

Notes

1   For more detail on the history of cooperation in education and training, see Pépin 2006 and the website of the DG-Education and Culture http://ec.europa. eu/education/index_en.htm).

2   There was certainly continuity between the 1990s and the post-2000 period, even though most authors consider 2000 as the beginning of 'policy'. Nóvoa (2001) provides an account of the Court of Justice's expansive understanding and definition of the concept of 'vocational training', which was already covered by European law and, in effect, amounts to virtually all forms of education that go beyond compulsory schooling. Similar points also apply to the recognition of professional qualifications, which is linked to education and training policy.

3   The key competencies 'necessary for personal fulfilment, active citizenship, social inclusion and employability in a knowledge society' are identified as follows: (1) Communication in the mother tongue; (2) Communication in foreign languages; (3) Mathematical competence and basic competences in science and technology; (4) Digital competence; (5) Learning to learn; (6) Social and civic competence; (7) Sense of initiative and entrepreneurship; (8) Cultural awareness and expression. (Council of the European Union 2010a).

4   Recommendation of the European Parliament and of the Council (2008) for the establishment of the European Qualifications Framework for Lifelong Learning and (2009) Recommendation for the setting up a European Credit System for Vocational Education and Training.

5 The Bologna Declaration signed in 1999 gave the name to the process and is
   considered as the primary document for the establishment of the 'framework for
   the modernization and reform of European higher education' (http://www.ehea.
   info/).

6 The European Qualifications Framework (EQF) agreed upon in 2008, is a
   'translation' instrument aiming to relate the qualification systems of different
   nations to a common European reference framework. It is a tool for promoting
   the mobility of learners and workers across the EU. It is made of 8 reference
   levels that describe different learning outcomes – what a learner knows or
   can do. It applies to academic as well as vocational qualifications, but also
   encourages the validation of 'non-formal and informal learning'. Member states
   are developing their own National Qualifications Frameworks based on such
   learning outcomes (http://ec.europa.eu/education/lifelong-learning-policy/).

7

Sub-Saharan Africa: Legacies and Innovations

Introduction

Sub-Saharan Africa is, in general, the least developed region in the world. The reasons for this are varied and complex – ranging from the lack of accommodation of much of the natural environment to human advancement, to the exploitation of physical and human resources by colonialism and neo-colonialism. The region exhibits educational problems that are unparalleled almost everywhere else in the world in terms of their complexity and intractability. The ways in which the trio of formal, non-formal and informal education need to come together to promote and support sustainable development are particularly difficult to realize. There are, however, some of the most innovative educational responses to the global challenge to be found in this region.

Only the south-east littoral of Sub-Saharan Africa enjoys the most favourable climate for humans: warm, temperate eastern margin. That is in the Republic of South Africa, the only country in the region that is regarded as semi-developed in terms of GDP, but the majority of its population do not share this privilege. Over most of the region soils are poor. This is a major constraint on development that is hardly appreciated, but was long ago pointed out by geographers (Hodder 1968). This is mentioned here because it refers to all parts of the humid tropics that make up almost all of Sub-Saharan Africa, including the lush and extensive tropical rain forests that are popularly and wrongly assumed to be indicators of fertility. In fact, they feed off the massive amount of organic detritus they shed themselves. Indigenous populations in the humid tropics and other parts of the region understand this and have developed forms of subsistence economy that maintain their survival if they are conflict-free.

This understanding is the core of indigenous education of an informal kind that has suffered under the influence of colonial incursions, mainly European but also Arab (Brown and Hiskett 1975). In many of the drier parts of the region, a combination of climate change and human-induced desertification (Grove 1977 and 2000) has further reduced the capacity of the environment to support populations that are also growing.

Cultural and colonial legacies

The origins of *Homo Sapiens* are generally accepted to have been in East Africa, whence migrations and subsequent adaptations occurred. The human populations that migrated through, and remained in, Sub-Saharan Africa may be roughly divided into Bantu and non-Bantu, on linguistic grounds. They overlap in West Central Africa, but together comprise over 1,000 languages (Nettle 1996) for the region overall. This makes it likely the most multilingual area in the world, even without the overlay of colonially derived media such as English, French and Portuguese, and lingua franca such as Creole in West Africa and Swahili in East Africa. This multilingual picture is not a static jigsaw but a dynamic one of ever changing ethnicities. Nettle quotes Otite (1990) as follows: 'The Nigerian ethnic map is a fast-changing picture created from changing manipulations and adaptations of surviving strategies in changing environments' (p. 36).

The adaptations referred to above would have been, and some still are, responses to a number of factors relevant to education. Nettle (1996) mentions four: physical isolation; political organization; transport; and trade. Of these, political organization is particularly relevant to education in all its forms and ranges from pre-colonial, through colonial to postcolonial periods. They involved territorial change through conflict from inter-tribal to inter-kingdom to inter-colonial. These opposing overlays led to the modern political geography of Africa, with all its problematic legacies for an already fragmented and fractious sub-continent. The political fragmentation created by European colonialism in Sub-Saharan Africa was much greater than in any other part of the world.

However, in respect of the religious dimension of culture, especially in west, and to some extent east, Africa, Islam was, and is, a considerable educational influence. So, we can already see that both geographical and historical factors combine to create complex and dynamic environments, physical and cultural, within which education has to operate. There have been few success stories at national level, such as Ghana (Mulholland 2012).

Yet, even Ghana retains some of the damaging legacies of colonialism, such as the placement of a national political boundary with neighbouring Togo that runs north–south straight through the territory of one of the region's major ethnic and linguistic cultures, that of the Ewe people. It must be remembered, though, that the Ewe people themselves had migrated several times in pre-colonial days. The educational legacy for the Ewe at the turn of the millennium has been researched by N'tchougan-Sonou (2000). The experience of the Ewe of a disrupted and fragmented educational legacy has countless parallels with their own unique characteristics all over Sub-Saharan Africa. Indeed, the process continues with the cessation of the southern, predominantly Christian, part of Sudan to create the world's newest country in July 2011, The Republic of South Sudan. Here, cultural, linguistic and political issues are to the fore in affecting the changing context within which education proceeds in all its forms. There are about 60 indigenous languages in the new country, which has a population of some eight million. English has been selected as the official language and medium of instruction for formal education. The current lingua franca, Arabic, is being supplanted by Swahili, widespread in east Africa, and South Sudan joined the East Africa Community of States, thus detaching itself from the Arab League, a major cultural turn.

Another country that, in 2008, has taken English on board as the official language and medium of instruction for formal education is the Presidential Unitary Republic of Rwanda. Traditionally, a territory ruled by a monarchical hierarchy, Rwanda became a German colony; then, in 1916 was taken over by Belgium, with French as the official medium, though the main indigenous language, Kinyarwanda was, and is, widely spoken. The country remains a member of 'La Francophonie', a community of French-speaking countries, but has joined the East Africa Community and the Commonwealth of Nations, despite never having been a British colony.

Rwanda shares with Southern Sudan the fact of being a landlocked country. Sub-Saharan Africa has more such nations than any other continental area, there being also: Burkino Faso, Botswana, Burundi, Central African Republic, Lesotho, Malawi, Uganda, Zambia and Zimbabwe. We might also include Chad, Niger and Mali, mainly Sahel countries but with their main concentrations of population being Sub-Saharan.

Education colonialism and conflict in sub-Saharan Africa

The indigenous peoples of Africa had their own forms of education in operation centuries before incursions by Arab or European explorers or colonizers brought them into contact with the outside world. So, as Brown and Hiskett (1975) observe:

> Schooling in the sense of institutionalised induction into the life of society is a comparatively recent development in Africa; education in the sense of initiation into the life of the adult community is a very ancient concept. In many parts of Africa this initiation has owed nothing to the influence of the world religions of Christianity and Islam (but) this ancient concept is still very much part of the complicated overall provision of education in Africa (p. 19).

In other words, formal schooling imparted by both Christian and Islamic colonizers, was always mediated by the numerous local cultures, languages and social structures at community level. Consequently, the full understanding of subsequent institutions and policies of education will be compromised if the ongoing effects of indigenous language, culture and informal education are not taken into account. Unfortunately, they rarely are. According to Brown and Hiskett (1975), the first full length account in English of informal African education of children, by Dudley Kidd in 1906, went under the title of '*Savage Childhood*'.

While not all approaches by Christian missions to institute formal schooling for the indigenous populations were so patronising (Holmes 1967), it was certainly the case that their major concern was to proselytize and convert. A related and influential concern was to compete, the outcome of which presented the newly independent nations of the region with a highly disparate legacy in terms of school location in relation to population distribution. This is clear from a major study by Johnson in 1967. Her introductory remarks are still pertinent nearly 50 years later:

> Mission stations are a widely dispersed, more or less permanent cultural feature of rural Africa. With their chapels, residences, dormitories, schools, dispensaries, gardens, utility buildings, water supply systems, and good access roads they stand in great contrast with their immediate surroundings. In the confrontation of Europeans with African ways of life these stations have been for the missionaries a refuge, a symbol of achievement, and a home; for the Africans they have been strongholds of alien ways from religion to agriculture, an intrusion, but also a promise of help, of learning, and of a better life (p. 168).

The final point above is echoed in a case study by Dada and Oshagbemi (2008) of their home town of Egbe in Western Nigeria, where they also indicate that 'there were codes of conduct solely for the white missionaries on their relationship with the blacks who were regarded as heathens' (p. 97). They mention that, on the one hand, there was a degree of fear as well as contempt for the indigenous culture on account of superstitions and secret societies. On the other hand, the missionaries understood the need to acquire local languages. This was a practical necessity on account of the innumerable vernaculars and dialects even within one locality.

By the 1930s and the impact of direct British government interest, the long period of mission involvement had shaped thinking about education in sub-Saharan Africa (Kallaway 2009) and helped to establish a distinctive culture of education. As far as the British government and the colonial service was concerned, little interest in education was taken until the early 1920s and 'was fast waning by the 1950s as various territories assumed increasing responsibility for the conduct of their own internal affairs as a prelude to independence' (Whitehead 2005, p. 441). This had been part of so-called 'Indirect Rule', as compared to the French 'Direct Rule' of their colonies. Ball (1983), however, claims that once having taken a direct interest, Britain adopted a strong political approach that included severely limiting access to secondary schooling. Whatever the reason, the extremely patchy availability of secondary schooling in almost all sub-Saharan countries has attracted much less interest than the drive to universal primary education and the development of higher education. There are exceptions, such as Lewin and Calloids (2001).

Functionality was also the initial purpose of the first university in Sub-Saharan Africa, Fourah Bay College in Sierra Leone, set up for the training of missionaries and teachers. Its foundation by the Church Missionary Society in 1827 lay between the abolition of the British slave trade in 1807 and of slavery itself in the British Empire in 1833. The existence of slavery on a large scale, involving both European Christian and Arab Islamic traders, in itself had a significant effect on education, especially in west and east Africa (Allen 2008). The arrival of freed slaves from the Americas and the Caribbean introduced a new external culture, that of the Krio-speaking elite, especially in Sierra Leone and Liberia. The latter founded in 1820 and becoming a Republic in 1847, was a totally new and independent country, long preceding nearly all others, arising from the late nineteenth century scramble for Africa that created its political geography.

Fourah Bay College widened its curriculum through its affiliation to the University of Durham, England in 1876, which continued until 1965, when the University of Sierra Leone was created. Throughout the later nineteenth and early twentieth centuries, this institution, plus emergent teachers colleges, often mission-run and elite secondary schools, provided a formal education for the elites. A prominent example is Achimota School, Ghana, established in 1927 as 'a model secondary school for African leadership', yet accommodating some African traditions by default (Yamada 2009). Bo School in Sierra Leone, already established by the British colonial governor, was also said to be for the purpose of serving and furthering an African elite, but was, according to Corby (1990), really to help the chiefs create a technical and administrative class. Nonetheless, all post primary institutions in practice became the pathways to the advancement of an African elite. Their educational experience was formative in its significance in that some became leaders of newly independent states from the 1950s to the 1970s and gave priority to investment in formal education in the belief that this would lead directly and swiftly to national economic development. Relative lack of investment in infrastructure, basic and non-formal education and unstable political and administrative institutions, plus neo-colonial exploitation (Tickly 2004) combined to thwart progress.

The colonial and cultural impact of Islam in this part of the region continues to be considerable.

The influence of Islam thus preceded that of western Europe in Africa by many centuries, and it was in no way extinguished by the subsequent European domination of the continent. In some respects, indeed, the colonial period tended to entrench and even to extend the sway of Islam and its culture. Today, Islam is far and away the most important of the world religions in Africa. Christianity was greatly advanced by European penetration in the nineteenth and twentieth centuries, but it has always remained the religion of a minority. Indeed, in only five countries can it claim the adherence of more than a third of the population – the Republic of South Africa Zambia, Malawi, Zaire (*now Democratic Republic of Congo*) and Uganda (Fage and Tordoff 2002, p. 143).

To this list may be added a sixth, the aforementioned Republic of South Sudan, the creation of which owes much to the tension between these two major religions, including their different views of education.

Islam is not just a religion, but a civilization. Encompassing all aspects of life as it does, its approach to education is holistic. This is evident in the Koranic schools, *mektabs* that have long existed in many sub-Saharan countries as both supplementary to, and in competition with, the primary schools of the official state systems. In many countries of the region, universal primary education has not yet been achieved and *mektabs* are all there is available, especially in remote locations. Even among some Islamic communities, especially in multilingual contexts, the additional burden of learning Arabic can be a constraint (Fisher 1975), but the next stage is to proceed to the *madrasa*. The degree to which there is a tolerance of such schools varies considerably from country to country and from place to place within countries. Frederick, later Lord, Lugard was Governor of the Northern Territory of Nigeria from 1899 to 1906 and the overall Governor of the colony from 1912 to 1919. His approach to control was to accommodate the educational interests of the local Islamic rulers as far as possible:

In the pursuit of indirect rule advanced by Lord Lugard, Native Authorities were created, in which Arabic schools were established with some secular subjects, after a realisation that the north of Nigeria was far behind the south in Western terms. Christians were excluded from such schools, but

Muslim children were encouraged by provision of food and pocket money to attract and retain them in the schools. Successful pupils went on into the post-primary schools (madrasas) for Islamic religious instruction at a higher level. Christians were not specifically encouraged, and as late as 1952 in Niger Province the percentage of Christians in school was 3 per cent as against 41 per cent Muslims (Brock et al. 2006, p. 224).

The shatter zone long since created across the Sahel zone by the rivalries between the ancient kingdoms and the advance of European colonization from the south has been the longest of many examples of conflict in Africa involving or affecting education. In Nigeria, the conflict was assiduously researched by Dada (1986), who found Christian and Muslim communities to be equally to blame for the wanton destruction of schools, colleges and massive loss of life. The violence has recurred periodically in the subsequent 25 years. Such large-scale violence has become an even greater problem with the added fervour of the Islamic group, Boko Haram, whose aim is to make the whole of Nigeria into an Islamic state with all that that implies for education.

Sub-Saharan Africa, in general, makes a major contribution to the catalogue of violence against schools, teachers and other educational personnel, with about a third of the country case studies in Brendan O'Malley's *Education Under Attack* (2010), from Chad to Zimbabwe. The legacies of both Western Christian colonialism and Arab Islamic colonialism have contributed hugely to this, but inter-European and inter-tribal rivalries have done so as well. Both stem from the strongest of the factors responsible for shaping education – the political. This is the factor concerned with decisions about education at all levels from the individual to the international, which may lead to conflict between parents, genders, communities, races and religions, but also between international agencies and African governments. These may not be violent conflicts such as those mentioned above, though some are, and have been a force of constraint on educational development in Sub-Saharan Africa.

Clive Harber (1989) identified a number of key themes in the politics of education in Africa, illustrated by a series of well-selected case studies: in relation to national unity in Nigeria; political socialization and education in Kenya; education for self-reliance in Tanzania; and education as a weapon of war in Zimbabwe. In all cases, serious situations of conflict occurred, ranging from constraint and coercion in the service of a political ideal in Kenya and

Tanzania, to a civil war between 'state' and 'nation' in Nigeria, to the role of education in the struggle for control of the former British colony of South Rhodesia.

The case of former Southern Rhodesia brings into discussion the issue of separate development, known as 'apartheid', in neighbouring South Africa and also operated in former South-West Africa. In 1965, the Government of Southern Rhodesia unilaterally declared independence in order to try to preserve the privileged situation of the white elite who controlled the economy.

> Education in Rhodesia, therefore, was geared primarily to the preservation of the socio-economic and political domination of a white colonial class. Black education was essentially for the production of low status technical, manual and domestic workers while whites held a monopoly of higher-level government and commercial posts. From the British conquest of Rhodesia in 1890 until independence in 1980, education was used by whites to avoid economic or political competition from the black majority (Harber 1989, pp. 98–9).

The changes in the political identity of Southern Rhodesia over a relatively short period of time were extraordinary and had severe implications for education in all its form and at all levels. Immediately prior to becoming the colony of South Rhodesia, the territory had been part of the Federation of Rhodesia and Nyasaland that comprised what are now Zambia, Zimbabwe and Malawi. The unrecognized state of South Rhodesia lasted from 1965 to 1975 amid a great deal of internal conflict and external pressure, including economic sanctions. It was, however, supported by the apartheid regimes of South Africa and its colony that is now Namibia, and also by the Portuguese colonies of Angola and Mozambique (until its independence in 1975). On its collapse in December 1979, Southern Rhodesia became 'Zimbabwe Rhodesia' until April 1980, when it became the Republic of Zimbabwe. The implications for school curricula alone were of rapid change, one illustrating the primacy of the political factor being the rewriting of history texts to suit the purposes of any new government. Since 1980, education in Zimbabwe has been fraught with violent internal conflict, with tribal and political party confrontation (O'Malley 2010).

A degree of international economic sanctions through much of the period since 1980 inevitably adversely affected investment in education, especially for the poorest communities. Changes in the external political geography caused by the independence of Mozambique, Angola and Namibia have served to intensify the problem of Zimbabwe being landlocked. Only The Republic of South Africa, since the end of *de jure* apartheid in 1992, has proved of limited support in terms of receiving significant numbers of refugees from Zimbabwe. According to Meldrum (2004), the repression and racially based exclusion practised in the former South Rhodesia, has become part of the colonial legacy. This is part of what Mangin (1990) refers to in the title of his book, *Making Imperial Mentalities: Socialisation and British Imperialism*.

From many standpoints, The Republic of South Africa is a special case within Sub-Saharan Africa. It is, by far, the most developed country in the region, being ranked as 'middle income' by the World Bank, yet has the greatest socio-economic disparities. It is the only country in the region to enjoy temperate climates in a substantial proportion of the territory. Yet, it has had a troubled history not least due to its deeply dislocated education profile. Part of this is due to a very mixed Europe-derived colonial experience with the white population split between, broadly, British and Boer components. Though mainly of Dutch origin, the Boer component also contained German, Flemish and French elements. In 1830, the Boers set off north-westwards from the British dominated Cape, and took over what became Natal, Transvaal and Orange Free State. Initially, farming communities with cheap Bantu labour, they employed Afrikaans as their own language but also imposed it as a kind of lingua franca. The British-derived white population employed English, and the two colonial populations clashed in the First Boer War of 1880–81, following the discovery of gold and diamonds in the interior during the previous 20 years. With black African labour migrating to the new urban mining locations and slum townships developing, the overall sociolinguistic melange had become complex. Following the second Boer War of 1901–02, demands for independence led to the formation of the Union of South Africa in 1910 and full independence in 1931. Education policy had long been appropriated and its delivery operated on a racial basis, as in former Southern Rhodesia. Substantial wealth in the hands of the white elites had already led to the foundation of eight universities by 1916, only the last of which, Fort Hare University, was for black Africans – in effect, the black elite. Fort Hare was only the second university in sub-Saharan Africa, after Fourah Bay College,

Sierra Leone, to cater for this elite and remained as such until appropriated by the apartheid policy in 1959. Apartheid had been developing in practice since the nineteenth century, but became compulsory national policy from 1948, by which time political power was firmly in the hands of the Afrikaner – speaking whites. In this, they were strongly supported by their religious upbringing. As explained by Penny (1988):

> ... it is necessary to appreciate two things about the Afrikaner. The first is that his religion, and in particular, the three Dutch Reformed Churches have exercised an important influence and control over the political and educational history of South Africa. Calvinist in origin, this religion, a gospel of predestination of an elite and the divine authority of the state over the individual, is preached in its more extreme forms, providing a theological justification for Apartheid. Frequently the Afrikaner is likened to the Israelites of old (p. 347).

There was considerable internal opposition from the black majority, led by the African National Congress (ANC), and some external pressure. Opposition was focused on many issues of concern to the black majority, one of which was the use of Afrikaans in schools. The Afrikaner-led government had, up to its complete demise in 1994, fragmented the national education system into 19 departments, based on race and ethnicity in the interests of separate development: 'White education was controlled by the white House of Assembly, Indian education by the Indian House of Delegates, coloured education by the Coloured House of Representatives, and African education in urban areas by the Department of Education and Education system' (Harber 2001, p. 12).

As a result of the first national democratic election in 1994, won by the ANC, a federal Ministry of Education was established to share responsibility with the nine new provinces created which, between them, covered the territory of the Republic of South Africa and had equal status, irrespective of the ethnic and racial make-up of their respective populations. In practice, it has been extremely difficult to effect a system free of the legacies of past classical, and then internal, colonialism. This was partly due to the previously socialist-inclined ANC, somewhat surprisingly, accepting the near global embrace of neo liberalism with all that that implies for the widening of educational disparity. Issues of language festered on and teachers found it extremely hard to live with these conflicting forces (Schweisfurth 2002). Harber (2001) recognized twelve, what he termed 'barriers', to effectively implementing the ANC reform of the system, ranging from cultural inertia to societal violence, to low teacher morale and quality, to inter-provincial disparity, to the HIV/Aids crisis, to the complex linguistic heritage (p. 86). Borien (2004) found many of these constraints operating in the poorest province, the Eastern Cape.

The situation of the Republic of South Africa (RSA) is significant for the whole of Southern Africa, especially the majority Commonwealth territories, which former Portuguese colony Mozambique has now joined. If the RSA can reach its potential economically, neighbouring poorer countries could also benefit. Until the education system can raise the level of knowledge and skills, further diversification and development of the economy will be difficult to achieve. All the legacies, mostly negative, of the colonial experience still combine to provide a strong force of inertia. The situations and circumstances in each country are unique, as Pape (1998) pointed out with respect to Zimbabwe and South Africa. Pape also highlighted the contrast between the 'British Cambridge' system of education in Zimbabwe, which enjoyed widespread international currency in academic recognition, and the apartheid 'Bantu Education' of South Africa, limited to low level technical training which had no external value, and little internal. In the north and, especially, north-west of Sub-Saharan Africa, Nigeria represents a similar potential for development. Here again, colonial legacies, maladministration and continued external exploitation of resources are powerful constraints. In the north-east of the region, the 'Horn of Africa', violent conflict, mass migration, environmental degradation and famine continue and intensify.

With the general situation being what it is in this region, it is not surprising that the EFA Global Monitoring Report of 2011, *The Hidden Crisis: Armed Conflict and Education,* reports that, of the 21 developing countries that spend more on the military than primary education, 13 are in Sub-Saharan Africa or the Sahel. The same report also indicates that half of the world's out-of-school primary-age children live in just 15 countries, eight of which are in this region (see Chapter 5). Nigeria easily tops the global list, with 8.6 million such children and even South Africa makes the list, with 0.5 million. Nigeria also makes the top 10 in terms of illiterate adults, some 35 million.

Sub-Saharan Africa seems unlikely to benefit from global physical climatic and environmental shifts that are predicted (Martin 2011) and, only in a few rare cases, to benefit from the more extraordinary cybernetic advances that seem possible. Nonetheless, the currently very low level of the mostly survival and subsistence economies also means that modest advances that are already attainable have a possibility of being met. But, that depends on radical changes in how education is perceived and progressed. Some of these changes have been prompted by post-conflict responses and others by genuine radical innovation.

Post-conflict realities and responses

In respect of the educational dimensions of conflict and post-conflict situations (Davies 2004), they are part of 'education in emergencies' that is, in turn, part of 'education as a humanitarian response' (Brock 2011a). A significant step in such a response in some countries has been the establishment of Truth and Reconciliation Commissions (TRCs) (Paulson 2011 a and b). Two such initiatives have been undertaken in sub-Saharan Africa, in South Africa (Johnson 2011) and Sierra Leone (Matsumoto 2011), and an alternative National Unity and Reconciliation Commission in Rwanda (Kearney 2011).

The South African TRC was set up in 1995 by the Government. Johnson's (2011) analysis of the outcome to date is not optimistic, stating that '. . . there are many who question whether the primary purpose of achieving restorative justice has been achieved in all communities' (p. 109). He investigates this further, with special reference to universities in South Africa, and finds that the issue of language has been a significant constraint. Serious innovation with regard to medium of instruction is still required, as this key component of culture is necessarily resilient. He concludes that:

> The effect of apartheid on South African higher education cannot be underestimated, nor should its legacy. The political functions of the universities, the divisions and segregation along ethno-linguistic lines and the huge inequalities and disparities in the funding of institutions and the opportunities they afforded their students continue to shape South Africa today. As was shown, even after the end of apartheid, access to and participation and success in higher education remained major issues for the black population (p. 122).

Johnson's analysis shows that underlying preconceptions and misconceptions of the intellectual aptitude of different racial and ethnic groups remain a resistant legacy not only of the specific effects of apartheid, but of the colonial experience overall. That, of course, has resonance throughout sub-Saharan Africa in terms of dependency culture. Beckford's (1972) view that 'the most intractable problem of dependent societies is the "colonised" condition of the minds of the people' (p. 235) applies there as well in his native Caribbean.

The conflict and post-conflict situation in Sierra Leone has particular regard to the civil war of 1991–2002. The so-called rebel force, the Revolutionary United Front (RUF), involved a grossly disproportionate number of children and young people. Most were coerced not only into fighting but also into committing and witnessing appalling atrocities. To some outsiders, this was a surprise in that, for reasons mentioned above, Sierra Leone had been regarded as the 'Athens of Africa' because of the historic role of Fourah Bay College and the high quality of prestigious secondary schools in Freetown. But, in fact, these largely benefited the Krio community, Christians descended from slaves freed from the West Indies and the United States of America. Indeed, the pre-1991 peaceful image of the country overlooks the little publicized massacre of Krios in 1898 and its aftermath (Corby 1990).

There are at least 16 major linguistic and tribal groups of interior, mainly Islamic, Sierra Leone. The civil war a century later began with incursions into the country from neighbouring Liberia, leading to an army demonstration against the corrupt President Momoh due to non-payment of salaries. Momoh fled, leaving the young officers in charge of the country in a bloodless coup. Intuitively, they appointed their former headmaster as Minister of Education. But the fighting in the interior descended into a situation of near anarchy over control of mineral deposits and inter-tribal rivalry under the name of a rebellion against the army and the military government. This was eventually brought to an end with the help of British and Nigerian troops. One factor underlying the conflict was the continued and extreme disparities in educational access that had continued to exist, even deepen, during direct colonial rule from 1896 to Independence in 1965. According to Matsumoto (2011), education had become a source of symbolic capital that collapsed as credentialism failed to translate into meaningful and gainful employment. The Sierra Leone Truth and Reconciliation Commission, set up after the conflict ended, reported in 2004 but its circulation was restricted and has had little positive effect on the education system since. Despite a number of reforms and major aid-supported projects, there is little progress to be seen. Redwood Sawyerr (2011) lists some post-conflict plans, but it is the socio-economic reality that must be recognized in Sierra Leone and all of sub-Saharan Africa, if formal education is to make any contribution to sustained survival and development.

Gender, education and development

In situations of violent conflict, the negative experiences of women and girls are often more severe than those of boys and men. Although males formed the majority of combatants, girls and young women were inevitably drawn in and often suffered more in consequence. Rape and other violations cause extreme psychological as well as physical conditions that have further reduced the potential contributions of females to the well-being of their families, communities and countries. This is probably the single most important factor in sub-Saharan Africa because, as Lalage Bown (1985) so succinctly put it: 'Without Women No Development'. She was writing in terms of 'the role of non-formal education for women in African development' (pp. 258–76). Her positioning of females at the heart of development was echoed by Davison and Kanyuka (1992), with reference to formal education in Africa, and Malawi in particular:

> ... increased evidence over the last decade suggests that the crucial problems precluding overall development, including shortfalls in food production, inadequate health care, and a rapidly increasing population, will not be solved unless women's pivotal role in the development process and unequal access to development benefits are addressed (p. 446).

Karin Hyde (1993) summarized the situation in the following terms:

> The factors that have affected girls' educational status in African countries include negative parental and community attitudes toward the Western education of girls; the opportunity cost of a girl's school time and, indirectly, of her mother's; general levels of wealth and development; disparities between urban and rural areas; unfavourable labour market opportunities; and low quality schools with limited curriculum choices (p. 126).

Given the problems of generating enough primary places to achieve EFA and the generally continuing rapid population increase, despite serious health issues, Hyde is on the right lines in following LalageBown's lead in suggesting that: 'One of the more fruitful approaches to increasing female schooling may be a strategy directed not at school-age girls themselves but at their mothers' (Bown 1985, pp. 126–7). Anthropologists, such as Todd (1987), have long identified the significance of the educational level of wives as compared to that of their husbands when it comes to decisions about the schooling, or otherwise, of their sons and, especially, their daughters. This has to do with levels of literacy rather than years of formal schooling. That is to say, the imperative of taking non-formal adult education as a priority.

In their DfiD research project into *Factors Affecting Female participation in Education in Seven Developing Countries*, Brock and Cammish (1997) included two sub-Saharan countries, Cameroon and Sierra Leone. While the educational profile of girls in the former was, in general, significantly better than the latter, two main adverse factors were found in both – namely, poverty and patriarchy. There were sharp disparities between urban and rural and, especially, between the capital cities and the rest of their respective countries. Other factors shown to be of significance included: health (including early marriage and teenage pregnancy); legal (disparities between traditional and modern law); political (lack of political will to prioritize this problem) and educational (inappropriate curricula and security problems faced by female teachers).

The 2003/4 EFA Global Monitoring Report went under the title, *Gender and Education for All: The Leap to Equality* – needless to say, an over-optimistic title. Data were given for 1990 and 2000, which showed some improvement over the decade, but the report also stated that: 'The number of African children out of school increased by 17 per cent over the decade' (p. 50). Furthermore, when disaggregated by countries, sub-Saharan Africa had 14 of the 22 countries in the world with under 80 per cent gross enrolment rates. In almost every country in the region, the rate for females at primary level was significantly lower than that for males.

Repeating years and retention are just as important as enrolment and the 2003/4 EFA GMR showed that while boys repeated more overall, girls repeated more at the same level. Consequently, more boys survived to grade 5 and had a chance to progress further. For example, in Malawi, 53 per cent of boys who enrolled in primary school made it to grade 5 but only 43 per cent of girls. In a few cases, girls exceeded boys, as in Lesotho, 67–80 per cent, where boys were required as herders in some parts of the country. In 2000, the Gross Enrolment Rates for secondary school showed sub-Saharan Africa to be by far the weakest region in the world, with 19 countries showing less than 30 per cent (of those who completed primary school) and another 9 countries between 30 per cent and 50 per cent. The problem for acquiring quality university standards showed how the attrition of talent continues with 28 sub-Saharan countries showing less than 15 per cent of secondary school students proceeding to the tertiary level. Even the Republic of South Africa showed less than 30 per cent, with most of those enrolled being from the white elite. The position of females gets progressively worse as the ages rise and early marriage and pregnancies take their toll and the acquisition of literacy falters. Both sexes are further depleted by the high incidence of HIV/Aids in the region (Biggs 2012).

The 2010 GMR was titled *Reaching the Marginalised* which, in sub-Saharan Africa, means 'the marginalized majority' (Brock 2011b). It showed that 20 of the lowest 30 countries in the world for 'gender parity' figures were in sub-Saharan Africa, and commented that even where the gender gap is narrowing, 'it is sometimes due to decreasing enrolment' (EFA GMR 2010, p. 66). It must be remembered that the position for boys, while generally better than that for girls, is only marginally so. While the report states that 'the transition from primary school to lower secondary school is hazardous for many children' (p. 75), the situation for those who do progress is not necessarily rewarding, for 'In Burundi, Cameroon, Kenya and Nigeria, youth with secondary and tertiary education have higher rates of unemployment than those with lower levels of attainment' (p. 83).

Many girls and boys between the ages of 7 and 14 in this region have regular daily work as well as going to school, as many as 50 per cent of those enrolled. This is especially onerous for girls. The persistence of these problems is not always due to a lack of political will in terms of government policy, but rather a lack of capacity to carry it through in the face of socio-cultural conservatism and economic poverty. The widespread appeal of 'gender mainstreaming' (Unterhalter and North 2010) as a policy faces a host of challenges, including for example, in Nigeria, having to combat 'sexist interpretations of Christian texts'. This is a parallel to the appropriation of aspects of the Koran by strong patriarchal forces in the same country and elsewhere. Neither Christianity nor Islam have sufficient female role models to assist the generally favourable attitude of missions of both these religions to the education of girls, at least in west Africa (Brock and Cammish 1997). More to the point is the innate conservatism of formal education itself, especially the dead hand of examinations. Ansell (2002) points out, as a result, a large percentage of girls leave, failing examinations and getting no qualifications. However, she concluded that there may be some hope in some parts of the region:

> There is an increasingly perceived need to cater for the majority of young people who leave school with no qualifications and remain economically inactive. This potential must be acted upon in the interests of rural girls, however, otherwise the response to these contradictions might simply be a contraction of secondary education. This is an answer that structural adjustment has proffered and that experience shows will hit rural girls first and hardest (p. 108).

If lack of political will and macro policies, like gender mainstreaming, are not going to be change agents for the better education of girls, then the task must fall to teachers. Unfortunately, as Davison and Kanyuka (1992) point out, in general, teachers are a conservative force and foster the gender specific socialization of communities in the marginalized majority of sub-Saharan Africa.

Teachers as change agents in sub-Saharan Africa

In all countries and regions of the world, teachers are uniquely at the interface between the providers and recipients of education at all levels and in all its forms. Before the 1990s, teachers could still be regarded as the main sources of information at all levels of formal education. In less than 20 years, the internet, in association with other forms of technology, has made much more information available, and even formal programmes may be followed online, leading to qualifications. This has rendered the role of teachers, especially in schools, as much one of facilitating learning as of imparting knowledge. In effect, there could be as many teachers as there are learners. So, we need to distinguish issues relating to teaching in the classroom from those relating to informal, almost involuntary, learning.

As mentioned in the previous section on gender and education, teachers in general, in sub-Saharan Africa, are a reactionary force. This is due to their sharing societal norms, to their training or lack of it, and due to the curricular constraints placed on them, by the governance of national systems that still operate, in part, as political and social control mechanisms. The formal training of teachers is mainly derived from colonial legacy and can be illustrated with regard to Sierra Leone.

The area around Freetown became a 'The Colony' in 1808, immediately after the abolition of the slave trade in the British Empire, and freed slaves from the Caribbean and United States of America settled as 'Krios'. The interior of the territory officially became a colony in 1896, and known as 'The Protectorate'. The Colony and Protectorate were unified in 1961, when Sierra Leone became independent. Idiosyncracies of political geography and administration abound in sub-Saharan Africa, and help to explain, in this case, why no teacher training institutions were established prior to independence. Fourah Bay College had set up both a Department and an Institute of Education on the bipartite model for English universities that followed the McNair Report of 1944. In 1964, Njala University College was founded in the interior in association with the University of Illinois, and so had a different curriculum, including for educational studies.

Meantime in 1963, Milton Margai College was founded in Freetown, for the training of secondary school teachers and during the 1960s, five teachers colleges were established for primary school training – at Bo, Bunumbu, Freetown, Makeni and Port Loko. Entry to any training institution was based on 'O' levels gained in secondary school, which necessarily excluded almost everyone, as by this time less than 50 per cent of boys and 40 per cent of girls were enrolled in primary schools and very few made it through to the secondary level. The many primary schools that had been founded by missions, chiefs and communities, as well as some by the government, were staffed largely by unqualified teachers. The staff of teachers' colleges were appointed on the basis of academic qualifications mostly gained elsewhere. Few had any experience of teaching in school, especially in the circumstances of poor rural communities. Consequently, the training programmes were highly theoretical. The overthrow of Momoh led to the World Bank funding a fourth IDA education project in association with the overall reform of the education system in 1993, the core of which was a plan to create universal basic education and training (Government of Sierra Leone 1994).

As far as the education and training of teachers was concerned, there were two priorities: (a) the radical rationalization of training programmes in the five primary colleges, the one secondary college and the two branches of the university (GOSL/World Bank 1994) and (b) a nationwide four year (1996–2000) in-service programme for the training and certification of the majority of teachers who were untrained (GOSL/World Bank 1995) (illustrated in Brock 1996). In order for the qualification arising from this project to be accepted as equivalent to the formal process, it was required that it had the same number of contact hours of study and the same number of weeks of school-based supervision. Consequently, the in-service plan for unqualified teachers would have 1620 college-based contact hours (taking place in school vacations) and 540 home-based study hours, making 2160 study hours over the four years, which equalled the 2160 college-based full-time study hours of the formal training programme. While that formal programme had 26 weeks of school practice, the plan for the unqualified teachers would have 22 weeks of formal supervision and 4 weeks in district centres. The unqualified teachers would anyway be teaching full time throughout the four years.

There would also be a radical difference in terms of who would be responsible for the overall supervision of the unqualified teachers, in that teachers college tutors would be engaged only in college-based knowledge acquisition. Teaching practice would be the responsibility of practising head-teachers supported by a national cadre of retired head-teachers who would travel round the schools. Given the relatively early retirement age of primary head-teachers at the time (55), there was shown to be a sufficient willing, and able, pool of retirees to carry out this task. They, and the current heads, had the kind of experience totally lacking in the majority of teachers college tutors. In the event, this World Bank Project had to be terminated in 1996 due to the civil war reaching its peak, with the virtual destruction of schools, killing of teachers and conscription of boys and girls as soldiers. Nevertheless, this remains a relevant model, as such 'on-the-job' (OTJ) approaches to teacher education in sub-Saharan Africa were commended by the 'Muster Project Report' (Department for International Development 2003). This was a research report examining teacher education in five countries, four of which were in sub-Saharan Africa.

The most significant innovation in respect of enhancing teacher quality in the region is the project 'Teacher Education in Sub-Saharan Africa' (TESSA). This is an innovation by a consortium of five institutions, all operating in distance/virtual mode and led by the Open University UK, under the direction of Professor Bob Moon. It 'seeks to roll out radical reform in this sector across the region in the decade 2005–15' (Brock 2011a, pp. 52–4). One of the consortium members is the Commonwealth of Learning, a leading agent of appropriate application of ICT to education in developing countries. An important concept of the Commonwealth of Learning in this regard is the identification of what it calls 'digital natives' and 'digital immigrants'. This is basic to the effective OTJ training of teachers in sub-Saharan Africa. In its contribution to the 2009 UNESCO World Congress on Higher Education (Commonwealth of Learning 2009), it included the following:

> Today's students (digital natives) have a different way of approaching and using technologies like cell phones and computers that their teachers (digital immigrants) still need to come to terms with. Educators need to gain an understanding of the virtual worlds that their learners move in so that they may better understand how to interest them in ways that make sense to digital natives (p. 3).

This is, in effect, a contemporary counterpart to the missions of colonial times needing to know the local languages of native communities.

Tertiary education, ICT and sustainable survival

Mention has been made above of the range of constraints, on the one hand, on socio-economic development in sub-Saharan Africa: the unhelpful physical environment; the colonial legacy of a derived political geography; imposed educational structures and related 'brain drain; economic exploitation, neo-colonialism and postcolonialism; widespread conflict, displaced peoples and further environmental degradation. On the other hand, there has been a remarkably rapid spread of informal education through some of the basic instruments of ICT, such as transistor radios, mobile phones and, in some areas, hand held solar-powered computers. This has meant the creation of a majority population of 'digital natives' in the region who are acquiring a new form of literacy. This could enhance their chances of meeting the urgent challenges they face in the twenty-first century, provided that four distinctive sources of educational innovation adapt their approaches appropriately. They are: governments, the private sector, NGOs and agencies of post-compulsory education, especially universities. Of these, most governments are unlikely to have the political will to release their control of formal schooling, as their control capacity may be enhanced by modern technology (Bird 2011). This means that radical curricular innovation likely to be able to respond to this urgent challenge is unlikely to derive from this source. Private initiatives to respond to the needs of the marginalized majority are championed by Tooley and Dixon (2005), though whether they are relating any more appropriately than governments in curricular terms to what Martin (2011) predicts as 'the worst crisis of human history' (p. 28) is not clear. Martin is referring to the developing phenomenon of climate change on a global scale. Some nations and parts of the world are likely to benefit, such as North America and Russia, but most will not, including sub-Saharan Africa. Such predictions also come from the United Nations Environmental Programme (2010), in its *Global Biodiversity Outlook 3*.

Sub-Saharan Africa will be among the losers and, so, its communities will have to learn, within a generation or at most two, to respond to this challenge merely to survive, and sustain their livelihoods. This could best be achieved by an alliance of the global and the local through ICT, which has been on the discourse agenda since the UNESCO Global Higher Education Conference of 1998. This resulted in a World Bank Task Force (2000) report on *Higher Education in Developing Countries*. In 2003, the Commonwealth Secretariat reported on a workshop held in 1997 in Langkawi, Malaysia, which highlighted the issue of partnerships between higher education institutions and basic education, mostly through 10 case studies, of which four were in sub-Saharan Africa: Botswana, Ghana, Tanzania and Zambia (Leach 2003). These initiatives related to the decline in multinational aid to higher education following the concentration on basic education after the Jomtien meeting in 1990.

In Botswana, it proved conducive to cooperation and even partnership. In that country, higher education was officially designated as 'all post-secondary education'. There was a high enrolment (83%) in primary school. The longstanding vocational innovation of the 'brigades' (Van Rensburg 1978) was also a positive contextual component. However, the Botswana contributor, Chengu Mannathoko (2003), concluded that, in general, higher education in Botswana had been reactive in response to the needs of primary schooling, and needed to be pro-active with initiatives to meet the challenges of the twenty-first century. In Ghana, Sutherland-Addy (2003) found a more active picture, there being more universities participating in EFA follow up, educational reform and development and gender issues. The Institute of Adult Education and the University of Cape Coast were addressing the related issues of adult literacy and primary enrolment and retention, and there was some inter Higher Education Institution (HEI) liaison. However, it was found that for university staff to publish on primary/basic education was counter-productive as such a topic was not seen by the universities as sufficiently academic to go towards promotion. For Tanzania, Mmari (2003) from the Open University of Tanzania, a member of the later TESSA consortium, found a strong national legacy for promoting EFA from the days of Julius Nyerere. In a country of some 25 million people, there were in 2003 only four universities, but they were supporting EFA by connecting with NGOs and linking higher education to basic education. The University of Agriculture, founded in 1987, was suitably active in helping to relate schooling to survival and development. For the Zambian case, Geoffrey Lungwangwa (2003) reported a mixed picture. On the positive side, basic education was defined as comprising both primary schooling and non-formal learning for young people and adults. This helps to link literacy acquisition between home, school and community. On the downside, he reported that there were only two universities, plus a number of teacher training colleges in the post-secondary sector.

Despite the subsequent creation of some HEIs, there were, in 2003, very few linkages within that sector and what the author terms 'the higher education-basic education divide' (p. 203). This he ascribes to the global and national policy focus on primary education after 1990, and called for universities in Zambia to provide consultancy, create data banks on education and demography, help form policy on basic education and provide short courses for teachers. All this is very much in line with the conclusion of the World Bank Task Force report of 2000 that noted, 'Without more and better higher education, developing countries will find it increasingly difficult to benefit from the global knowledge-based economy' (p. 9).

Despite the relative dearth of higher education provision in sub-Saharan Africa, and the modest quality of most of it outside South Africa, universities and other post-secondary institutions can play a vital role through such connections as they have with the global knowledge network. They need to focus on the third role of all universities everywhere after teaching and research, which is to serve their local community. Through their ICT connections and understanding, they need to adapt knowledge and expertise from elsewhere to the nature and needs of local communities seeking to survive. Such linkages could be made through schools and NGOs who understand the local needs. These may well not be addressed by a derived curriculum model even if they have access to schooling.

Universities and other HEIs represent a vital resource everywhere in meeting the challenge to education posed by the approaching tipping point towards global environmental catastrophe (Brock 2012). They are even more crucial in the world's poorest region, sub-Saharan Africa. Universities in this region and other poor developing countries are poorly served by the international obsession with university rankings. Their academics struggle to get published in the so-called quality journals, rather than generating local and regional publication streams that would have greater relevance for their countries and communities. In 2009, the World Bank issued a report on tertiary education and economic growth in sub-Saharan Africa. It is summarized by its co-author, William Saint, in *International Higher Education* 54 (Winter 2009), who recognizes the key role of universities in the region and indicates that the analysis 'softens the long-standing confrontation between basic and higher education' (p. 14). The report is projected at the national level and government policies regarding higher education. Saint mentions the most difficult challenge being to effect pedagogical reform.

Such new pedagogies are not yet evident in all universities in industrialized countries, but as sub-Saharan universities need to be increased in number as well as quality, perhaps this would provide the context for pedagogical innovation. But, is the weak and undersized secondary sector in most countries in the region going to be able to send enough suitably qualified students? Will the plethora of new private universities be an asset or an irrelevance? As Saint (2009) indicates: 'relevance is the key', but in respect of which goal? National, economic, or local survival?' (p. 5).

Conclusion

Despite the range of multiple disadvantages faced by sub-Saharan Africa, there are certainly some positive developments, but these are hard won in the continued face of a generally unhelpful physical environment, constraining colonial legacies and aggressive neo-colonial exploitation. Only two countries have the potential to be powerhouses for the region: Nigeria for west Africa and South Africa for southern Africa. The former is riddled with internal conflict and the latter still struggling to throw off the debilitating legacies of apartheid, not least in education. East and central Africa are currently stricken by famine and violent conflict respectively. Some states with valuable natural resources and little conflict, such as Angola, are emerging impressively in terms of national indices of development. But, for most, the goal of sustainable survival through the twenty-first century led by innovative education may prove elusive.

8

Rising Stars: Brazil, Russia, India and The People's Republic of China (The BRIC States)

Introduction

The BRIC countries are the four new 'global giants' in terms of emergent economic power and influence, as well as in terms of size of their populations. The intention in this chapter is not, of course, to cover education in these countries in any comprehensive presentation. Rather, we aim to illustrate some of the themes that we have raised in earlier chapters by making broad comparisons across two or more of the BRIC states.

The first dimension that is common in all these four countries is their large scale, with all the challenges and possibilities that this entails. With more than 1.3 billion people, China is the most populous country on earth, followed by India, with 1.21 billion, and which is expected to surpass the Chinese population by 2025. These two countries together make up almost 40 per cent of the total world population. Brazil and Russia are certainly smaller in terms of number of people, but they are very large in terms of space, with Brazil being the largest South American country and Russia being the largest country in the world, spanning 11 time zones. But, size is not the only thing these countries share. They all host within their borders multiple nationalities, ethnicities, languages and religions. China is the most homogenous in ethnic terms, and Brazil the most homogenous in terms of language. In Russia, there are more than 160 nationalities, while in India, there are an estimated 2000 ethnic groups and 18 officially recognized languages. This population diversity in the BRIC countries, together with their increasing economic power and influence on the world stage, their size and the spatial distribution of people, make for particularly challenging issues when it comes to planning and providing education.

The second element of similarity is the economic growth and expansion the BRIC countries have achieved. The political systems in these countries vary considerably and, in conjunction with growing and changing economies, this has differential impact on investment in education. Two, Brazil and India are republics. Russia can be described as a transitional political economy, but China is more difficult to characterize, with the Chinese Communist Party forming the government since 1949. After 1978, China began a process of slow, but radical, reform of its economy, which led to periods of internal political conflict but also waves of slower and faster changes in both politics and the economy. The vastness of the country, with at least half the population still living in rural areas, the diversity of the population, rapid overall economic growth and modern technology, all make a strict centralized control increasingly problematic. The economic reforms of the 1980s signified a transition to a changing economy that produced a consistent rise in average living standards. But, there are still sharp regional inequalities and local disparities in the distribution of incomes, with political change only at the level of the local government and still under the strict control of the Chinese Communist Party (Galbraith et al. 2003).

China invests a significant amount of its public expenditure on education (about 16.3%). This represented 3.3 per cent of the country's GDP in 2008, significantly lower than the OECD average of 5.9 per cent. The amount spent per student from primary to tertiary education is low, compared to Brazil and to Russia, and far below the EU average. In tertiary education, even though only 5 per cent of the 25–64 year-olds have a degree, there has been considerable progress, with the proportion of the population enrolling in tertiary programmes doubling in the last 30 years. Moving from relatively low levels of tertiary attainment, China has expanded far greater in that measure than most OECD countries. Based on OECD data, an estimated 65 per cent of young Chinese today complete upper secondary education (the OECD average is 82 per cent), with a gender gap that is smaller than that within the EU and the United States of America (OECD 2011c). However, women have suffered a deterioration of status, according to Xiangmin Chen (2002), due to the underlying legacy of patriarchy, now that central controls have been relaxed.

Brazil is a fast growing economy and a democracy, with one of the most advanced service industries in Latin America. It is, at present, the seventh-largest economy in the world, with a high rate of economic growth that has transformed the country from a regional to a global power in the first decade of the new millennium. Some of this growth has been accompanied by issues of environmental concern, such as deforestation in the Amazon basin. Brazil is also an interesting example of a fast developing economy, where economic growth was achieved while, at the same time, there was a strong commitment to the reduction of poverty. This was achieved under the administration of President Lula (2003–10) and is being continued by his successor, Dilma Rousseff. The fast economic growth of Brazil has seen a corresponding growth in education investment (World Bank 2011b). In the period 2000–08, Brazil increased expenditure per student from primary to upper secondary education by 121 per cent, which meant that, at the tertiary level, there was not enough capacity to meet rising demand. The country's spending on education as a share of GDP rose from 3.5 per cent in 2000 to 5.3 per cent in 2008, a significant increase but still slightly below the OECD average (5.9%). This increase in investment has seen a dramatic rise in both the numbers of students participating in secondary education as also in the attainment levels of upper-secondary school students (OECD 2011a). Significantly, though, the compulsory sector of public education is still rather weak.

India has also seen significant economic growth since the mid-1990s and a reduction in poverty by about 10 per cent. However, similarities end there since, in absolute terms, poverty in India is a much more serious and extended problem, with an estimated 700 million people still living on less than US$2 per day by the end of 2011. Social mobility is also much slower in India than in Brazil, partly due to the socially institutionalized caste system of the Hindu majority that, together with language and religion, still seem to be major determinants of social mobility and political organization. Education investment, including government spending on it, is on the rise. In 2010, the *Right of Children to Free and Compulsory Education* Act was passed. It aims to achieve universal enrolment and retention in elementary education. So, the political commitment is to have free and compulsory education of all children between the ages of 6–14 and the infrastructure to make this possible. Successive projects, from Operation Blackboard (Dyer 2000), through the

District Primary Education Project (DPEP) to the present, have all worked towards Universal Primary Education (UPE). Similarly, the government is trying to achieve universal lower secondary school attendance, and an increase of participation in the tertiary sector. In 2008–09, public spending on education was 3.8 per cent of the GDP, similar to that of China, and lower than Brazil and most other OECD countries (2011d).

Russia is still undergoing stress in its economy and political system, since the radical change in the 1990s of moving from a centrally planned economy to a free market system. This transition resulted in increased disparity in income and wealth, and a huge increase in poverty and unemployment (Spryskov 2003). These trends in Russia were expected by economists, but they continued far longer than anticipated (Klugman and Braithwaite 1998). Compared to China, Russia is considered to be the 'polar opposite' in terms of smoothness of economic transition, experiencing a chaotic liberalization process as opposed to a steady and more sustained economic growth. But, both have seen a sharp rise in economic and social disparity (Galbraith et al. 2003, pp. 87–8). In China, the reaction to the political upheavals of the last few decades has been one of strengthening central control, military confrontation and harsh responses to requests for openness and change. In Russia, in terms of education, expenditure saw a rise from about 3.7 to 4.6 per cent of GDP between 2002 and 2009, but in part, due to a general reduction of the GDP rather than an increase in the education spending. The economic crisis of the late 2000s 'affected neither the size nor the geography of education spending' (Sinitsina 2011). The education system has produced almost 100 per cent literacy, accompanied by remarkable achievements in the spheres of mathematics, science and technology. Nonetheless, Russia's performance in the latest PISA study was somewhat modest, and there is a recurrent criticism of the education system for encouraging rote learning at the expense of critical evaluation and analysis of information (OECD 2009).

The BRIC countries exemplify some of the themes in this book in particularly eloquent ways. One of these refers to the very topical theme of 'transition' to a different economic or political system and its implications for education, and we shall review some key issues here, drawing on Russia and China. The second theme that we shall explore is that of poverty and inequality and, here, we shall draw from all four countries. This is a theme that often represents the 'other side' to economic modernization and development, and has serious consequences for the delivery of schooling and for its outcomes. The third section in this chapter will deal with developments in the higher education sectors, where changes are responding to the influence of globalization, including that of multinational and international organizations, neo liberalism and privatization.

Transition, modernization and reform

China and Russia have both been considered as 'transition' societies, a term usually referring to the transformation of a centrally controlled, sometimes communist, system to a market economy. The states of the former Soviet Union and Eastern Europe fall within this definition, but China also 'qualifies' as a country that is communist at the official level of government but has moved to a 'socialist market economy' (Bray and Borevskaya 2001, p. 350). In all transition societies and economies, there are fundamental changes to the role of the state in providing and regulating education (McLeish and Phillips 1998). In China, significant reforms began in the late 1970s, while in Russia, it was the 1990s. Despite the many differences between the systems in these countries, their education policies in the pre-transition period shared:

a. A commitment to universality (evidenced by the high literacy rates amongst the population, and high participation rates of students from nursery to secondary schools). But, whereas in Russia, there was also a high commitment to equity, China has been characterized by elitism in favouring 'key' schools and technical/scientific higher education;

b. High degrees of centralization of most dimensions of school life and organization (financing, regulation, provision, curricula and assessment);

c. A rural–urban divide in terms of investing resources that, in both countries resulted in higher investment in schools in urban areas. (Ngok 2011; Pavlova 2010; Zajda 2003)

In both countries, schooling was traditionally provided almost entirely by the state (with contributions from state enterprises) and, with some exceptions in China, free of charge. Since the reforms of the 1980s and 1990s, there has been a significant challenge to these principles of organization, in an attempt to rapidly 'modernize' education (in Russia), or to slowly, transform the system (in China).

As already discussed, the term 'modernization' is loaded with theoretically and politically contentious issues. Still, we observe its continuous use in the reform of 'transition' economies, such as that of Russia. Interestingly, China used throughout the 1990s the term 'modernization' with similar connotations, where education was seen as core in the process of social progress, and a distinct communist interpretation of the term. Education is expected to serve the socialist economy by developing industry, agriculture, science and defence. Modernization in the Chinese context of the post-Mao era has been all about economic transformation. As Hu Kaixuan, former Minister of Education, said in the 1990s: 'Education is closely linked with the economy, and has become an organic component and key content of the plans for economic and social developments' (in Ngok 2011, p. 144).

Most reports on Russia that emerge from within the World Bank and the OECD begin with short 'praise' of past performances of the Russian education system in terms of population literacy and scientific and technical achievements, then move sharply to the criticisms of the 'rigid' and 'over centralized' system inherited from the Soviet Union (Canning 2004). Education in Russia has been criticized for investing heavily in human capital while, at the same time, producing the 'wrong skills for a market economy', since the system was geared to the skills needed by the former Soviet economy (Fan et al. 1999). The transformation of the labour market, and the economic crisis that followed, meant that possessing high-level human capital did not necessarily 'translate' into better income. As a result, throughout the 1990s and early 2000s, young people did not have the incentives to pursue further education or training, something that may have long implications for commitment to education of at least one more generation (ibid.). Under the 'advice' of international organizations, Russia launched an ambitious (and highly criticized) programme to 'modernize' its education system (Zajda 2003). The reforms that began in the early 1990s aimed to change curricula, school pedagogy, the ideology underpinning the teaching and learning process, as well as the way the system was governed and funded. The new 'model' of education shifted emphasis away from the ideals of equality, citizenship and political/civic focus of the curriculum, the underpinning pillars of the Soviet education system, towards a perceived 'westernized' model that concentrated on a tight coupling between the now free, marketized economy and schooling (Pavlova 2010). In the Russian context, modernization had a distinct political as well as economic transformational element. The key elements of that reform for Russia and, to a large extent, also China, can be summarized as 'system governance' and 'content reform'.

In Russia, the first aim of the reform was to be accomplished by changing the funding and management of schools and, in particular, introducing decentralization to the system. This measure meant that responsibilities of education have been transferred from the central government to the regions. A typical criticism of the earlier system was that the school directors had to follow and execute federal regulations with little or no financial, or other, autonomy at the level of the school. The economic crisis that followed the early 1990s political transitions, and the rapidly declining pupil population, resulted in a new 'per-capita' funding system that was introduced in 2001 as part of the *Education Modernization Program*. The aim of this part of the reform was to introduce efficiency and accountability into the system and to provide school directors with incentives to manage their budgets in a way that improved the quality of education and attracted more students (Kataoka 2011). Part of the shift to financing students rather than schools had to do also with the great discrepancy of available funding to schools of different regions. This also had to do with massive variations in population distribution and density, with some regions in poor or remote areas facing serious problems in terms of being able to provide education of comparable quality to that in major urban concentrations. The per-capita financing scheme introduced in Russia was modelled on 'western' examples. In particular, in the 2004 World Bank report on the *Modernisation of Education in Russia*, the example of England is highlighted as a 'particularly useful model for Russia in its efforts to implement a scheme with many of the same features' (Canning 2004, p. 36) – a clear example of policy borrowing. Decentralization of school funding took place also in China, but in a less dramatic form because of China's unitary type of state, as opposed to the federal Russian one. The weight of decision-making and management of school finances passed from the central to the county, town and village levels. But, China differed from Russia in some significant ways. According to Bray and Borevskaya (2001), the Chinese central government, since the 1970s, had already placed much of the weight of school financing on local communities, 'on the grounds that the people's education should be run by the people' (p. 361). This was unparalleled in Russia, where the central state was the only actor in education. China also was ready to fund more generously selected elite schools and universities whereas, in Russia, the dominant ideology was still to distribute resources more evenly, even if thinly. Interestingly, in both countries, financial decentralization was accompanied by a decrease of central government expenditure on education – a response to the scarcity of resources available. In both countries, but particularly in China, this has led to serious challenges to the principle of 'free' compulsory education.

These changes were not merely the products of financial necessity, but also ideological repositioning. In China, there has been a steady development of the notion of education as an item of consumption, which, together with the rise of individualism to be found in an increasingly competitive marketized economy, is now seen as a key to social mobility (Chan and Wang 2009). This view of education as a private good and investment in human capital easily led to the principle and practice of charging fees in the Chinese education system. According to Ngok (2011), these ideological shifts in combination with the state's limited capacity to fund an increasingly expanding education sector, have led the central government to relax its control over education and to invite other sectors and stakeholders (local authorities, parents etc.) in the financing, provision and regulation of education.

In Russia, a second set of reform themes attempted to increase the quality of general education in line with a westernized modernization programme, and focused on curriculum, assessment and pedagogy. The new Russian curriculum for a 12-year schooling, adopted in 2003, aimed to shift emphasis to 'outcomes'-based assessment of students, focusing on their skills and competencies and establishing national standards for assessment as a way of improving school performance (Zgaga 2003). These reforms were a response to the criticism that education was not 'relevant' to the needs of the labour market and that it did not 'sufficiently reflect modern ideas on what kinds of learning outcomes are relevant for the knowledge economy and society' (Canning 2004, p. 6).

The education reforms in China and Russia followed different trajectories and rationales, but had some common features. The 'new' elements of privatization – and controlled decentralization in China, and a more rushed decentralization in Russia – entailed both: (a) ideological elements – a shift in thinking towards education as human capital investment, but also investing highly in the education of an elite and: (b) pragmatic economic reasoning – lack of financial capacity of the central state to meet the demands of education. The roles of the central state have changed in both countries. They have become more regulatory states rather than provider states – which in China, was not a particularly new feature, but in Russia, constituted a radical change since the central state had traditionally been the sole provider of education.

Educational inequality and poverty

High levels of deep poverty exist in all of the BRIC countries. The proportion of people who survive on less than $1.25 per day are about 5 per cent in Brazil, 16 per cent in China, and 35 per cent in India. In Russia, in 2011, the official poverty rate was 14.9 per cent. The geography of poverty is important. In Brazil, the poverty rate is higher in the interior states and the north-east. These include large concentrations of urban poor in illegal *favelas* or 'shanty towns'. It was here that Paulo Freire developed his literacy programmes based on *The Pedagogy of the Oppressed*. In China, despite limited success in dealing with poverty in the countryside, not much progress has been made to tackling urban poverty. Rural poverty for millions still remains high in China while, in India, by the mid-2000s, social policy has managed to equalize the proportions of the poor in rural and urban areas. However, as in Brazil, this has much to do with urbanization – the drift of the poor from the countryside to towns and cities. While some progress has been made in terms of poverty reduction, income inequality has increased in all of the BRIC countries with the exception of Brazil, but where it is still high (OECD 2010). In times when political and economic circumstance meant that the BRIC countries were reducing the already limited social protection that would shield the poor from the worst consequences, such poverty levels coincided with radical reforms towards economic liberalization and marketization of services in general and education in particular.

As with all reforms, we can observe positive and negative consequences on different parts of the population and at different times. The policies of decentralization and marketization described above in Russia and China have had both. In China, controlled decentralization produced huge new resources that have come into the education system, from non-state and non-education actors. At the same time, it has led to a 'remarkable disparity and inequality of educational development' (Ngok 2011, p. 146) since the resources available for primary education in particular depend on the local economic circumstances, which vary from locality to locality. Already well-developed regions have benefited substantially from decentralization, but at the expense of the less developed, usually rural areas. China's rural population counts for about 65 per cent of the total, but by the late 1990s, they would get less than half of the education resources. Compared to the urban areas, rural schools have higher drop-out rates, lower enrolment rates, poorer infrastructure and conditions of work for teachers. These disparities, and the inequalities they produce, have become systematically worse since the decentralization reforms of the late 1970s (ibid.). Towards the middle of the 2000s, the Chinese government recognized the problems of disparity and inequality, and pledged to increase education spending on rural primary and secondary schools. It has also promised to eliminate gradually the fees for rural students in an attempt to redress the rural–urban divide. This has signalled that, post 2010, we may begin to see the central government strengthening its role over education (ibid.).

Significant inequalities in education in China can also be attributed to the post-1982 policy of privatization, when the limited resources of the state have resulted in a number of non-state actors supporting academic programmes, or running schools (the so called *minban* – people-run – schools, ranging from kindergartens to higher education institutions), which have considerable autonomy to determine their curricula, pedagogy and recruitment of teachers. This was accompanied 10 years later by schemes of privatization of existing public schools, where the ownership would remain public, but administration was contracted out to individual actors, businesses or social organizations (Chan and Wang 2009). Since then, many different types of *minban* educational institutions (with varying degrees of blurred boundaries between the state and the private contribution to the running, regulating and financing) have emerged. They constitute a significant parallel sector to that of public schools. In 2002, the *Minban Education Promotion Law* stated that investors would be allowed to make a 'reasonable economic return' out of the running of such schools, giving rise to even further deepening of private involvement in the provision of education (ibid.).

In Russia, the inequalities of education provision and quality between rural and urban areas need to be seen in the wider context of the events of the 1990s. The collapse of the Soviet Union produced 'chaos, hyperinflation, industrial collapse and privatisation', that saw significant material impoverishment while still in political transition (Galbraith et al. 2003). In China, the acceleration of economic reforms in combination with the strong one-party rule saw economic growth and improvement in average living standards. But, in both China and Russia, economic liberalization was accompanied by sharp rises in economic and social inequalities, creating dramatic regional disparities in poverty and welfare. Because of the economic crisis, the government in Russia has reduced its expenditure, something that has disproportionately, and adversely, affected the poor regions and households. High unemployment and ad hoc or limited social assistance put certain groups in the population, such as families with children, in a particularly precarious situation (Kislitsyna 2003).

Against, given this context of liberalization in the early 1990s in Russia, there was significant interest in the new freedom to set up a private sector. But, the financial instability meant that a lot of these institutions had to rely on informal networks, 'sometimes criminal in nature' (Lisovskaya and Karpov 2001, p. 43). They comprised four types of private schools: 'ethnic', 'religious', 'special needs' and 'elite', the last finding themselves paradoxically overshadowed by the elite schools developed in the public sector. A somewhat similar quandary faced post-Soviet adult education (Zajda 1999) that, since 1993, saw supportive policies, but also faced 'enforced commercialization' and has had to 'mop-up disaffected youth' as well as 'demobilised armed forces personnel and former prisoners seeking retraining' (ibid., p. 157).

In Brazil, poverty is a serious problem that affects children participating in school in both rural and urban areas. In 2005, UNESCO reported 12 per cent of children between the ages of 5 and 15 not going to school, or combining school with work, mainly in agriculture or in *favellas*. But, low attendance in parts of the country has been attributed not only to the necessity for many pupils to take part in productive labour activities, but also to the poor quality of schooling (OECD 2010). Until the last two decades, the reactionary policies of the military regimes of the previous period, with their restrictive imposition of the doctrine of 'national security' (Brock 1980a), had blunted the more progressive effects of the support from the USA's 'alliance for progress' in the 1960s. Reforms that took place throughout the 1990s attempted to deal with this by clarifying the roles of the federal, state and municipal levels, increasing state funding to schools, giving poor parents a 'conditional cash transfer' for enrolling children in school instead of putting them to work, changing the curricula, and by a process of democratization of school governance and decentralization of funding and to schools. Brazil, even during the first decade of the new millennium, faced a problem of infrastructure that had direct implications for the quality of schooling and achievement. The low performance of the country in the 2000 and 2003 PISA studies pinpointed two major problems in Brazilian schools: (a) the low levels of completion of secondary education and (b) the absence of full day schools, where the daily school schedule is only 4 hours long because a significant number of schools have 2 or even 3 'shifts' every day. That is to say, three complete schools occupying the same site and facilities in succession every working day. The plan for the establishment of full-day schools everywhere has been set as a progression over the next 10 years, since it is currently not feasible. Surprisingly, this is in a country that spends 5.2 per cent of its GDP on education. The OECD in the 2010 publication, *Education at a Glance,* attributed this to the distribution of funding to various sectors of education. The burden of primary education funding still falls disproportionately on the local, municipal level. So, primary education receives six times less spending per student than higher education, which, the report concludes, results in some first class public universities that few public school graduates are eligible to enter. In addition, almost all of the higher socio-economic groups send their children to private schools (Soares 2004). As a result, there is a very large disparity in the achievement of pupils, depending on the socio-economic make up of any given locality. Parental background seems to be the key factor determining educational achievement, with a clear positive relationship between high achievement and students who are male, white, from the south-east of the country and from private schools (Guimarães and Sampaio 2011).

After sub-Saharan Africa, South Asia exhibits the largest concentration of the world's 'marginalized majority' (Brock 2011a; Siddique 2012), though China is not far behind. As mentioned, the caste system within the Hindu majority (80 per cent of the population) is still a significant constraint on overall development, depriving many of the lowest caste children of any schooling at all. Even below that are the 'scheduled' and 'unscheduled tribes'. All groups exhibit their own informal education traditions that mostly relate to family and community survival and are conducted in one of the 1,500 languages in operation.

The 25 States and seven Union Territories have diverse combinations of characteristics in respect of cultural mix, colonial legacy and political ideologies. These three indicators may come together in a positive combination, or may not, as indicated by the differential situation regarding the education of women and girls (Brock 2002). With an overall federal responsibility for public education, each state, nonetheless, has its own minister of education, linguistic profile and variant on the national system. According to Parekh (1995), there has long been a tension between 'modernist' and 'traditionalist' approaches to development. This has ebbed and flowed according to major shifts in policy between successive federal governments, and affected decisions regarding official medium of instruction which, in most states, is neither Hindi nor English but regional languages such as Bengali, Oriya and Punjabi. Populations are so large in most areas that the main subdivisions of each state, known as districts, become the practical unit of operation and identity as far as public education is concerned. Within districts are blocks, and within them, local communities or 'Panchayati Raj'. It is at this level that decisions are made regarding the schooling of children, though parents make the definitive school choice. Rao (2010) described and analysed this process at village level. She found significant disparity even at this micro-level of scale, where educational choices operate 'at multiple levels' and are experienced differently depending on people's location in the 'power' and 'gender hierarchies' (p. 182).

The issue of non-state schooling provision in relation to the marginalized majority has long been a feature of Indian education. A variety of approaches are being tried to deal with some of these issues; some involve philanthropic style arrangements (Day-Ashley 2006), the charging of low fees for girls in private schools (Srivastava 2006) or implementing various forms of privatized schooling for the poor (Tooley and Dixon 2006). None of these provides the single answer to the entrenched problems created by poverty and social inequality but do effect a degree of amelioration for some.

Higher education and development

Higher education today is clearly a massively globalized phenomenon, with expansion having contributed to an increase of education opportunities for many social groups in the majority of countries. Internationalized policies and practices of universities are increasingly observable in relation to such areas as knowledge acquisition, gaining commercial advantage and organizing exchange programmes for staff and students. At a time when globalization processes continue to accrue further wealth, knowledge and power to the already advantaged, internationalization processes within higher education 'compound existing inequalities' (Altbach and Knight 2007, p. 291). As David (2011) argues, the expansion of higher education, both in terms of institutions and numbers of students, is characterized by 'structural and systemic inequalities, . . . also between and across the global north and the global south' (p. 160). The huge expansion of higher education is particularly relevant to the BRIC countries. The highest growth in numbers of students in higher education is expected to come over the coming years from India and China. In the year 2011, together, they already contained about 35 per cent of the world's higher education student population.

China

The changing context within which the tertiary sector has developed in China has been an unusually turbulent one, reaching its nadir in the years of Mao's anti-intellectual and violent 'cultural revolution' of 1966–76.[1] By 1980, the remarkable turn under Deng Xiaoping had begun to enable higher education to play its part in the emerging socialist market economy that has brought China to its place as the world's second largest economy (Hayhoe 1996). The higher education sector in China was 'opened up' and exposed to multiple sources of income. Universities themselves have been encouraged to undertake roles in the private sector, including consultancies for individual profit (Oh 2002) as well as establishing their own companies. An example of that has been the 'tripartite' enterprise involving a university or college, a research institute and one or more 'production units' (Law 1995), where profits can be retained by the university and used to invest in staff development, infrastructure and equipment. In addition, a gradual opening of admissions to fee-paying students in the mid-1980s led to a complete change in the system in 1994, when students were charged fees for studying, with the exception of certain academic disciplines. This process has produced a system that is larger than before, but also significantly unequal, with disadvantages in access for students from low socio-economic backgrounds and particular regions in the country (Wang 2011).

Greater curricular variety has also resulted in interdisciplinary studies, a western trend aiming to broadening the knowledge base. At the same time, there has been a concerted drive to get China's top universities, such as, Tsinghua and Fudan, into the top 100 in the world rankings. This has been achieved by focusing on the key research activities that meet the main criteria, namely: (a) science and technology, which attracts optimum research funding and publishing in the most highly rated journals and (b) mostly operating in English for research purposes. These rankings, though questionable, are a feature of the competitive dimension of globalization, which means accepting, at least in part, the neo-liberal mantra of marketization.

Another element of internationalization that has a longer history in Chinese universities is the flow of students into the country from outside, and the even greater exodus to study overseas, especially in the United States of America and United Kingdom. There are now at least 1000 universities in China with students from overseas. This helps to build ties with other countries and also earns considerable income, with China having trained, between 1995 and 2000, more than 360,000 international students in 'science and technology, education, diplomacy, and administration' (Kai Jiang and Xueni Ma, 2011, p. 7). The outflow of Chinese students is more problematic, creating a 'brain drain' as the most successful academics gain well-paid posts in western institutions (Altbach and Wanhua Ma 2011).

It is certainly the case that, in the period since 1978, Chinese higher education has played a significant part in social and economic development from local, through regional to national levels (Zhong 2006), but the country is so vast that hundreds of millions have yet to benefit. Yet, this in itself is a measure of massive potential.

Russia

We find in Russia a similar situation to that of China, where the relatively low level of public resources that go to the financing of universities has resulted in a rapid commercialization of the sector to fill the gap. This includes the expectation that students be liable to pay high fees for their tuition. The co-existence of public and private higher education institutions and the high cost of tuition fees for an increasingly large number of students, as also the cost of private tutoring preparing school pupils for university entrance, means that the social gap has been getting increasingly wider in terms of university access. At the same time, the quality of training has been in doubt (Kolesnikov et al. 2005). In the Soviet period, young people were allocated to jobs on the basis of the needs of the economy and in accordance to their qualifications. This close correspondence between school, vocational and higher education graduates and a centrally planned system of work allocation was disrupted in the early 1990s. This, in turn, led to a paradox of a system geared up to train young people for jobs that no longer existed. Walker (2007) exemplifies this particularly eloquently in relation to the vocational education system in Russia, where the shift to a 'knowledge economy' has 'taken severe forms, resulting from the fundamental dislocation of an entire "transition infrastructure" from the economy around which it was built' (p. 514). The relative decline of the industrial and agricultural sectors of the economy, and the lack of alternatives, has hit young people from lower socio-economic backgrounds particularly hard, since these were the traditional routes for their post-school transition to employment (ibid.).

Today, in Russia, there are over 8.25 million students in over 1100 institutions of higher education. As in the secondary and adult education sectors mentioned above, this massive number has inevitably meant a radical revision of funding regulations and mechanisms, where 'free' education is no longer the assumption (Smolentseva 2005). It is not only expansion in student numbers that has put pressure on structural reforms. While the traditional five-year undergraduate specialist diploma has been retained for the majority – about 90 per cent – the 'western' model of a shorter Bachelors degree followed by a Masters has also been introduced. This creates a university elite, entry to which is regulated by state funding being available according to test scores: 'In social terms the link between "individual government financial obligation" and test scores limits the higher education access of many vulnerable socio-economic groups in society with less opportunity for test preparation' (ibid., p. 22). For the Bachelors degree, such funding is only available to less than 200 students per 10,000 candidates. The Masters degree is even more exclusive, with support for only an elite few, with other students depending on corporate funding or family.

Even though the Russian economy is far from being 'knowledge-based', both rhetoric and government policies seem to be employing a discursive repertoire that accompanies neo-liberal reforms in the Russian higher education marketplace, and mask the increasingly large inequalities of access and participation in university education.

Brazil

In Brazil, in the year 2009, 36 per cent of the population of tertiary age are in tertiary education and that represents roughly 4.5 million students (31 per cent men, 42 per cent women) educated in just over 2000 higher education institutions (UNESCO 2011a). But, of this large number of students, over two-thirds are enrolled in private universities. At the same time, the public system has remained small, modestly funded but highly academically selective, and connected to the social elite. Schwarzman (2009) examines the problem of what is, in effect, mass exclusion from the federally funded higher quality universities that tend to educate the students from wealthy backgrounds in highly prestigious academic subjects. The alternative higher education for poorer students is offered by less prestigious public universities or the private sector that offer less competitive courses (that, in turn, lead to lower status jobs, such as teaching, social work and nursing).

One response by the state was to consider a quota system to help the poorer and 'ethnic' groups in the population ('black' and 'coloured' people constituting about 50 per cent of the population). Such positive discrimination is unlikely to be effective, since to do so, it would need to rely on (a) much higher quality basic and secondary education (Schwarzman, ibid.) and (b) political and social consensus, something far from achievable, given that the 'Brazilian elite perceives the prestigious public institutions as their exclusive grounds' (Tessler 2011, p. 24). At the same time, there is a huge expansion in the private higher education sector, with institutions that do little or nothing to enhance the prospects of their already mostly disadvantaged clientele (Durham 2004; Castro 2004).

As has been the case in South Africa, a reforming socialist regime in Brazil has embraced the neo-liberal influence of globalization, especially in relation to meeting the demand for post-secondary education. Sobrinho and de Brito (2008) have observed that global supporters, such as the IMF/World Bank, are favourable to such developments while, at the same time, strongly recommend that public resources are redirected to basic education (compulsory stage) instead of higher education (Bertolin and Leite 2008). Leite (2010) argues that the Brazilian university is losing its 'national' character (which was originally formed by a foreign Humboldtian model) to become an example of an 'isomorphous' global university, driven by private interests (p. 221).

What does this mean for quality? Over the last few decades, Brazilian universities have had to shift away from internal and participatory evaluation processes, towards external procedures that, even though driven by national regulation, aimed at convergence with international accreditation practices (ibid.). In response to such global influences, in 2004, Brazil established 'The National System of Higher Education Assessment' to cover both public and private sectors. This accreditation system governs the evaluation of the institution, the programmes and student performance, and has been used widely (and sometimes abused) in producing information about the higher education sector, but also programme and university rankings, with all the connotations this entails (Pedrosa 2011).

India

Even though India had its own traditional patterns of higher education and learning, the British Empire left its stamp in the creation of the modern higher education system in the country (Altbach 2004; Brock 2007; Eisemon 1984), which is compatible with the late nineteenth and early twentieth centuries' interaction between India and Britain on many educational matters (Day Ashley 2006).

In the early twenty-first century, the picture is very different. In response to massive increases in population over the intervening 100 years, the landscape of Indian higher education has radically changed. This is also in response to the influences of globalization, but, despite the expansion, today the country ranks lower than the other BRICs in terms of the proportion of its young people of university age enjoying a tertiary education. According to Agarwall (2010), between 2005 and 2010 alone, 200 new universities and 8,000 new colleges were founded. This has created a massive problem of widely variable quality, which has triggered the formulation of an Accreditation Law. This is based on the American accreditation model of not-for-profit, independent external agencies that are ignored by the majority of Indian higher education institutions, since accreditation is not linked to government funding (ibid.).

There is also the variable political influence of the 27 states, with their sometimes changeable policies from one election to the next, an unavoidable feature of a democratic polity. Some of the Indian states have a very strong and stable political profile that directly affects this issue. In the southern state of Kerala, a long and inclusive educational tradition has developed, based on a combination of matriarchal kinship systems, Christian missions and socialistic politics. The long-standing governing Communist Party is highly critical of both the unbridled expansion of the tertiary sector and the new accreditation law mentioned above: 'The overriding criticism involved the underlying commitment in the reform to linking Indian higher education to global trends of commercializing higher education, and uncritically linking India to the global knowledge economy' (Altbach and Mathews 2010, p. 17).

Another dimension of this, perhaps, unfortunate linkage is the Indian government's desire to have its universities, or at least the elite of the system, appearing in the international university ranking tables, or as Altbach and Jayaram (2009) put it: 'India's effort to join twenty-first century higher education'. The government has been planning to reach a target of 30 'world class universities' by expanding the sector and creating new Institutes of

Technology. But, the creation of a 'research culture' has been a challenge, with no institution considered as 'research intensive' (ibid.).

Conclusion

That formal, and especially higher, education relates to the rise of the BRIC states is not in dispute, but an increasing range of disparities creates problems for all four. These can threaten social and national cohesion, especially as the increasing demand for education from growing populations is being met by private providers. With the presence of endemic poverty for significant parts of the growing population in all four BRICs, there are serious issues of quality of secondary education, and an increasingly privatized, and in parts low quality, higher education available. Well over 50 per cent of university students in Brazil and India are in the private sector (Altbach et al. 2009) while 'about 50 per cent of university faculty worldwide have only a Bachelors degree' (Brock 2012, p. 17).

Also, for India and China, and to some extent Brazil, the issue of many of the most able graduates, as well as some undergraduates, choosing to study in another country is a double-edged sword. Those who return can contribute high social and economic 'returns', but many never return and instead become part of the knowledge 'capital' in such countries as the United States of America, United Kingdom, Canada and Australia.

Whether, despite their progress by conventional economic indicators, the almost footloose education sectors of these countries can meet the twenty-first century challenge of human and environmental survival remains in the balance.

References

Agarwal, P. (2010), India's New Accreditation Law. *International Higher Education* 61: 16–17.

Aldrich, R. (2002), *The Institute of Education 1902–2002: A Centenary History.* London: Institute of Education, University of London.

— (2006), *Lessons from the History of Education.* London: Routledge.

— (2010), Education for survival: An historical perspective. *History of Education* 39(1): 1–14.

Alexander, R., Osborn, M. and Phillips, D. (eds) (2000), *Learning from Comparing: New Directions in Comparative Educational Research* (Volumes One and Two). Wallingford: Symposium Books.

Alexiadou, N. (2002), Social inclusion and social exclusion in England: tensions in education policy. *Journal of Education Policy* 17(1): 71–86.

— (2005a), Europeanisation and education policy, in D. Coulby, C. Jones and E. Zambeta (eds), *World Yearbook of Education 2005: Globalisation and Nationalism in Education.* London: Falmer Routledge, pp. 128–46.

— (2005b), Social exclusion, and educational opportunity: the case of British education policies within a European Union context. *Globalisation, Societies and Education Journal* 3(1): 103–27.

Alexiadou, N. and Brock, C. (eds) (1999), *Education as a Commodity.* London: John Catt Educational.

Alexiadou, N. and Jones, K. (2001), Travelling policy/local spaces. Paper presented at the *Congrès Marx International III: Le capital et l'humanité,* Université de Paris-X Nanterre-Sorbonne, 26–29 September 2001.

Alexiadou, N. and Lange, B. (2013), Deflecting EU influence on national education policy-making: The case of the United Kingdom. *Journal of European Integration* 35(1): Forthcoming.

Allan, J. (2010), Questions of inclusion in Scotland and Europe. *European Journal of Special Needs Education* 25(2): 199–208.

Allen, J. (2008), Slavery, colonialism and the pursuit of community life: Anglican mission education in Zanzibar and Northern Rhodesia 1864–1940. *History of Education* 37(2): 207–26.

Altbach, P. G. (2004), The past and future of Asian universities: Twenty-first century challenges, in P. G. Altbach and T. Umakoshi (eds), *Asian Universities: Historical*

Perspectives and Contemporary Challenges. Baltimore and London: The John Hopkins University Press.

— (2011), Rankings season is here. *International Higher Education* 62: 2–4.

Altbach, P. G. and Jayaram, N. (2009), India's effort to join 21st century higher education. *International Higher Education* 54: 17–19.

Altbach, P. G. and Kelly, G. P. (1978), *Education and Colonialism*. New York and London: Longman.

Altbach, P. and Kelly, G. (eds) (1986), *New Approaches to Comparative Education*. Chicago and London: The University of Chicago Press.

Altbach, P. G. and Knight, J. (2007), The internationalisation of higher education: Motivations and realities. *Journal of Studies in International Education* 11(3/4): 290–305.

Altbach, P. G. and Mathews, E. (2010), Kerala: The dilemmas of equality. *International Higher Education* 61: 18–22.

Altbach, P. G. and Ma, W. (2011), Getting graduates to come home: Not easy. *International Higher Education* 63: 8–9.

Altbach, P. G., Peisberg, L. and Rumbley, L. E. (2009), *Trends in Global Higher Education: Tracking an Academic Revolution*. Executive Summary, World Conference on Higher Education. Paris: UNESCO.

Anand, S., Segal, P. and Stiglitz, J. E. (eds) (2011), *Debates on the Measurement of Global Poverty*, Initiative for Policy Dialogue Series. Oxford: Oxford University Press.

Anderson, C. A. (1961), Methodology of comparative education. *International Review of Education* 6: 1–23.

Anderson, R. D. (2004), *European Universities from the Enlightenment to 1914*. Oxford: Oxford University Press.

Ansell, N. (2002), Secondary education reform in Lesotho and Zimbabwe and the needs of rural girls: Pronouncements, policy and practice. *Comparative Education* 38(1): 91–112.

Archer, D. and Costello, P (1990), *Literacy and Power: The Latin American Battleground*. (reissued by Taylor and Francis in 2009).

Armytage, W. H. G. (1968), *The French Influence on English Education*. London: Routledge and Kegan Paul.

Arnove R. F. and Torres, C. A. (1999), *Comparative Education: The Dialectic of the Global and the Local*. New York: Rownal and Littlefield.

Arreman-Erixon, I. and Holm, A-S. (2011), Privatisation of public education? The emergence of independent upper secondary schools in Sweden. *Journal of Education Policy* 26(2): 225–42.

Augier, R. and Irvine, D. (1998), The Caribbean Examinations Council, in M. Bray and L. Steward (eds), *Examinations Systems in Small States: Comparative*

Perspectives on Policies, Models and Operations. London: Commonwealth Secretariat, pp. 145–61.

Bahry, S. A. (2005), 'Travelling policy and local spaces in the Republic of Tajikistan: A comparison of the attitudes of Tajikistan and the World Bank towards textbook provision. *European Educational Research Journal* 4(1): 60–78.

— (2007), *Education plc: Understanding Private Sector Participation in Public Sector Education.* Abington: Routledge.

Ball, S. J. (1983), Imperialism, social control and the colonial curriculum. *Journal of Curriculum Studies* 15(3): 237–63.

Ball, S. (1998), Big Policies/Small World: An introduction to international perspectives in education policy. *Comparative Education* 34(2): 119–30.

Baldacchino, G. and Farrugia, C. J. (eds) (2002), *Educational Planning and Management in Small States: Concepts and Experiences.* London: Commonwealth Secretariat.

Ballantyne, J. H. and Hammack, F. M. (2011), *The Sociology of Education: A Systematic Analysis.* New Jersey: Prentice Hall.

Barber, B. R. (1972), Science, salience and comparative education: Some reflections on social scientific enquiry. *Comparative Education Review* 16(3): 424–36.

— (1995), *Jihad vs. McWorld: How Globalism and Tribalism are Reshaping the World.* New York: Ballantine.

— (1996), *Jihad vs McWorld: How Globalism and Tribalism are Reshaping the World.* New York: Ballantyne Books.

Barro, R. and Lee, J. (2011), Educational attainment in the world, 1950–2010. *VoxEU/Centre for Economic Policy Research,* http://www.voxeu.org/index. php?q=node/5058.

Bassanini, A. and Scarpetta, S. (2001), Does human capital matter for growth in OECD countries? Evidence from pooled mean-group estimates. *Economics Department Working Papers.* No. 282 ECO/WKP(18), Paris: OECD.

Becher, T. (1989), *Academic Tribes and Territories: Intellectual Enquiry and the Cultures of Disciplines.* Milton Keynes: SRHE and the Open University Press.

Becker, G. (1962), Investment in human capital: A theoretical analysis. *Journal of Political Economy* 70(5): 9–49.

Beckford, G. L. (1972), *Persistent Poverty: Underdevelopment in Plantation Economies of the Third World.* Oxford: Oxford University Press.

Bell, R. and Grant, N. (1977), *Patterns of Education in the British Isles.* London: George, Allen and Unwin.

Beller, W., d'Ayala, P. and Hein, P. (eds) (1990), *Sustainanble Development and Environmental Management of Small Islands.* Carnforth UK, and Park Ridge NJ/ USA: Parthenon Publishing, and UNESCO.

Benedict, B. (1967), *Problems of Smaller Territories*. London: Athlone Press.

Bereday, G. Z. F. (1964), *Comparative Method in Education*. London and New York: Holt, Rinehart and Winston.

Bertolin, J. and Leite, D. (2008), Quality evaluation of the Brazilian higher education system: Relevance, diversity, equity and effectiveness. *Quality in Higher Education* 14(2): 121–33.

Biggs, N. A. (ed.) (2012), *Education and HIV/AIDS*. London: Continuum Books.

Bird, L. (2011), Promoting resilience: Developing capacity within education systems affected by conflict, in *Commonwealth Secretariat Commonwealth Education Partnerships*. London: The Commonwealth Secretariat, pp. 94–6.

Bizony, J. (2011), *Science: The Definitive Guide*. London: Quarcus.

Blaug, M. (1987), *The Economics of Education and the Education of an Economist*. New York: New York University Press.

Bonal, X. (2004), Is the World Bank education policy adequate for fighting poverty? Some evidence from Latin America. *International Journal of Educational Development* 24: 649–66.

Borien, K. M. (2004), *Education in Transition: From Policy to Practice In Post-Apartheid South Africa 1994–99*. DPhil Thesis: University of Oxford.

Bowles, S. and Gintis, H. (1975), The problem with human capital theory: A Marxist critique. *The American Economic Review* 65(2): 74–82.

Bown, L. (1985), Without women no development: The role of non-formal education for women in African development, in K. M. Lillis (ed.), *School and Community in Less Developed Areas*. London: Croom Helm, pp. 258–76.

— (2000a), Lifelong learning: Ideas and achievements on the threshold of the 21st century. *Compare* 30(3): 341–51.

— (2000b), *Preparing the Future: Women, Literacy and Development*. London: Action Aid.

Boyd, W. and King, E. J. (1995), *The History of Western Education*. Lanham: Barnes and Noble Books.

Bray, M. (1992), *Educational Planning in Small Countries*. Paris: UNESCO.

— (2007), Scholarly enquiry and the field of comparative education, in M. Bray, B. Anderson and M. Mason, M. op. cit. pp. 341–62.

— (2011), The small states paradigm and its evolution, in M. Bray and M. Martin (eds), *Tertiary Education in Small States*. Paris: UNESCO/IIEP, pp. 37–72.

Bray, M., Adamson, B. and Mason, M. (2007), *Comparative Education Research: Approaches and Methods*. Comparative Education Research Centre: University of Hong Kong/Springer.

Bray, M. and Borevskaya, N. (2001), Financing education in transitional societies: Lessons from Russia and China. *Comparative Education* 37(3): 345–65.

Bray, M. and Fergus, H. (1986), The implications of size for educational development in small countries: Montserrat, a Caribbean case study. *Compare* 16(1): 91–102.

Bray, M. and Thomas, R. M. (1995), Levels of comparison in educational studies: Different insights from different literatures and the value of multi-level analysis. *Harvard Educational Review* 65(4): 472–90.

Bray, M., Anderson, R. and Mason, M. (eds) (2007), *Comparative Education Research: Approaches and Methods*. Hong Kong: Comparative Education Research Centre, University of Hong Kong.

Brine, J. (2002), *The European Social Fund and the EU: Flexibility, Growth, Stability*. London: Continuum Press.

Brock, C. (1980a), Education in Latin America in the mid-twentieth century. *International Journal of Educational Development* 1(1): 50–64.

— (1980b), Problems of education and human ecology in small tropical island nations, in C. Brock and R. Ryba (eds), *A Volume of Essays for Elizabeth Halsall*. Hull: University of Hull, Institute of Education, pp. 71–83.

— (1984a), Junior secondary innovations in Nigeria and St Lucia, in B. Gorwood (ed.), *Intermediate Schooling*. Hull: University of Hull Institute of Education, pp. 64–75.

— (1984b), *Scale, Isolation and Dependence: Educational Development in Island Developing and Other Specially Disadvantaged States*. London: Commonwealth Secretariat.

— (1985), Comparative education and the geographical factor, in K. Watson and R. Wilson (eds), *Contemporary Issues in Comparative Education: A Festschrift in Honour of Emeritus Professor Vernon Mallinson*. London: Croom Helm.

— (1988), Comparative education: What do we think of it so far?, in T. E. Corner (ed.), *Learning Opportunities for Adults (Section One: Comparative Education: The State of the Art)*. Glasgow: British Comparative Education Society/University of Glasgow.

— (1992), *The Case for a Geography of Education*. PhD Thesis: University of Hull.

— (1996), Changing patterns of teacher education in Sierra Leone, in C. Brock (ed.) *Global Perspectives on Teacher Education*. Wallingford: Triangle Books, pp. 103–22.

— (2002), Gender, education and change: The case of India, in R. Griffin (ed.), *Education in Transition: International Perspectives on the Politics and Processes of Change*. Wallingford: Symposium, pp. 259–77.

— (2007), Historical and societal roots of regulation and accreditation of higher education for quality assurance, in *Higher Education in the World 2007. Accreditation for Quality Assurance: What is at Stake?* (GUNI Series on the Social Commitment of Universities) Basingstoke: Palgrave Macmillan, pp. 24–36.

— (2008), Perspectives on higher education in the anglophone Caribbean, in F. S. Segrera, C. Brock and J. D. Sobrinho (eds), *Higher Education in Latin America and the Caribbean*. Caracas: UNESCO/IESALC, pp. 93–112.

— (2010), Spatial dimensions of Christianity and education in Western European history, with legacies for the present. *Comparative Education* 46(3): 289–306.

— (2011a), *Education as a Global Concern*. London and New York: Continuum.

— (2011b), Education and conflict: A fundamental relationship, in J. Paulson (ed.), *Education, Conflict and Development: Oxford Studies in Comparative Education*. Didcot/Wallingford: Symposium Books, pp. 17–32.

— (2012), Perspectives on the contribution of higher education to education as a humanitarian response. *Journal of Comparative and International Education* 1(1): 13–22.

Brock, C. and Cammish, N. K. (1997), *Factors Affecting Female Participation in Education in Seven Developing Countries*. London: DfID.

Brock, C. and Parker, R. (1985), School and community in situations of close proximity: The question of small states, in K. M. Lillis (ed.), *School and Community in Less Developed Areas*. London: Croom Helm, pp. 42–56.

Brock, C. and Smawfield, D. (1988), Education and development: The issues of small states. *Education Review* 40(10): 227–39.

Brock, C., Dada, J. and Jatta, T. (2006), Selected perspectives on education in West Africa with special reference to gender and religion, in R. Griffin (ed.), *Education in the Muslim World: Different Perspectives*. Didcot: Symposium Books, pp. 211–38.

Brown, G. N. and Hiskett, M. (eds) (1975), *Conflict and Harmony in Education in Tropical Africa*. London: George Allen and Unwin.

Burbules, N. C. and Torres, C. A. (2000), *Globalisation and Education: Critical Perspectives*. London: Routledge.

Cable, V. (2009), *The World Economic Crisis and What it Means*. London: Atlantic Books.

Cahill, T. (1998), *How the Irish Saved Civilisation*. New York: Doubleday.

Camilleri, C. (1986), *Cultural Anthropology and Education*. Paris: Kogan Page/UNESCO.

Cammish, N. K. (1985), Educational issues in small countries: The case of the Seychelles, in C. Brock (ed.), *Educational Issues in Small Countries,* Occasional Paper No. 2. Hull: British Comparative and International Education Society, pp. 22–9.

Canning, M. (2004), *The Modernization of Education in Russia*. World Bank Document/Public Information Centre in Russia, http://www.worldbank.org/eca/rer (Accessed April 2012).

Carnoy, M. and Samoff, J. (1990), *Education and Social Transformation in the Third World*. Princeton: Princeton University Press.

Castells, M. (1996), *The Rise of the Network Society*. Oxford: Blackwell.

Castro, M. H. (2004), The state and the market in the regulation of higher education in Brazil, in C. Brock and S. Schwartzman (eds), *The Challenges of Education in Brazil*. Didcot: Symposium Books.

Chan, R. K. H. and Wang, Y. (2009), Controlled decentralisation: Minban education reform in China. *Journal of Comparative Social Welfare* 25(1): 27–36.

Chevalier, A., Harmon, C., Walker, I. and Zhu, Y. (2004), Does education raise productivity, or just reflect it?. *The Economic Journal* 114: 499–517.

Chubb, J. E. and Moe, T. M. (1990), *Politics, Markets and America's Schools*. Washington DC: The Brookings Institution.

Clarke, C. and Payne, T. (eds) (1987), *Politics, Security and Development in Small States*. London: Allen and Unwin.

Colclough. C., Al Samarri, S., Rose, P. and Tembon, M. (2003), *Achieving Schooling for All in Africa: Costs, Commitment and Gender*. Aldershot: Ashgate.

Cole, M., Gay, J., Glick, J. A. and Sharp, D. W. (1971), *The Cultural Context of Learning and Thinking: An Exploration In Experimental Anthropology*. London: Methuen.

Coles, E. K. T. (1969), *Adult Education in Developing Countries*. Oxford: Pergamon.

Commonwealth of Learning (2009), *ICTs for Higher Education*. Paris: UNESCO.

Corbett, A. (2011), Ping pong: Competing leadership for reform in EU higher education 1998–2006. *European Journal of education* 46(1): 36–53.

Corby, R. A. (1990), Educating Africans for inferiority under British rule: Bo school in Sierra Leone. *Comparative Education Review* 34(3): 314–49.

Council of the European Union (2000), *Presidency Conclusions*. Lisbon: European Council, 23 and 24 March 2000.

— (2009), Council Conclusions of 12 May 2009 on a Strategic Framework for European Cooperation in Education and Training (ET 2020). *Official Journal C.119*.

— (2010a), *Joint Progress Report of the Council and the Commission on the implementation of the 'Education & Training 2010' work programme*. Brussels 18 January 2010, EDUC11, SOC21.

— (2010b), *Draft Joint Report on Social Protection and Social Inclusion 2010*, 6500/10. Brussels, 15 February 2010.

Cox, B. and Forshaw, J. (2009), *Why Does E = MC²? And Why Should We Care?*. Cambridge, MA: Da Capo Press.

Crossley, M. and Watson, K. (2003), *Comparative and International Research in Education: Globalisation, Context and Difference*. London: Routledge/Falmer.

— (2011), Comparative and international education: Policy transfer, context sensitivity and professional development, in J. Furlong and M. Lawn (eds), *Disciplines of Education: Their Role in the Future of Education Research*. London and New York: Routledge, pp. 103–121.

Crossley, M., Bray, M. and Packer, S. (2011), *Education in Small States: Policies and Priorities.* London: Commonwealth Secretariat.

Crouch, C. (1999), *Social Change in Western Europe.* Oxford: Oxford University Press.

Dada, J. A. (1986), *Educational Development and Religion in Northern Nigeria, with Special Reference to Kwara State.* PhD thesis: University of Hull.

Dada, J. and Oshagbemi, T. (2008), *Egbe History and Culture.* Bury St. Edmunds: Arima Publishing.

Dale, R. (1999), Specifying globalization effects on national education policy. *Journal of Education Policy* 14(1): 1–17.

— (2005) Globalisation, knowledge economy and comparative education. *Comparative Education* 41(2): 117–49.

Dalton, B. (2012), Grade level and science achievements: US performance in cross-national perspective. *Comparative Education Review* 56(1): 125–54.

Daly, M. (2006), EU social policy after Lisbon. *Journal of Common Market Studies* 44(3): 461–81.

Daly, M. and Silver, H. (2008), Social exclusion and social capital: A comparison and critique. *Theoretical Sociology* 37: 537–66.

Daniels, B. C. (1979), *The Connecticut Town: Growth and Development 1635–1790.* Middletown, CT: Wesleyan University Press.

David, M. (2011), Overview of researching global higher education: Challenge, change or crisis?. *Contemporary Social Science* 6(2): 147–63.

Davies, L. (2004), *Conflict and Education: Complexity and Chaos.* London: Routledge/ Falmer.

— (2005), Schools and war: Urgent agendas for comparative education. *Compare* 35(4): 357–72.

— (2011), Learning for state-building: Capacity development, education and fragility. *Comparative Education* 47(2): 157–80.

Davison, J. and Kanyuka, M. (1992), Girls' participation in basic education in southern Malawi. *Comparative Education Review* 36(4): 446–66.

Day-Ashley, A. (2006), Inter-school working involving private school outreach activities and government schools in India. *Compare* 36(4): 481–96.

Diamantopoulou, A. (2002), European integration and governance: challenges and opportunities. *Address to the Institute of European Studies*, University of Montreal, 25 April 2002.

DiMaggio, P. J. and Powell, W. W. (1983), The iron cage revisited: Institutional isomorphism and collective rationality in organisational fields. *American Sociological Review* 48(2): 147–60.

Dodge, M. and Kitchin, R. (2001), *Mapping Cyperspace.* London and New York: Routledge.

Dodgshon, R. A. (1987), *The European Past: Social Evolution and the Spatial Order.* Basingstoke: Macmillan.

Douglas-Scott, S. (2002), *Constitutional Law of the European Union.* Harlow: Pearsons Education Limited.

Durham, E. R. (2004), Higher education in Brazil: Public and private, in C. Brock and S. Schwartzman (eds), op. cit., pp. 147–78.

Dyer, C. (2000), *Operation Blackboard: Policy Implementation in Indian Elementary Education.* Wallingford: Symposium.

Easterby, W. (2006), *The White Man's Burden: Why the West's Efforts to Aid the Rest Have Done So Much Ill and So Little Good.* New York: Penguin Books.

Eisemon, T. O. (1984), Autonomy and authority in an Indian university: A Study of the University of Bombay. *Compare* 14(1): 59–68.

European Commission (2011a), *Progress Towards the Common European Objectives in Education and Training: Indicators and Benchmarks 2010/2011,* SEC(2011), 526.

— (2011b), Supporting Growth and Jobs: An Agenda for the Modernisation of Europe's Higher Education Systems. *Communication from the Commission to the European Parliament, the Council, the European Economic and Social Committee and the Committee of the Regions,* COM(2011), 567 final.

Fage, J. D. and Tordoff, W. (2002), *A History of Africa.* London: Routledge.

Fan, C. S., Overland, J. and Spagat, M. (1999), Human capital, growth and inequality in Russia. *Journal of Comparative Economics* 27: 618–43.

Farrell, J. P. (1979), The necessity of comparisons in the study of education: The salience of science and the problem of comparability. *Comparative Education Review* 23(1): 3–16.

Findlow, S. (2008), Islam, modernity and education in the Arab States. *Intercultural Education* 19(4): 337–52.

Finegold, D., McFarland, L. and Richardson, W. (eds) (1992 Part 1), *Something Borrowed, Something Blue: A Study of the Thatcher Government's Appropriation of American Education and Training Policy.* Wallingford: Triangle Books.

Finegold, D., McFarland, L. and Richardson, W. (1993 Part 2), *Something Borrowed, Something Learned? The Transatlantic Market in Education and Training Reform.* Washington, DC: The Brookings Institution.

Fisher, H. J. (1975), The modernisation of Islamic education in Sierra Leone, Gambia and Liberia: Religion and language, in G. N. Brown and M. Hiskett (eds), op. cit., pp. 187–99.

Fletcher, L. (1974), Comparative education: A question of identity. *Comparative Education Review* 18(3): 348–53.

Forde, C. D. (1939), *Habitat, Economy and Society: A Geographical Introduction to Ethnology.* London: Methuen.

Fordham, P. (1980), *Participation, Lifelong Learning and Change: Commonwealth Approaches to Non-Formal Education*. London: Commonwealth Secretariat.

Fosberg, F. R. (ed.) (1963), *Man's Place in the Island Ecosystem*. Honolulu: Bishop Museum Press.

Freire, P. (1970), *The Pedagogy of the Oppressed*. New York: Continuum Books.

Furlong, J. (1992), Disaffected pupils: Reconstructing the sociological perspective. *British Journal of the Sociology of Education* 12(3): 293–309.

Furlong, J. and Lawn, M. (2011), *Disciplines of Education: Their Role in the Future of Education Research*. London: Routledge.

Galbraith, J. K., Krytynskaia, L. and Wang, Q. (2003), The experience of rising inequality in Russia and China during the transition. *The European Journal of Comparative Economics* 1(1): 87–106.

Gewirtz, S. and Cribb, A. (2009), *Understanding Education*. Cambridge: Polity Press.

Gezi, K. (1971), *Education in Comparative and International Perspectives*. New York: Holt Rinehart and Winston.

Giroux, H. (2010), Paulo Freire and the crisis of the political. *Power and Education* 2(3): 335–40.

Goldin, C. and Katz, L. F. (2008), *Race between Education and Technology*. Cambridge: Harvard University Press.

Goudie, A. (2006), *The Human Impact on the Natural Environment: Past, Present and Future*. Oxford: Blackwell.

Government of Sierra Leone/World Bank (1994), *Developing Basic Education and Training in Sierra Leone: A National Education Action Plan 1995–2000*. Freetown: Department of Education.

— (1995), *New Education Policy for Sierra Leone*. Freetown: Department of Education.

Grant, N. (1964), *Education in the Soviet Union*. Harmondsworth: Penguin.

— (1969), *Society, School and Progress in Eastern Europe*. Oxford: Pergamon.

Grant, N. and Bell, R. E. (1977), *Patterns of Education in the British Isles*. London: Allen and Unwin.

Grayling, A. C. (2001), *The Meaning of Things: Applying Philosophy to Life*. London: Pheonix.

Grek, S. (2009), Governing by numbers: The PISA 'effect' in Europe. *Journal of Education Policy* 24(1): 23–37.

Griffin, R. (2001), *The Mediation of Market-Related Policies for the provision of Public second Level Education: An International Comparative Study of Selected Locations in England Ireland and the USA*. Unpublished DPhil Thesis: University of Oxford.

— (ed.) (2002), *Education in Transition: International Perspectives on the Politics and Processes of Change*. Wallingford: Symposium Books/Continuum.

Grove, A. T. (1977), Desertification. *Progress in Physical Geography* 1(2): 296–310.

— (2000), The African environment: Understood and misunderstood, in D. Rimmer and A. Kirk-Green (eds), *The British Intellectual Engagement with Africa in the Twentieth Century.* Basingstoke: Macmillan, pp. 179–206.

Guimarães, J. and Sampaio, B. (2011), Family background and students' achievement on a university entrance exam in Brazil. *Education Economics* 1–22.

Halász, G. (2006), *European Co-ordination of national education policies from the perspective of the new Member Countries.* National Institute for Public Education, http://www.oki.hu/oldal.php?tipus=cikk&kod=english-art-Halasz-European (Accessed November 2011).

Halász, G. and Michel, A. (2011), Key competencies in Europe: Interpretation, policy formulation and implementation. *European Journal of Education* 46(3): 289–306.

Halls, W. D. (1977), Comparative studies in education 1964–77: A personal view. *Comparative Education* 13(4): 81–6.

Hans, N. (1949), *Comparative Education: A Study of Educational Factors and Traditions.* London: Routledge and Kegan Paul.

Harber, C. (1989), *Politics in African Education.* London and Basingstoke: Macmillan.

— (2001), *State of Transition: Post-Apartheid Educational Reform in South Africa.* Wallingford: Symposium Books.

Hatcher, R. and Jones, K. (eds) (2011), *No Country for the Young.* London: The Tufnell Press.

Hawking, S. (2011), *The Grand Design.* London: Transworld Publishers.

Hayhoe, R. (1996), *Chinese Universities 1895–1995: A Century of Cultural Conflict.* New York: Garland.

Heckman, J. (2008), Schools, Skills and Synapses. *Discussion Paper* No. 3515, http://www.heckmanequation.org/content/resource/schools-skills-synapses.

Held, D., McGrew, A., Goldblatt D. and Perraton, J. (1999), *Global Transformations: Politics, Economics and Culture.* Stanford: Polity and Stanford Press.

Higginson, J. H. (1979), *Selections from Sir Michael Sadler: Studies in World Citizenship.* Liverpool: Dejall and Meyorre.

Hingel, A. (2001), *Education policies and European governance, Contribution to the Interservice Groups on European Governance*, March, DG EAC/A/1 Brussels: European Commission Directorate-General for Education and Culture, http://ec.europa.eu/governance/areas/group12/contribution_education_en.pdf (Accessed November 2011).

Hodder, B. W. (1968), *Economic Development in the Tropics.* London: Methuen.

Holmes, B. (1965), *Problems in Education.* London: Routledge and Kegan Paul.

— (1967), *Educational Policy and the Mission Schools: Case Studies from the British Empire.* London: Routledge and Kegan Paul.

Hopper, W. (1968), A Typology for the classification of education systems. *Sociology* 2: 29–46.

Hummel, R. C. and Nagle, J. M. (1973), *Urban Education in America*. New York: Oxford University Press.

Hurst, M. (ed.) (1986), *States, Countries, Provinces*. Bourne End: The Kensal Press.

Hyde, K. A. L. (1993), Sub-Saharan Africa, in E. M. King and M. A. Hill (eds), op. cit., pp. 100–35.

Iverson, K. (1978), Civilization and assimilation in the colonized schooling of Native Americans, in P. G. Altbach and G. P. Kelly (eds), op. cit., pp. 149–80.

Jakobi A. P., Martens K. and Wolf, K. D. (eds) (2010), *Education in Political Science: Discovering a Neglected Field*. London and New York: Routledge/ECPR.

Johnson, D. (2011), A cloud over the rainbow nation? Language, national reconciliation and educational transformation in post-Apartheid South Africa, in J. Paulson (ed.), (op. cit. 2011a), pp. 103–25.

Johnson, H. B. (1967), The location of Christian missions in Africa. *Geographical Review* LVII: 168–202.

Johnston, R. J. (1981), The political element in suburbia: A key influence on the urban geography of the United States. *Geography* 66(4): 286–96.

Jones, K., Cunchillos, C., Hatcher, R., Hirtt, N., Innes, R., Johsua, S. and Klausenitzer, J. (2008), *Schooling in Western Europe: The New Order and its Adversaries*. Basingstoke: Palgrave Macmillan.

Jones, P. E. (1971), *Comparative Education: Purpose and Method*. St Lucia, Brisbane: University of Queensland Press.

Jones, P. W. (1990), *Literacy and basic education for adults and young people: A review of experience*. Paris: UNESCO.

— (2006), *Education, Poverty and the World Bank*. Rotterdam: Sense Publishers.

Jiang, K. and Ma, X. (2011), Overseas education in China: Changing landscapes, *International Higher Education* 63: 6–8.

Kallaway, P. (2009), Education, health and social welfare in the late colonial context: The International Missionary Council and educational transition in the inter-war years with specific reference to colonial Africa. *History of Education* 38(2): 217–46.

Kandel, I. (1933), *Studies in Comparative Education*. London: Harrap.

Karlsen, G. E. (2002), Educational policy and educational programmes in the European Union, in J. A. Ibanez-Martin and G. Jover (eds), *Education in Europe: Policies and Politics*. Dordrecht: Kluwer Academic Publishers.

Karpinska, Z. (ed.) (2012), *Education, Aid and Aid Agencies*. London: Continuum Books.

Kataoka, S. (2011), Per capita financing of general education in Russia, in J. D. Alonso and A. Sánchez (eds), *Reforming Education Finance in Transition Countries: Six Case Studies in Per Capita Financing Systems.* The World Bank, http://issuu. com/world.bank.publications/docs/9780821387832?mode=window&pageNumbe r=276 (Accessed April 2012).

Kazamias, A. M. and Massialas, B. (1965), *Tradition and Change in Education: A Comparative Study.* New York: Prentice Hall.

Kearney, J. (2011), A unified Rwanda? Ethnicity, history and reconciliation in the Ingando peace and solidarity camp, in Paulson (ed.), (op. cit. 2011a), pp. 151–77.

King, E. J. (1958), *Other Schools and Ours.* London and New York: Holt, Rinehart and Winston.

— (1965), *Society, School and Progress in the USA.* Oxford: Pergamon Press.

— (1968), *Comparative Studies and Educational Decision.* London: Methuen.

King, K. (1991), *Aid and Education in the Developing World: The Role of Donor Agencies in Educational Analysis.* Harlow: Longman.

King, L. and Schielman, S. (eds) (2004), *The Challenge of Indigenous Education: Practice and Perspectives.* Paris: UNESCO.

Kislitsyna, O. (2003), Income inequality in Russia during transition: How can it be explained? *Economics Education and Research Consortium, Working Paper Series,* No. 3/08, http://econpapers.repec.org/paper/eerwpalle/03–08e.htm (Accessed April 2012).

Klees, S. (2010), Aid, development, and education. *Current Issues in Comparative Education* 13(1): 7–28.

Klugman, J. and Braithwaite, J. (1998), Poverty in Russia during the transition: An overview. *The World Bank Research Observer* 13(1): 37–58.

Kok, W. (2004), Facing the Challenge Ahead: The Lisbon Strategy for Growth and Employment. *Report from the High Level Group* (Chair W. Kok), Brussels: European Commission.

Kolesnikov, V. N., Kucher, I. V. and Turchenko, V. N. (2005), The commercialisation of Higher Education: A threat to the national security of Russia. *Russian Education and Society* 47(8): 35–48.

Kosack, S. (2009), Realising education for all: Defining and using the political will to invest in primary education. *Comparative Education* 45(4): 495–523.

Lacey, C. (1971), *Hightown Grammar: The School as a Social System.* Manchester: Manchester University Press.

Lafontaine, O. (2009), *Together for Change in Europe, Platform of the Party of the European Left for the elections to the European Parliament* 2009, http://www. spokesmanbooks.com/leftparties.pdf (Accessed April 2012).

Lange, B. and Alexiadou, N. (2007), New forms of European Union governance in the education sector? A preliminary analysis of the Open Method of Coordination. *European Educational Research Journal* 6(4): 321–35.

— (2010), Policy learning and governance of education policy in the EU. *Journal of Education Policy* 25(4): 443–63.

Lanot, G. and Chevalier, A. (2002), Financial transfers and educational achievement. *Education Economics* 10(2): 165–81.

Lauglo, J. (1995), Forms of decentralisation and their implications for education. *Comparative Education* 14(1): 5–29.

Law, W. W. (1995), The role of the state in higher education reform: Mainland China and Taiwan. *Comparative Education Review* 39(3): 322–55.

Leach, F. (ed.) (2003), *Partnerships in Education for All: The Role of Higher Education in Basic* Education. London: Commonwealth Secretariat.

Leite, D. (2010), Brazilian higher education from a post-colonial perspective. *Globalisation, Societies and Education* 8(2): 219–33.

Lewicka-Grisdale, K. and McLaughlin, T. (2002), Education for European identity and European citizenship, in J. A. Ibanez-Martin and G. Jover (eds), op. cit.

Lewin, K. and Calloids, F. (2001), *Financing Secondary Education in Developing Countries: Startegies for Sustainable Growth*. Paris: UNESCO/IIEP.

Lewin, K. M. (2008), Strategies for sustainable financing of secondary education in sub-Saharan Africa. *World Bank Working Paper 136*, Washington DC, World Bank.

— (2011), Policy dialogue and target setting: do current indicators of Education for All signify progress?. *Journal of Education Policy* 26(4): 571–87.

Lindblad, S. and Popkewitz, T. (2000), Educational governance and social inclusion and exclusion: Some conceptual difficulties and problematics in policy and research. *Discourse: Studies in the Cultural Politics of Education* 21(1): 5–44.

Lingard, B. and Rawolle, S. (2011), New scalar politics: Implications for education policy. *Comparative Education* 47(1): 489–502.

Lisovskaya, E. and Karpov, V. (2001), The perplexed world of Russian private schools: Findings from field research. *Comparative Education* 37(1): 43–64.

Lowenthal, D. (1957), The population of Barbados. *Social and Economic Studies* 6(4): 445–501.

Lundahl, L. (2011), Paving the way to the future? Education and young Europeans' paths to work and independence. *European Educational Research Journal* 10(2): 168–79.

Lundahl, L., Erixon-Arreman, I., Lundström, U. and Rönnberg, L. (2010), Setting things right? Swedish upper secondary school reform in a 40-year perspective. *European Journal of Education* 45(1): 46–59.

Lungwangwa, G. (2003), Zambia, in F. Leach (ed.), op. cit., pp. 191–205.

Madison, J. (1787/2011), Objections to the Proposed Constitution From Extent of Territory Answered, November 30, 1787. *The Federalist*, No. 14. http://www. whatwouldthefoundersthink.com/federalist-no-14.

Mahieu, R. (2006), *Agents of Change and Policies of Scale: A policy Study of Entrepreneurship and Enterprise in Education*. Doktorsavhandling I Pedagogiskt arbete Nr 9, Umeå University.

Mallinson, V. (1957), *An Introduction to the Study of Comparative Education*. London: Heinemann.

— (1980), *The Western European Idea of Education*. Oxford: Elsevier.

Mangin, J. A. (ed.) (1990), *Making Imperial Mentalities: Socialisation and British Imperialism*. Manchester: Manchester University Press.

Mannathoko, C. (2003), Botswana, in Leach F. (ed.), op. cit., pp. 19–38.

Martin, J. (2011), Fasten your seatbelts: There's turbulence ahead. *Oxford Today* 23(3): 28–30.

Martin, M. and Bray, M. (eds) (2011), *Tertiary Education in Small States:The Context of Globalization*. Paris: IIEP/UNESCO.

Maseman, V., Bray, M. and Manzan, M. (2007), *Common Interests, Uncommon Goals: Histories of the WCCES and its Members*. Hong Kong: University of Hong Kong/ Springer.

Matsumoto, M. (2011), Expectations and realities of education in post-conflict Sierra Leone: A reflection of society or a driver for peace-building?, in J. Paulson (ed.), (op. cit. 2011b), pp. 119–44.

McDade, D. F. (1982), The things that interest mankind: A commentary on thirty years of comparative education. *British Journal of Educational Studies* XXX(1): 72–84.

McLeish, E. A. and Phillips, D. G. (eds) (1998), *Processes of Transition in Education Systems*. Wallingford: Symposium Books.

McPartland, M. F. (1979), The emergence of an education system: A geographical perspective. *Compare* 9(2): 119–31.

Meldrum, A. (2004), *Where We Have Hope: A Memoir of Zimbabwe*. London: John Murray.

Meyer, H-D. and Rowan, B. (2006), Institutional analysis and the study of education, in H-D. Meyer and B. Rowan (eds), *The New Institutionalism in Education*. Albany: State University of New York Press.

Mmari, G. (2003), Tanzania, in F. Leach (ed.), op. cit., pp. 161–73.

Moutsios, S. (2010), Power, politics and transnational policy-making in education. *Globalisation, Societies and Education Journal* 8(1): 121–41.

Mulcahy, D. (2001), *The role of the Bush presidency (1989–93) in U.S. educational policy*. Educational Studies Association of Ireland Conference: Limerick, mimeo, p. 6.

Mulholland, J. (2012), In 10 years' time, Ghana may not require any aid at all'. *The Observer*, 15th February, pp. 36–7.

Mundy, K. (2006), Education for all and the new development compact, in J. Zajda, S. Majhanovich and V. Rust (eds), *Education and Social Justice*. Dordrecht: Springer, pp. 13–38.

— (2007), Global governance, educational change. *Comparative Education* 43(3): 339–57.

Nettle, D. (1996), Language diversity in West Africa: An ecological approach. *Journal of Anthropological Archaeology* 15: 403–38.

Ngok, K. (2011), Chinese education policy in the context of decentralization and marketization: Evolution and implications. *Asia Pacific Education Review* 8(1): 142–57.

Noah, H. J. and Eckstein, M. A. (1969), *Toward a Science of Comparative Education*. London: Collier-Macmillan.

Nóvoa, A. (2001), The restructuring of the European educational space: Changing relationships among states, citizens and educational communities, in A. J. Fink, G. Lewis and J. Clarke (eds), *Rethinking European Welfare*. The Open University, London: Sage.

Nóvoa, A. and deJong-Lambert, W. (2003), Educating Europe: an analysis of EU educational policies, in D. Phillips and H. Ertl (eds), *Implementing European Union Education and Training Policy*. Dordrecht: Kluwer, pp. 41–72.

N'tchougan-Sonou, C. (2000), *Values Learned Through Formal Education: A Comparative Study of Anglophone and Francophone Ewes in Ghana and Togo*. DPhil thesis: University of Oxford.

OECD (2010), Tackling inequalities in Brazil, China, India and South Africa, *Position Paper*, November 2010, http://www.oecd.org/dataoecd/22/41/46459969.pdf (Accessed April 2012).

— (2011a), Brazil: Encouraging lessons from a large federal system, in *Strong Performers and Successful Reformers in Education: Lessons from PISA for the United States*, OECD Publishing, http://dx.do.org/10.1787/978926096660-en (Accessed April 2012).

— (2011b), *Education at a Glance 2011: Country Note – China*, OECD Publishing. http://dx.doi.org/10.1787/eag-2011-2n (Accessed April 2012).

— (2011c), *Education at a Glance 2011: Highlights*. OECD Publishing.

— (2011d), Improving access and quality in the Indian education system. *Economics Department Working Papers*, No. 885, ECO/WKP(2011)54.

— (2011e), *OECD Employment Outlook 2011*. OECD Publishing.

Oh, S-A. (2002), *From Ivory Tower to Knowledge Factory: The Impact of University-Industry Links on Universities in China and England*. Unpublished DPhil Thesis: University of Oxford.

Öhrn, E. (2011), Class and ethnicity at work: Segregation and conflict in a Swedish secondary school. *Education Inquiry* 2(2): 345–57.

O'Malley, B. (2010), *Education Under Attack*. Paris: UNESCO.

Orr, D. W. (1994), *Earth in Mind: On Education, Environment and the Human Prospect*. Washington DC: Island Press.

Otite, O. (1990), *Ethnic Pluralism and Ethnicity in Nigeria*. Ibadan: Shaneson.

Ozga, J. and Lingard, B. (2007), Globalisation, education policy and politics, in B. Lingard and J. Ozga (eds), *The RoutledgeFalmer Reader in Education Policy and Politics*. London: Routledge.

Pangle, L. S. and Pangle, T. L. (1993), *The Learning of Liberty: The Educational Ideas of the American Founders*. Lawrence Kansas: University Press of Kansas.

Pape, J. (1998), Changing education for majority rule in Zimbabwe and South Africa. *Comparative Education Review* 42(3): 253–66.

Parekh, B. (1995), Jewarharlal Nehru and the crisis of modernisation, in U. Baxi and B. Parekh (eds), *Crisis and Change in Contemporary India*. New Delhi: Sage, pp. 21–56.

Paulson, J. (2011a), *Education and Reconciliation: Exploring Conflict and Post-Conflict Situations*. London: Continuum

— (2011b), *Education, Conflict and Development*. Didcot/Wallingford: Symposium.

Paulston, R. G. (ed.) (1996), *Social Cartography: Mapping ways of Seeing Social and EducationalChange*. New York and London: Garland.

Pavlova, M. (2010), The modernisation of education in Russia: Culture and markets, in D. Johnson (ed.), *Politics, Modernisation and Educational Reform in Russia: From past to present*. Oxford: Didcot.

Peach, C. (1975), *Urban Social Segregation*. London and New York: Longman.

— (1980), Ethnic segregation and intermarriage. *Annals of the Association of American Geographers* 70(3): 371–81.

Pedrosa, R. H. L. (2011), Assessing higher education outcomes in Brazil. *International Higher Education* 63: 24–6.

Peers, R. (1958), *Adult Education: A Comparative Study*. London: Routledge.

Penny, A. (1988), Afrikaner identity and educational policy in South Africa, in W. F. Tulasiewicz and C. Brock (eds), *Christianity and Educational Provision in International Perspective*. London: Routledge, pp. 345–74.

Pépin, L. (2006), *The history of European cooperation in education and training: Europe in the making – an example*. Luxembourg: Office for Official Publications of the European Communities.

— (2011), Education in the Lisbon strategy: Assessment and prospects. *European Journal of Education* 46(1): 25–35.

Pereyra, M. A., Kotthoff, H. and Cowen, R. (eds) (2011), *PISA Under Examination: Changing Knowledge, Changing Tests, and Changing Schools*. Rotterdam/Boston/Taipei: Sense Publishers.

Perkinson, H. J. (1976), *Two Hundred Years of American Educational Thought.* New York: David McKay Company Inc.

Phillips, D. (2006), Michael Sadler and comparative education. *Oxford Review of Education* 32(1): 39–54.

Phillips, D. and Ochs, K. (2004), Researching policy borrowing: Some methodological challenges in comparative education. *British Educational Research Journal* 30(6): 773–84.

Phillips, D. and Schweisfurth, M. (2008), *Comparative and International Education: An Introduction to Theory, Method and Practice.* London: Continuum Books.

Phillips, D. G. (1989), Neither borrower nor a lender be? The problem of cross-national attraction in education. *Comparative Education* 25(3): 267–74.

— (1994), Periodisation in historical approaches to comparative education: Some considerations from the examples of Germany and England and Wales. *British Journal of Educational Studies* 42(3): 261–72.

— (2002), Comparative historical studies in education: Problems of periodisation reconsidered. *British Journal of Educational Studies* 50(3): 363–77.

Phillips, D. G. and Kaser, M. (1992), *Education and Economic Change in Eastern Europe and the Former Soviet Union.* Wallingford: Triangle Books.

Pollack, E. (1993), Isaac Leon Kandel (1881–1965). *Prospects* 23(3/4): 775–87.

Postlethwaite, T. N. (1999), Overview of issues in international achievement studies, in B. Jawaorski and D. Phillips (eds), *Comparing Standards internationally.* Wallingford: Symposium Books, pp. 23–60.

Psacharopoulos, G. and Patrinos, H. A. (2002), Returns to investment in education: A further update. *World Bank Policy Research Working Paper,* 2881.

Pyle, J. L. and Forrant, R. (eds) (2002), *Globalization, Universities and Issues of Sustainable Human Development.* Cheltenham UK: Edward Elgar.

Ramirez, F. O. (2006), Growing commonalities and persistent differences in higher education: Universities between global models and national legacies, in H-D. Meyer and B. Rowan (eds), op. cit.

Rao, N. (2010), Aspiring for distinction: Gendered educational choices in an Indian village. *Compare* 40(2): 167–83.

Ravi, K. and Sumner, A. (2011), Poor countries or poor people? Development assistance and the new geography of global poverty. *CEPR Discussion Paper 8489,* CEPR.

Redwood Sawyerr, J. A. S. (2011), Rebuilding the Athens of West Africa: Education in twenty-first century Sierra Leone, in *Commonwealth Education Partnerships 2011/12.* Cambridge: Nexus Strategic Partnerships, pp. 87–90.

Rees, T. and Singh, G. (1998), South Pacific Board for Educational Assessment, in M. Bray and L. Steward (eds), op. cit. pp. 162–80.

Robertson, S. (2010), The EU, 'regulatory state regionalism' and new modes of higher education governance. *Globalisation, Societies and Education* 8(1): 23–37.

Robertson, S. and Keeling, R. (2008), Stirring the lions: Strategy and tactics in global higher education. *Globalisation, Societies and Education* 6(3): 221–40.

Robertson, S., Novelli, M., Dale, R., Tikly, L., Dachi, H. and Ndebela, A. (2007), *Globalisation, Education and Development: Ideas, Actors And Dynamics*. London: DFID, No. 68.

Rogers, C. (2007), *Parenting and Inclusive Education: Discovering Difference, Experiencing Difficulty*. Houndmills: Palgrave Macmillan.

Rostan, M. (2011), English as 'lingua franca' and the internationalisation of academe. *International Higher Education* 63: 11–13.

Ruegg, D. (ed.) (1992), *A History of the University in Europe*. Cambridge: Cambridge University Press.

Sachs, J. D. (2005), *The End of Poverty: Economic Possibilities for Our Time*. New York: Penguin Books.

Saint, W. (2009), Tertiary education and economic growth in Sub-Saharan Africa. *International Higher Education* 54(Winter): 14–15.

Samoff, J. (2003), Institutionalizing international influence. *Safundi* 4(1): 1–35.

— (2007), Education quality: the disabilities of aid. *International Review of Education* 53: 485–507.

Scharpf, F. (2001), European governance: common concerns vs the challenges of diversity. *Jean Monnet Working Paper*, No. 6/01, New York University. http://www.jeanmonnetprogram.org/papers/01/010701.rtf.

Schwartzman, S. (2009), Student quotas in Brazil. *International Higher Education* 56: 11–13.

Schweisfurth, M. (2002), *Teachers, Democratisation and Educational Reform in Russia and South Africa*. Wallingford: Symposium Books.

Seddon, T. (2005), Introduction: Travelling policy in post-socialist education. *European Educational Research Journal* 4(1): 1–4.

Selwyn, P. (ed.) (1975), *Development Policy in Small Countries*. London: Croom Helm.

Shain, F. (2012), 'Getting on' rather than 'getting by': ethnicity, class and 'success against the odds'. *British Journal of Sociology of Education* 33(1): 153–63.

Shand, R. T. (ed.) (1980), The island states of the Pacific and Indian oceans: Anatomy of development. *Development Studies Centre Monographs:* No. 23, Australian National University, pp. 369–79.

Shavit, Y., Blossfeld, H-P. (1993), *Persistent Inequality: Changing Educational Attainment in Thirteen Countries*. Boulder CO: Westview Press.

Shavit, Y., Yaish, M. and Bar-Haim, E. (2007), The persistence of persistent inequality, in S. Scherer, R. Pollak, G. Otte and M. Gangl (eds), *From Origin to Destination: Trends and Mechanisms in Social Stratification Research, Essays in Honour of Walter Müller*. Frankfurt/New York: Campus Verlag.

Siddique, M. (2012), Education and disadvantaged children in India, in M. Matsumoto (ed.), *Education and Disadvantaged Children and Young People*. London and New York: Bloomsbury/Continuum (forthcoming).

Silova, I. (2005), Travelling policies: Hijacked in Central Asia. *European Educational Research Journal* 4(1): 50–9.

Silver, H. (1994), Social exclusion and social solidarity: Three paradigms. *International Labour Review* 133(5–6): 531–72.

Simons, M. (2007), To be informed: Understanding the role of feedback information for Flemish/European policy. *Journal of Education Policy* 22(5): 531–48.

Sinclair, M. (2001), Education in Emergencies, in J. Crisp, C. Talbot and D. B. Cipillone (eds), *Learning for a Future: Refugee Education in Developing Countries*. Geneva: UNHCR, pp. 1–84.

Sinitsina, I. (2011), Public expenditures on education and health in Russian Federation before and during the global crisis. *CASE Network Reports*, No. 103/2011, http://www.case-research.eu/sites/default/files/publications/CNR_2011_103.pdf (Accessed April 2012).

Smawfield. D. (ed.) (2012), *Education and Natural Disasters*. London: Continuum Books.

Smolentseva, A. (2005), Will there be free higher education in Russia? *International Higher Education* 40: 22–3.

Soares, F. (2004), Quality and equity in Brazilian basic education: Facts and possibilities, in C. Brock and S. Schwartzman (eds), *The Challenges of Education in Brazil*. Oxford Studies in Comparative Education. Didcot/Oxford: Symposium Books.

Sobrinho, J. D. and de Brito, M. R. F. (2008), Higher education in Brazil: Main trends and challenges, in F. L. Segrera, C. Brock and J. D. Sobrinho (eds), *Higher Education in Latin America and the Caribbean*. Caracas: UNESCO/IESALC, pp. 235–54.

Spring, J. (1978), *American Education: An Introduction to Social and Political Aspects*. New York and London: Longman.

Spryskov, D. (2003), Below the poverty line: Duration of poverty in Russia. *Economics Education and Research Consortium, Working Paper Series*, No. 03/04.

Srivastava, P. (2006), Private schooling and mental models about girls' schooling in India. *Compare* 36(4): 497–514.

Steiner-Khamsi, G. (ed.) (2004), *The Global Politics of Educational Borrowing and Lending*. New York: Teachers College, Columbia University.

Steiner-Khamsi, G. and Stolpe, I. (2005), Non-traveling 'best practices' for a traveling population: The case of nomadic education in Mongolia. *European Educational Research Journal* 4(1): 22–35.

Stiglitz, J. E. (2001), Development theory at a crossroads. *Proceedings from the Annual Bank Conference on Development Economics in Europe*, June 2000, J. F. Richard.

— (2011), Rethinking development economics. *The World Bank Research Observer*, 19 July 2011, http://wbro.oxfordjournals.org/content/26/2/230.full (Accessed October 2011).

Streeck W. (1999), Competitive solidarity: Rethinking the 'European Social Model', Presidential address to the Conference. *Globalisation and the Good Society*, organised by the Society for the Advancement of Socio-Economics (SASE), Madison, Wisconsin, USA, July 8–11, 1999.

Stromquist, N. (1996), Mapping gendered spaces in Third World Educational Interventions, in R. G. Paulston, op. cit., pp. 223–47.

Stromquist, N. P. (1997), *Literacy for Citizenship: Gender and Grassroots Dynamics in Brazil*. Albany NY: State University of New York Press.

Sultana, R. (2008a), Looking back before moving forward: Building on 15 years of comparative educational research in the Mediterranean. *Mediterranean Journal of Educational Studies* 13(2): 9–25.

— (2008b), *The Challenge of Policy Implementation: A Comparative Analysis of Vocational School Reforms in Albania, Kosovo and Turkey*. Peer Learning 2007, European Training Foundation.

Sutherland-Addy, E. (2003), Ghana, in F. Leach (ed.), op. cit., pp. 39–61.

Sweetland, S. R. (1996), Human capital theory: Foundations of a field of inquiry. *Review of Educational Research* 66(3):341–59.

Taylor, C. (2009), Towards a geography of education, *Oxford Review of Education*35(5):651–69.

Tessler, L. R. (2011), The pursuit of equity in Brazilian higher education. *International Higher Education* 63: 23–5.

Thomas, R. M. and Postlethwaite, T. N. (eds) (1984), *Schooling in the Pacific Islands*. Oxford: Pergamon.

Thomas, W. I. (1956), *Man's Role in Changing the Face of the Earth*. Chicago: Chicago University Press.

Todaro, M. and Smith, S. (2008), *Economic Development*. 10th Edition, Boston: Addison Wesley.

Todd, E. (1987), *The Causes of Progress: Culture, Authority and Change*. Oxford: Blackwell.

Tooley, J. and Dixon, P. (2005), *Private Education is Good for the Poor*. Washington DC: Cato Institute.

— (2006), *De-facto* privatisation of education and the poor: Implications of a study from sub-Saharan Africa and India. *Compare* 36(4): 443–62.

Torche, F. (2010), Economic crisis and inequality of educational opportunity in Latin America. *American Sociological Association* 83(2): 85–110.

Torres, C. A. and Schugurensky, D. (2002), The political economy of higher education in the era of neoliberal globalization: Latin America in comparative perspective. *Higher Education* 43: 429–55.

Tickly, L. (2004), Education and the new imperialism. *Comparative Education: Special Edition on Post-colonialism and Comparative Education* 40(2): 173–98.

— (2011), Towards a framework for researching the quality of education in low-income countries. *Comparative Education* 47(1): 1–23.

Trethewey, A. R. (1976), *Introducing Comparative Education*. Oxford: Pergamon.

Tulasiewicz, W. and Brock, C. (2000), Introduction: The place of education in a united Europe, in C. Brock and W. Tulasiewicz (eds), *Education in a Single Europe*. London: Routledge.

UNEP (2010), *Global Biodiversity Outlook 3*. Secretariat of the Convention on Biological Diversity, Montreal.

UNESCO (2004), *Gender and Education for All: The Leap to Equality, EFA Global Monitoring Report 2003/4*. Paris.

— (2010), *Reaching the Marginalised, EFA Global Monitoring Report*. Paris.

— (2011a), *Country Brazil*, Institute for Statistics, http://stats.uis.unesco.org/ unesco/TableViewer/document.aspx?ReportId=121&IF_Language=eng&BR_ Country=760&BR_Region=40520 (Accessed April 2012).

— (2011b), *World Data on Education*, VII Ed. 2010/2011.

UNICEF (2007), *Promoting the Rights of Children with Disabilities*. Innocenti Digest No. 13, http://www.unicef-irc.org/publications/pdf/digest13-disability.pdf

United Nations Development Programme (2010), The real wealth of nations: Pathways to human development. *Human Development Report*, UNDP, http://hdr. undp.org/en/reports/global/hdr2010/ (Accessed October 2011).

Unterhalter, E. and North, A. (2010), Assessing gender mainstreaming in the education sector: Depoliticised technique or a step towards women's rights. *Compare* 40(4): 389–404.

Van Rensburg, P. (1978), *The Sorowe Brigades: Alternative Education in Botswana*. Basingstoke: Macmillan/Brenard Van Leer Foundation.

Van Zanten, A. (2005), New modes of reproducing social inequality in education: The changing role of parents, teachers, schools and educational policies. *European Educational Research Journal* 4(3): 155–69.

Walker, C. (2007), Navigating a 'zombie' system: Youth transitions from vocational education in post-Soviet Russia. *International Journal of Lifelong Education* 26(5): 513–31.

Wallerstein, I. (1974), *The modern world-system: Capitalist agriculture and the origins of the European world-economy in the 16th century.* New York: Academic Press.

— (2004), *World-systems analysis: An introduction.* Durha: Duke University Press.

Wang, L. (2011), Social exclusion and inequality in higher education in China: A capability perspective. *International Journal of Educational Development* 31: 277–86.

Watros, J. (2010), UNESCO's Programme of Fundamental Education 1946–59. *History of Education* 39(2): 219–37.

Watson, K. (1992), Language, education and political power: Some reflections on North-South relationships. *Language and Education* 2(4): 99–121.

— (2010), Contrasting policies towards (mainly) Christian education in different contexts. *Comparative Education* 46(3): 307–23.

— (2011), Education and language policies in South-East Asian countries, in C. Brock and L. P. Symaco (eds), *Education in South-East Asia.* Wallingford: Symposium Books, pp. 283–304.

Whitehead, C. (2005), The historiography of British imperial education policy, part II: Africa and the rest of the colonial empire. *History of Education* 34(4): 441–54.

Whitty, G., Power, S., Edwards, T. and Wigfall, V. (2003), *Education and the Middle Class.* Maidenhead: Open University Press.

Wirt, F. M. (1986), Comparing educational policies: Theory, units of analysis, and research strategies, in P. G. Altbach and G. P. Kelly (eds), op. cit., pp. 275–92.

World Bank (2000), *Higher Education in Developing Countries: Peril and Promise.* Washington DC.

— (2009), *Accelerating Catch-Up: Tertiary Education for Growth in Sub-Saharan Africa.* Washington DC.

— (2011a), *Learning for All: Investing in People's Knowledge and Skills to Promote Development.* World Bank Group Education Strategy 2020.

— (2011b), *World Bank Education Statistics-Brazil at a Glance,* http://devdata. worldbank.org/AAG/bra_aag.pdf (Accessed April 2012).

Xiangmin, C. (2002), An old issue in a new era: Educated women in China's transition from a command economy to a market economy, in R. Griffin (ed.), op. cit., pp. 223–38.

Yamada, S. (2009), 'Traditions' and cultural production: Character training at the Achimota school in colonial Ghana. *History of Education* 38(1): 29–60.

Young, M. and Willmott, P. (1957), *Family and Kinship in East London.* London: Routledge and Kegan Paul.

Zajda, J. (2003), Educational reform and transformation in Russia: Why education reforms fail. *European Education* 35(1): 58–88.

Zambeta, E. (2003), *School and Religion.* Athens: Themelio.

Zgaga, P. (2003), *Bologna Process, Between Prague and Berlin, Report to the Ministers of Education of the signatory countries.* Report commissioned by the Follow-up Group of the Bologna Process, Berlin.

— (2005), *The Importance of Education in Social Reconstruction.* A report on the contribution of the Task Force Education and Youth/Enhanced Graz Process to the Development of Education in South-east Europe, Ljubljana: Centre for Educational Policy Studies.

Zhong, Z. (2006), *A Critical Analysis of Chinese Higher Education in the Context of its Contribution to China's Development.* Unpublished DPhil Thesis: University of Oxford.

Index